WOMAN WITH A MOVIE CAMERA

CONSTRUCTS

The Constructs series examines the ways in which the things we make change both our world and how we understand it. Authors in the series explore the constructive nature of the human artifact and the imagination and reflection that bring it into being.

Series Editors
H. Randolph Swearer
Robert Mugerauer
Vivian Sobchack

WOMAN
with a MOVIE
CAMERA

Marina Goldovskaya

Translated by *Antonina W. Bouis*
Foreword by *Robert Rosen*

University of Texas Press ◆ Austin

Requests for permission to reproduce material
from this work should be sent to:
  Permissions
  University of Texas Press
  P.O. Box 7819
  Austin, TX 78713-7819
  www.utexas.edu/utpress/about/bpermission.html

∞ The paper used in this book meets the minimum requirements
of ANSI/NISO Z39.48-1992 (R1997) (Permanence of Paper).

Library of Congress Cataloging-in-Publication Data

Goldovskaia, Marina Evseevna.
  [Zhenshchina s kinoapparatom. English]
  Woman with a movie camera : my life as a Russian filmmaker / Marina Goldovskaya ;
translated by Antonina W. Bouis ; foreword by Robert Rosen. — 1st ed.
     p.   cm. — (Constructs)

ISBN-13: 978-0-292-71343-7

  1. Goldovskaia, Marina Evseevna.   2. Motion picture producers and directors—Soviet
Union—Biography.   3. Motion picture producers and directors—Russia (Federation)—
Biography.   4. Women motion picture producers and directors—Soviet Union—Biography.
5. Women motion picture producers and directors—Russia (Federation)—Biography.
I. Title.   II. Series.
PN1998.3.G645A3   2006
791.4302′32092—dc22
[B]
                                                                    2006009472

To my parents

Contents

Foreword

I FIRST MET Marina Goldovskaya during the period of perestroika in the Soviet Union when I was part of a delegation of scholars sent to Moscow to negotiate formal cultural relations between our two countries in the field of film studies. Here was a filmmaker whose courageous documentary films on past abuses of power were hailed as nothing less than events of nationwide importance. She was a woman who had climbed to the top of her field in a male-dominated television industry, and a film artist who wrote scholarly books embodying the much-vaunted but seldom-achieved ideal of uniting theory and practice. And, most of all, I met a gracious, generous, and articulate individual whose commitments and humanistic sensibilities came from the heart. I knew then that I desperately wanted Marina to come to UCLA to build our documentary program, to teach our students, and especially to serve as a role model for what it means to be an engaged filmmaker. In retrospect I still cannot believe how profoundly lucky we are that this actually came to pass.

As a maker of documentary films, Marina embraces a unique mixture of seemingly contradictory characteristics that are in fact complementary. Others may praise her work for different reasons, but, personally, what I admire most is the dialectical tension between a humanistic sensibility that is intensely personal and a critical awareness that is broadly social. In *The House on Arbat Street* (1993), she manages to capture in their full integrity the beliefs and idiosyncratic personalities of a score of people who had lived in a large Moscow apartment building over a period of more than seventy-five years. But when integrated into the overall context of the film, these separate testimonies add up to a whole that is far greater than the sum of its parts—nothing less than a masterful summary of the history of the Soviet Union from its inception through its demise, with all of the tragic contradictions laid bare. *The Prince Is Back* (1999) is an intimate and sympathetic portrait of a blindly idealistic dreamer, restoring an abandoned ruin in the hope of reclaiming his prerevolutionary family identity. But true to Marina's dialectical agenda, the personal once again provides a window onto the social, in this instance a period of unrest and street demonstrations when disquieting uncertainty about the future results in an escapist nostalgia for an irretrievable past. *The Shattered Mirror* (1992) may be Marina's most unapologetically personal essay, focusing warmly on many of her dear friends, but what I took away from the film most of all was the vision of a woman with a movie camera braving danger in the streets of Moscow to record and, by her filmmaking, to protect Russia's fragile hold on newfound political rights. I do not believe it is a coincidence that Marina selected Peter Sellars as the subject of her most recent film—a wildly creative, boundary-breaking theater director for whom artistic, humanistic, and ideological objectives are inextricably intertwined.

These same intriguing complexities define Marina as a person as well. Warmly personable, considerate, and exceptionally loyal to her friends, students, and colleagues, she also displays an iron-willed commitment to honesty and the integrity of her work. Over the years, I have seen her anguish about whether or not a particular shot did justice to the motivations of a person or the complexity of an event. I have witnessed the intensity of her quest for an underlying narrative thread that would tie hundreds of hours of footage into a coherent story, but never at the sacrifice of truth.

I am proud to have known Marina Goldovskaya for more than a decade as friend, colleague, mentor, and film artist. *A Woman with A Movie Camera* will enable you to get to know her too. Her story is one worth telling.

Robert Rosen
Dean of the UCLA School of Theater, Film, and Television

Acknowledgments

I WANT TO express my deepest gratitude to the people without whom this book would not have been possible. In the first place, to the people who appear in my films. They sparked the ideas for my films, and they inspired me. I cherish the memory of those who are not with us anymore. I am proud that their stories and their images will not be lost to history.

I am grateful to my peers with whom I worked for many years: Marina Krutoyarskaya, my closest friend and composer, and her husband, Sasha Zaitzev; Sasha Hassin, my sound engineer; Tanya Samoilova, my editor; Alexander Lipkov, Sergei Muratov, Yuri Bogomolov, Aleksei Gusev, and Masha Muratov; and many, many others. Their advice was always invaluable.

I wouldn't have written this book if not for my students, both in Russia and America. I felt the temperature of their interest when communicating with them, and this interest inspired me greatly. I hope that this book will help some young documentarians understand "the secrets" of our complex profession.

My most sincere thanks go to the University of California, Los Angeles, and especially to the UCLA School of Theater, Film, and Television, which became my home in the United States. Here I found a wonderful community of professors, staff, and students whose nourishing atmosphere gave me strength and support to adjust to completely a new life and work conditions.

My very special thanks go to Vivian Sobchack, who believed in my work and supported me all the way through, and to Bob Rosen, Michael Heim, Roberto Peccei, Ivan Berend, and Maja Manojlovic. I will never forget their generous help.

I am more than grateful to Nina Bouis. She was not only a brilliant translator but also a wonderful adviser who became a friend for life.

And of course my thanks go to my husband, George Herzfeld, for his patience, tolerance, immeasurable help, and endless support.

Introduction

On September 11, I woke very early, thanks to jet lag. I had returned to Los Angeles from Moscow the night before. I sat down at my desk to jot a few notes, as usual.

I was in a marvelous mood. Over the summer in Russia I had seen all my friends, spent two weeks in Borovsk, near Kaluga, and had filmed a lot—and I liked what I had filmed. The film was taking shape.

Suddenly, my husband shouted from the bedroom, "Marina, come here! You wanted to hear the Orson Welles broadcast? I think they're playing it."

He had turned on the radio while he did his exercises. Something incredible was on the air.

I ran into the room and listened. No, it wasn't Welles . . . although the sense of horror was probably what people experienced in 1938, when America almost lost its collective mind, listening to the Mercury Theater's radio version of H. G. Welles's *War of the Worlds*, presented as live coverage of a Martian invasion.

I rushed to the television set. What I saw looked like a Hollywood action thriller. But it wasn't fiction. It was live reporting on CNN about what was actually happening—happening in New York, happening in Washington, D.C. I saw a plane hitting a tower of the World Trade Center; this was the second attack. I had been on that roof six months earlier, enjoying the view of the city, and I had been too lazy to bring my camera. I was so sure I'd have plenty of time to film from that vantage point. But I didn't.

I stuck a cassette in the VCR: it's instinctive for me to tape everything important—for work, for memory, for future films. Sometimes I don't even know why I do it. I just feel I must. It was clear that this was a historic moment.

American television is brilliant at reporting live, showing things from different points of view, in a detailed and multifaceted way, with very precise commentaries. I kept switching channels. The scenes were shocking: fire, destruction, people buried alive. And more and more new horrible details . . .

Before that day, I had felt a comparably powerful emotional response only to events in Russia. You have the deepest feelings for events in your own house. I was a guest in America, after all, albeit a guest for ten years. But now I experienced the pain as if it were my own.

I looked at my watch: it was 7 a.m. By 10, I was at the university. I felt I had to be there. Maybe I could help someone, do something, run an errand.

The semester hadn't started yet, and the classrooms were practically empty. I saw only a few of my co-workers, and they were all stunned. We had no idea what to do. We tried to find out where we could donate blood, thinking that it would be important and could help the survivors of the collapse of the 110-story towers. But it turned out that no one was accepting blood; we couldn't find a place to donate. The next day I made some calls, found the locations, drove there, and saw enormous lines at all the hospitals. People stood in line five or six hours to give blood. And it was clear by then that it probably would not be of any use. What a bizarre situation—a mix of nightmare and absurd reality.

A major change had occurred: everyone understood that we were living in a different world. It's a banal thing to say it now—the sentiment is repeated daily—but that feeling became part of me, and I will live with it to the end of my days.

Everything that happened afterward—the letters with anthrax, the constant stream of news on television (which you couldn't not watch: it both mesmerized and agitated), the monstrous terrorist hostage-taking of an entire theater in Moscow, the war in Iraq—made me feel over and over that I was a creature connected to my environment. Wherever I am, Russia or America, I feel that connection acutely, even morbidly.

Life had always been clear to me. I tried to do my work well and to do what I thought was right. I taught with pleasure and joy. I spent as much time as I could with students and friends. I made the films I wanted to make and didn't film the ones I didn't want to make. I knew what interested me and didn't take on a project until it was clear what I could, and wanted to, say in it. I lived at peace with myself, feeling no sense of duality that comes from doing one thing but thinking another, saying yet something else, and living yet another way. Whenever I deviated from the natural course of my life, I fell into a depression, my internal braking system kicking in: something is wrong, stop and think. However hard it was, I broke my way out of the situations that were wrong for me. Things seemed to be in their places, or at least clearly defined.

And now I felt total confusion. My value system, developed over the course of my life, was shot to hell. There was no more solid ground under my feet. So many people were frightened in those days, but I experienced something else. I must have used up all my reserves of fear in the previous fifteen years. I had spent them on the brink of a nervous breakdown, constantly trying to balance—perhaps not between life and death but certainly between catastrophe and survival.

Even in America, where everything seemed tranquil, settled, and stable, I couldn't rid myself of that feeling of anxiety.

Even though physically I had been spending more time in America, I still felt part of Russia, and everything that went on there was close to me. Russian newspapers arrive in Los Angeles once a week; I made the two-hour round-trip to Sunset Boulevard to pick up *Moskovskie Novosti (Moscow News)*, *Literaturnaya Gazeta (Literary Gazette)*, *Komsomolskaya Pravda*, and *Izvestiya* to keep me in reading for the week. Then I started getting Russian news on the Internet, and I spent every evening at my computer, living in virtual Russia in America.

But 9/11 made me feel American. A Russian American. Apparently, what unites you with your surroundings is shared grief. The catastrophe that befell America bound me to the country.

I had spent the last ten years living a marvelous life—or rather, two lives. One in America, where I had family and interesting work that I loved. The second in Russia, where I go like a visitor coming home, even though for only short stays: two to three months in the summer, a month in the winter, and sometimes I manage another two or three weeks in the spring.

Both lives are interesting in their own way, totally unalike. When I fly into Moscow, I'm nervous, as if hurrying to an important meeting. I try to see from the airplane what changes there have been or if everything is still the same. Stepping onto Russian soil is a very emotional experience for me. Everything binds me to Russia—my country, my friends, my memories, my childhood, my parents' graves. When I step onto my native soil, I feel as if I've never been away, as if America did not exist. That life goes into deep background, like a dream that might not be real at all. But transatlantic phone calls back to America put everything in place for me: the other life is also mine.

Friends usually ask how I'm managing in America and if I've adjusted to life here. Honestly, I don't feel much difference. There's enough work for me in America, and that's the main thing for me; wherever my work has meaning, I feel at home. I quickly switch gears, caught in the whirlwind of work, and it no longer matters what language I'm speaking or what scenery surrounds me.

My summer's trip to Russia had been very intense that year. I continued working on a film I began many years ago. It's not even a film but a chronicle of Russian life. People talk about themselves, their past and future, what they feel and what plans they're making. I shot some street scenes too, based on today and therefore unique. I filmed memorable events, plays that touched my heart, people I love and sometimes those I don't like—street rallies by supporters of radical right-wingers like Anpilov and Zhirinovsky and representatives of other strange parties. These are also signs of the times and must be preserved. I've been doing this for the last fifteen years. I collect scenes and people. I ponder how to use them in a future film with the working title *Russian Chronicles: A Diary of Change*. Film is most importantly a comprehension of what is happening around us. Every one of my films, at least for me, has been an attempt at such an understanding.

But after 9/11 everything changed. Maybe the film I was shooting with such hope and love over the summer was not needed? Maybe I should be making a completely different film now? I think I'll set aside all my footage for a while.

What happened to America is not only an American tragedy. It is a world tragedy. The cancerous growth had been latent for decades, and now it came, the horrible, paradoxical explosion. How much hatred had to collect in the hearts of the men who committed that terrible crime. America had lived as if on another planet for so many years, protected from the storms and misery of the rest of the world. And then came this shock. The last drop of evil broke through the dam, but how many drops had accumulated over the years!

I often think of the tragic experiences of Russia in the last fifteen years. They were the result and continuation of the long chain of crimes committed by the totalitarian state, and not only Stalinism.

I always considered myself lucky. People of my generation didn't experience what our parents did when they were young. We did not have to go through pogroms, revolutions, civil war, and the Stalin terror. We only learned of these things from our seniors. World War II also bypassed me; I was too little to remember much. Everything that tormented my parents' lives was but distant thunder to me. I did not have to fear a knock at the door at night, the way people did in the years of Yezhov's and Beria's secret police. I did not have to worry constantly over the fate of relatives, as everyone did in the years of the Civil War and World War II. Everything was comparatively calm. Sometimes things were upsetting, sometimes vile and disgusting, and occasionally intolerable, but nothing demanded a choice that would cost me my life.

Perestroika changed it all. Life became so complicated and so terrifying. It seemed that we were on the brink of civil war. Fortunately, we avoided that terrible path and survived without much bloodshed. But the mass of evil that had accumulated in our enormous country over a century did not leave without a trace. It was reflected in a loss of moral values and a crisis of liberal ideas, not to mention the decline of standards of living and other social woes.

A snowball rolling down a mountain will crush you if it is not stopped in time.

September 11 drew a line in my life. It was time to stop and take stock.

But I physically cannot tolerate not working. I fall into depression, losing interest in the entire world. What could be more interesting than talking with young people, you would think. I've been teaching for almost ten years at the UCLA School of Theater, Film, and Television. I communicate with students almost every day, discovering new things, some I had never even thought about before. And it's even more interesting meeting young people in a new country, in a new life. But now I felt that I was losing interest even in that.

I had never intended to write a memoir. It's not my genre, and I thought, why would anyone else care whether I had lived or not? My business is making films. Documentaries. That is what I have been doing all my life and what I love more than anything else.

But now I felt the need to write this book. I wanted it to be not so much about me but about the events I had witnessed, what I had learned, and how I tried to explain in my films what I had seen. About the people I filmed. About what truly had become the most important thing in my life: documentary film.

Once in February 1992, for my film *The Shattered Mirror,* I shot an episode at a Moscow gas station, where there was a long line. Most people in Moscow probably do not remember the three- to four-hour wait for gas in those days. While waiting for my turn, I picked up the camera. A man looked out from his car and asked me what I was doing.

"Filming."

"What are you filming?"

"Well, how we live today."

"Then you should film this line for gas."

"I did."

"What for?"

"For history, really."

"For history? That's noble. I photograph my family for history; you film reality."

"Well, I'm a documentary maker. I have to do it."

"You're right. It's your duty."

I used that piece in my film. I often return to it in my mind. It is my duty to tell about what I see and feel. Not that what I see and what I feel is so important. I am but a small particle in a huge world, but that world is reflected in me. I filmed and continue to film everything that seems interesting, symptomatic, or important.

Now it is important for me to write this book. To lay out my life. To understand what was good, what was bad, what was joyful, and what was disgusting. To understand myself. To understand history. I experienced a lot of things in my life that today's generation missed. The Stalin years, the years of the Thaw. The years of the development and flowering of television documentaries.

When the period of change began, I had the fortune to participate. Then my life changed completely. At a mature age, at fifty, I changed my personal life and my country of residence. This stage was filled with discoveries. Country, people, culture—all different. I was fortunate; I had more than enough to experience and feel.

And I always had my camera with me.

It was in 1993. I was making *The House on Arbat Street.*

The picture was born this way: I was traveling around the United States, giving lectures, with my screenwriter friends Masha Zvereva and Leonid Gurevich. Masha and I shared a hotel room, and we stayed up late talking. One night we mentioned Nikolai Gubenko, the actor who had unexpectedly been named Russia's minister of culture.

"I visited him recently," Masha said. "I walked into his office, he rose from his desk, and I realized that his desk was right where my crib used to be. I was stunned. It was our old apartment. I recognized the view from the window— I used to see it as a child."

"Masha," I said, "That's a fantastic theme. Let's make a film."

We began discussing it.

"We had twelve neighbors in our communal flat," Masha recalled. "One was a Party official; another was an economist who was arrested during the Stalin purges. The third was my aunt, with whom I lived. She had been married to a KGB man at first, but divorced him later. There was Auntie Marusya, my nanny . . ."

She listed them all and told me all about them. Each one represented a stratum of Soviet society.

"So, we'll make the film?" I asked.

"We should . . . while they're still alive."

When we came back to Moscow, we wrote a proposal, and I started offering it around. Masha called a few of our future subjects and learned that some were still alive and we had to film them right away. So we did. But many had already died, some could no longer remember anything, and the letters that one of the residents kept in a shoe box under the couch had disappeared. Our concept began to change. Now we were making a film not about an apartment but about the whole building.

By then I had gotten financing from the French Canal+, and work was moving along. We had a lot of people for the film, and we chose the most interesting. And, as usually happens, we were finding extraordinary archival materials. The concept was growing, taking on flesh.

But besides a concrete story and characters, a film needs a message—what I want to say with my film. I knew what my film was about: the fate of the people who had lived in this building and, through them, what had happened to us and our country from the turn of the century when the house was built. That was clear. But why was I making the film now? How did it relate to the way we were living now? That question always nags me; there is never just a single, final answer. And I have to find the answer. Without it, the film will have no energy, no point, no meaning.

In order to learn the fate of some of the characters whose lives came to an end in the late 1930s, I went to the press center of the KGB. The doors were just opening a crack in those days, and it was possible to learn things from their documents.

The director of the press center rose to greet me when I came in—an elegant man of forty or so. He knew me from my film *Solovki Power* (1988) about the Stalinist Gulag, the network of prison camps. To tell the truth, I was a bit leery of going to the KGB, thinking that my picture could not have pleased the institution and that I would not be particularly welcome. But no. The director was incredibly polite and helpful. He said that he had helped people find files on their relatives.

"And I thought maybe I would be able to see my father's case," I said.

"Well, why not? Of course."

He wrote down my phone number and promised to call as soon as he located it. I wasn't expecting him to call, but a week later I came home and heard the following message on my machine: "Marina Evseyevna, I found your father's file. Come over whenever it's convenient for you. Just give me a call first."

I asked my son, Seryozha, "Do you want to go with me?"

"Of course."

It took me a couple of days to gather up the courage to call.

"Alexei Georgiyevich, I can come over."

"When is it convenient?"

"What's good for you?"

"Come tomorrow at five. I think two hours will be enough. I'm at the office until seven."

My son and I went to Lubyanka, the KGB headquarters, unable to overcome the anxiety this building creates in every Russian who lived during the Stalin era.

We approached the entrance, the door gave way reluctantly, and we squeezed inside. We were met by a military man, very polite (it's unbelievable how gracious everyone is in that place!). He asked whom we wanted to see.

I told him.

"Come in. He's expecting you."

We went up to the second floor. The director of the press center met us, shook our hands, and smiled.

"I am in a meeting—please forgive me," he said. "I'll take you to the conference room. You can sit there and read."

He picked up a thin file. The cover was stamped "Keep Forever" and bore the name "Goldovsky Evsei Mikhailovich." My stomach turned over.

We were taken to a large room, with a table near the door, a lamp glowing on it. We were brought two cups of coffee, good cookies, and fresh fruit. This kind of reception was the last thing I had expected.

With trembling hands, I opened the file. The first thing I saw was an envelope. I looked inside—Oh, God! Photographs of Father, front and profile. And his eyes—so remote. I burst into tears.

Then I started reading. He was arrested on March 13, 1938, and released on August 31 of the same year. He was thirty-five. I knew that he had returned without any teeth and with lifelong insomnia. He had not slept a single night in the five and a half months he was in the infamous cells of the Lubyanka prison, located in the very same building where I was now reading his file. At night they hauled him out for interrogation, the corridors were very noisy, and he could hear shouts and screams—impossible to fall asleep. And they didn't let people sleep during the day. The guards would bang on the door if they saw through the peephole that a prisoner was asleep.

I knew that his arrest had to do with the Shumyatsky case. Shumyatsky was the minister of cinema then. At the time of his arrest, Father was his technology deputy. Father had told me a few things. He told me that once he had been brought in for a personal confrontation with Shumyatsky. They were being set up to be charged as a terrorist group. Allegedly, Father's boss had been the leader, and he was one of the main organizers; several other people were being charged in the same case. It involved the construction of the movie theater in the Kremlin—the one that was later re-created in Konchalovsky's film *Inner Circle* (1991).

Father was only remotely associated with the theater's construction. Alexei Ivanovich Molchanov, an engineer who had worked with Dziga Vertov on the sound of his film *Enthusiasm: Symphony of the Donbas* (1930), was in charge. As a top manager, Father was supposed to sign off on the work, and as the head of the ministry of cinema's film technology department, he had to oversee the installation of the projection system. He visited the site a few times, and when the work was done, he signed the certificate.

The opening of the theater was planned for November 7, 1937. On November 6, during the rehearsal, a mercury lamp exploded. There was nothing special about that—things happen. The bulb was replaced, and the projection ran beautifully. Stalin watched films and was pleased, but suddenly Shumyatsky was arrested, and the secret police began building a case. Allegedly, agents for Japan (my father had never seen a Japanese person until the 1960s) had intended to poison all the members of the politburo with mercury vapor. Molchanov claimed that my father had brought him in on this assassination attempt and that Shumyatsky had recruited my father. Shumyatsky confirmed it all.

During five and half months of interrogation, Father denied every charge. I read the transcripts: "no," "never heard that before," "it can't be," "I know nothing," "I never discussed anything like this with Shumyatsky," "never gave Molchanov any orders," 'I don't believe it could have happened," "this is impossible." He never referred to anyone else and did not mention any names.

A curious sidelight: During the interrogation, the investigator kept trying to find out why my father, a recognized scientist occupying such high positions, was not a member of the Communist Party. The official was trying hard to find a reason.

"Do you think that if I were a Party member, things would be easier for me now?"

The investigator was taken aback but agreed, "I believe you're right."

The file was thin: a few transcripts of interrogations, a transcript of the personal confrontation with Shumyatsky. Father had told me about that:

"I was already seated in the investigator's office. The door opened, they brought Shumyatsky in, and the investigator said: 'You'd better confess. There's nothing you can do anyway.'

"I simply did not recognize Shumyatsky. He had always been such a robust, strong, confident man. And suddenly I saw him, broken, hunched, the light in his eyes gone. He didn't even look at me. They placed him opposite me in a chair. He was wearing very light, almost white pants, either pajama bottoms or long underwear, tied at the ankle, and shoes without laces. When he crossed his legs, I could see that his skin was absolutely white. And I understood. They were beating him through wet sheets: This way the bruises don't show. You can't mistake it for anything else."

Father told me that he thought that it was Shumyatsky's self-confidence that had destroyed him. He apparently had started making independent decisions, which was something the Boss (as people referred to Stalin) did not like. For the same reason, Stalin later got rid of Dukelsky, who had replaced Shumyatsky as minister of cinema. He then appointed Bolshakov, who suited him much better. Bolshakov would never dare express his own opinion before he learned Stalin's point of view. Old filmmakers used to recall his simple-minded expression: "I don't know yet what I think about this film."

Stalin, like Lenin, considered cinema the most important of all arts. He himself censored all the scripts and watched every film, documentaries included. The fate of each film was completely dependent on his judgment.

My father told me that back then, in the investigator's office, Shumyatsky looked extremely exhausted. Arms crossed, staring at the desk, looking at no one, he answered the questions.

"Do you know Goldovsky?"

"Yes."

"Did you recruit him?"

"Yes."

"Did you give him an assignment?"

"Yes."

He answered all the questions with "yes."

Father burst out, "Boris Zakharovich, what are you saying! There was never any such conversation. You never said that to me! I don't believe that you could have ever said that to anyone. What are you doing, Boris Zakharovich? Why are you accusing yourself?"

At these words, Shumyatsky suddenly looked at him, with the expression of a completely crazed man, and suddenly a glint of life crossed his face. Something wild came into his eyes, but he immediately lowered his gaze and continued replying, "Yes," "Yes," "Yes."

Father said no to everything he was asked.

At the end of their confrontation, Father signed the transcript, and they were taken away.

This took place sometime in late July—Father had lost track of the time. After that, he was left alone, not called in for interrogation. On August 31 at five in the morning, a soldier came into his cell.

"Goldovsky, take your things to the exit!"

Father was sure that this was the end. Either the hard-labor camps or something worse. He got up and started walking.

He was brought to the interrogator, who greeted him with these words: "Comrade Goldovsky, you are free!"

The interrogator made Father sign a promise not to reveal anything about prison life. He was given his things, and then Father realized that he was really free.

Father, of course, never knew the facts I learned from his file.

An hour after their confrontation, Shumyatsky had asked to give additional statements in which he denied everything he had said about Father. He said that Goldovsky had not been part of the conspiracy.

Shumyatsky's fate was not known for many years. Some said that he had committed suicide in prison; another version was that he had been shot. Now all doubts are cleared up. The published transcripts reveal that "a group of terrorists under the direct supervision of Shumyatsky had planned to assassinate members of the Politburo by shattering a projection lamp containing poisonous mercury vapor in the theater of the Kremlin." Shumyatsky was also accused of performing treacherous actions against the signing of the 1918 Brest-Litovsk Peace Treaty, working for Japanese and British intelligence, and participating in rightist Trotskyite organizations.

The accusations did not mention the most horrible offense: Shumyatsky had allegedly refused to join a toast in honor of Stalin at a New Year's reception at the Kremlin on the night of December 31, 1937.

Shumyatsky's sentence was pronounced on August 1, 1938, one month before Father's release: "Execution and confiscation of all property."

I was stunned by what I had read and couldn't function appropriately. I can't forgive myself for not having taken any notes nor asking for a copy of the file.

When I returned the material to the director of the press center, he smiled guiltily. I think he found such situations uncomfortable—he seemed to be a decent man.

I said, "Thank you. I am very grateful. But I have two requests. Could I get Father's photographs, and could I find out what happened to the other six men who were charged in this case?"

"All right. When I know, I'll call you."

About ten days later, he left a new message on my answering machine, and I called back.

"I have copies of the photographs," he said, "and you can pick them up. Excellent copies. And as for your second question, alas, all the people in your father's case were shot." In 1939, Stalin changed the leadership of the secret police. Beria, the new chief, arrested his predecessor, Yezhov, for abusing his power and sentencing innocent people. Yezhov was shot, as were many of his predecessors in that job, and as Beria eventually was as well. Incidentally, Beria became Yezhov's first deputy in 1938, nine days before my father was released. Maybe the two events were related in some way? Maybe Father's release was one of those actions by which a new boss was trying to demonstrate his powers to establish himself as the man in charge.

Yezhov's regime was at an end, but Beria turned out to be no better.

My father had been one of the very few who had the strength not to sign false accusations. I wondered what miracle had saved him. How did he manage to deny any guilt? He was a very gentle and sensitive man. Where did he find the resolve? The strength to resist? If he had wavered just a little bit, he would not have lived, nor would I, for I was born after his release.

Here are more glimpses into my father's story. I learned them from him and from his former students.

Father lived with his mother in a communal flat in Moscow on the Sofiiskaya Embankment, still a bachelor. In December 1937 he got a three-room apartment in a new house on Bolshaya Polyanka Street. He left the old residence and handed in his identity papers to the superintendent of the new building for registration. The night of March 12, the secret police came looking for him in the old place on the Sofiiskaya Embankment. They came for him, but he was not there. And they probably suspected that he was trying to hide or was out performing terrorist acts.

At nine the next morning, when Father was in his office in Gnezdnikovsky Lane, three men in civilian clothes entered, searched the office, and said, "Get dressed. You are coming with us." Father understood at once what it meant. No one was surprised by arrests in those days. As he was going down the stairs, one of his students ran up to him.

"Evsei Mikhailovich! Wait! Are you going to the Film School? Could you give me a lift?"

"I don't think we're going in the same direction today, thank God," Father said, not losing his sense of humor even under these circumstances.

When he returned from prison, Father found that the police had sealed two rooms in his apartment, leaving only one for Grandmother to live in. He took off the seals, went into his study, and discovered among all the papers the police had scattered during their search a little locked leather case close to his desk. "What's this?" he wondered.

It turned out that his aunt who lived in a communal flat in Podolsk, a little town twenty miles away from Moscow, had dropped off the case two days before his arrest, after asking his mother if she could leave it there.

"Sofia Alexandrovna, could you keep this case for a few days? One of my neighbors in the apartment is a real thief. I'm afraid she'll steal it."

"You can leave it, Marusya."

The case remained in the study. Why didn't anyone search it? How could the police miss it?

Father opened the case. It was full of gold jewelry and coins.

Aunt Marusya came from a wealthy family. Her husband, an engineer, had a very modest salary, and yet she never worked. Until her dying day, she lived by selling family jewelry she had inherited in prerevolutionary times.

"Good Lord, I clearly was born under a lucky star" was the only thing Father could say. "If they had opened that case, nothing would have saved me. You can't imagine more incriminating evidence."

After the meeting at the KGB I came home, parked the car, walked into the house, and stopped. I simply couldn't walk upstairs, even though it was only one flight. It was the same house on Polyanka, the very same apartment, to which Father had returned in 1938.

Father had told me that he had been released from Lubyanka around five thirty in the morning. It was summer, August. The trolleys weren't running yet, Moscow was empty, no one was in the streets, and he was wearing his black winter coat with a fur collar, the same one he had worn when he was taken away in March. He walked through the empty streets. He reached the building. It was six by then. All was still very quiet. Everyone was asleep. He didn't want to wake his mother. He walked into the entrance and stood there waiting. Somewhere upstairs a door slammed—someone was off to work. It was time. He walked up the stairs, rang the doorbell, and in less than a second heard his mother's voice.

"Senechka, is that you?"

Now I stood in the dark entry. It was an old building, long in need of repair, smelling of cats, and I felt that I could not walk. A door slammed somewhere, and I walked up the stairs—the elevator was broken. I put my key in the lock and suddenly understood what my new film would be about.

Nothing in life vanishes without consequence.

And nothing happens for nothing.

Our today is the sum of our yesterday, the day before yesterday, and the days before that.

There are no trifles in life. I always believed that. The slightest event, however insignificant, spawns another, possibly more important. Everything has a beginning and a continuation.

That is why I always try to avoid things that will later make me feel bitter or ashamed. What goes around comes around.

Two days later I met Anya Belova and decided that she would definitely be in my film. She had multiple sclerosis; she could barely walk and spoke slowly with a thin, trembling voice. But she told me what I had been looking for since we began work on *The House on Arbat Street*. She went over to the wall and pointed at the photograph of a beautiful woman, eighteen years old and full of life.

"I was so carefree then! I fluttered like a butterfly, thinking of nothing," she said. "And now I am immobile . . . Maybe I am this way now because I never thought about what could happen to me. Nothing passes without a trace. Everything in the world is interrelated. The present flows out of the past."

Those words expressed just what I wanted to say.

I knew that my film would be about that.

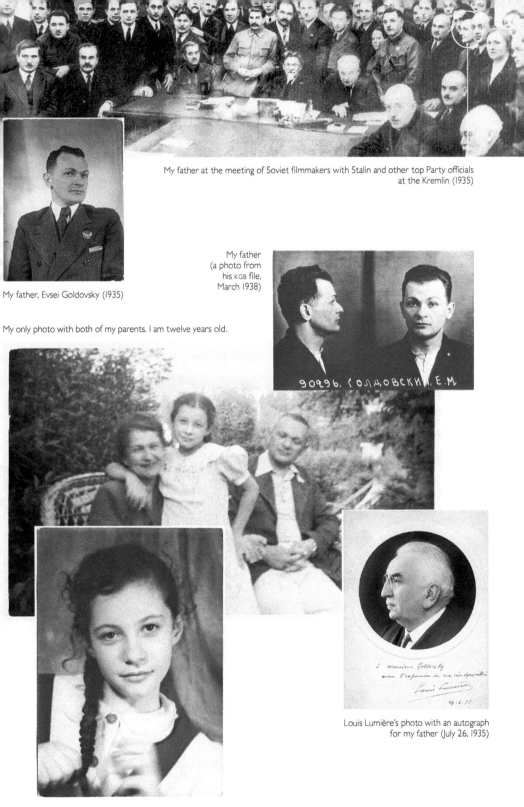

My father at the meeting of Soviet filmmakers with Stalin and other top Party officials
at the Kremlin (1935)

My father, Evsei Goldovsky (1935)

My father
(a photo from
his KGB file,
March 1938)

90296, ГОЛДОВСКИЙ, Е.М.

My only photo with both of my parents. I am twelve years old.

Louis Lumière's photo with an autograph
for my father (July 26, 1935)

And in this photo I am only nine.

Editing

Shooting a Communist Party conference in the Kremlin

Luba Kovaleva, weaver

Alexander Vishnevsky, surgeon

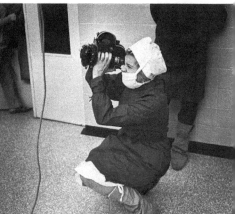

Filming *Surgeon Vishnevsky* (1969)

With miners of the Russia's Far North (summer 1963)

Slava Zaprudnov, glassblower (1972)

Raissa Nemchinskaya, circus actress (1970)

Yuri Zavadsky, theater actor and director (1971)

The seals and me (1983)

While shooting *Before the Harvest*

Deniska, the hero of my film (1976)

With documentary legend Roman Karmen (1976)

Arkady Raikin, stand-up comedian (1975)

Natan Eidelman, writer (1981)

Saluting *Antarctica* (1983)

PILOT
12

Father

My father was back. He had been rehabilitated. He immediately re-turned to work at VGIK (All-Union State Institute of Cinematography, which everyone referred to as the Moscow Film School), where he had taught since 1924.

The first thing he did was go to the library.

"Where are my books?" he asked. He had published close to fifteen works by then.

"We were forced to remove them," the librarian said.

"Well, and what did you do with them? Throw them away?"

I knew that librarian, from the time when I was a student. She was an old woman, very amusing.

"No, no . . . We hid them . . ."

"Put me back on the shelves. I'm back."

Later, the legendary Soviet filmmaker Sergei Eisenstein, with whom Father worked at VGIK, jokingly referred to him as the Prisoner of Chillon—not because of any Byronic romanticism about Father but because of the Lubyanka prison, whose facilities Father had enjoyed, alas. Eisenstein anticipated arrest several times in his life, and he used Father's sorrowful experience (or, depending on your point of view, exceptionally lucky one) as a yardstick for himself. Whenever anyone asked him what it was like, Father used to reply with a chuckle, "Not like a resort, that's for sure."

Father wasn't supposed to talk about it, but he did, rather fearlessly. He told some people about Shumyatsky—only a few glimpses, never the whole story. After Father's death, I asked my mother, "Did he ever talk to you about his imprisonment?"

"Never," she replied.

He didn't tell her, and he didn't tell me.

I don't know why she had never asked him. I do know why I didn't ask. I didn't want to traumatize him. He wouldn't have lied, of course, and I didn't want to make him talk about his beatings.

In the late 1940s, Father was walking down Ordynka Street and bumped into the interrogator who had been in charge of his case at Lubyanka. The man was on a bicycle, and when he saw Father, he stopped and gleefully waved. "Evsei Mikhailovich, hello!" he cried.

They shook hands. He said something. Father said something, trying to be polite.

When he got home, he exclaimed, "God, can you believe who I met today! It was horrible!"

I remembered that, even though I was only six or seven then.

In late 1952, at the peak of the anti-Semitic campaign when everyone was expecting the worst—arrests, pogroms, mass deportation to Siberia—the same interrogator called up on the telephone out of the blue.

"Evsei Mikhailovich, my daughter just graduated from college. She needs a job. Can you help, please?"

At the time, Father was heading the research department at NIKFI (the Film Technology Research Institute).

"Sorry, but we don't have any openings at this time," he said. "I can't help you."

At home, he commented to Mother, "Why did I have to be so abrupt? I don't know. It just came out. I couldn't say anything different. What is going to happen now?"

But, fortunately, there were no repercussions.

Father died in 1971 at the age of sixty-eight—by today's standards, a young man. He was very strong physically, but the doctors said that the insomnia that had tormented him throughout his life had undermined his health. He never slept more than three or four hours a night, and always with very strong drugs. After his sixty-third birthday, he began having heart attacks. I am sure that they were the result of his incarceration in 1938 and the always-present threat of a new arrest during the years of Stalin's dictatorship.

He also worked very hard, to the point of exhaustion—holding at least two jobs at the same time. He was head of the cinema technology laboratory at NIKFI and a department head at VGIK. He was an adviser on many projects and worked on the development of Russian sound film. Later, in the 1950s and 1960s, he created Soviet wide-screen systems, including Cinerama and Circarama. He was also in charge of designing and installing the famous ruby stars that to date adorn the Kremlin towers.

Every morning, he was at his desk by six. He had ninety-two books published, two of them posthumously. One of his books was a profile of Louis Lumière, whom Father met in 1935 during the first visit made to France by a Soviet delegation of filmmakers.

Perhaps this is why, as a child, I had already developed such a strong feeling for the art of filmmaking. I had the privilege of growing up among the people who shaped this art from the beginning.

Even when I was very little, Father used to tell me, "Darling, you must work. You must do all kinds of work. No work is ever wasted. It will always have some use."

"Papa, but why do you write so many books? Why do you torture yourself?"

"I'll die, but the books will remain."

The books did remain. But I don't know if anyone reads them these days.

Now I blame myself for not having talked more to my father—not only about his incarceration in Lubyanka but about everything.

Nowadays I tape the video memoirs of old filmmakers—but I never filmed my own parents or seriously questioned them. Yet I could have learned so much from them!

There didn't seem to be enough time to ask Father anything. He was at work from morning till night. And when I was young, I had no time for conversations. My head was empty, and whatever my elders had to say was by definition boring. Later I was too busy with work, family, and friends.

The only things Father liked talking about and I liked listening to were stories of his own childhood and life in the tiny Ukrainian town of Nikopol. "When I was a little boy," he would begin, and then came reminiscences of what marvelous apricots and tomatoes the people had there, the delicious aroma of the sausage that cost only two kopecks, how you could buy a cow for a ruble, and where he went to school. All those trifles settled in my brain, but we never got around to the important things.

Childhood

I was born at the most inconvenient time—July 15, 1941. Mother told me (during the only interview I ever videotaped of her) that I was born in the middle of an air raid, bombs falling, horrible noise outside, and she begged the midwife to take me away. "Please, please! Take her to a bomb shelter."

The midwife placed me in my mother's arms and said, "I'm not taking her away from you. You two have one fate. Whatever happens, you must be together."

For a long time I did not know who my grandparents were. Mother's passport gave her birthplace as Kaunas, in Lithuania. Later, my mother admitted that she was born in Moscow.

"Then why does it say Kaunas on your passport?"

"Because my parents were wealthy people. If it said Moscow, everyone would understand that I came from a rich family. Only rich Jews were given permission to live in Moscow. Your grandmother 'corrected' my documents by bribing the authorities."

An interesting detail: Before the revolution, my grandmother had a safe-deposit box in a bank where she kept her jewelry. When the Bolsheviks took over and it became clear that they were there to stay, she wanted to retrieve it. But this was easier said than done. To get it, she had to "convince" the guard, a Red Army soldier, to help her.

She told him, "If you get it for me, I'll give you half." He didn't argue. He got the box, and he got his share.

So even at the euphoric idealistic height of the revolution, there were no incorruptibles. Mother's story was a revelation to me. All my life I had been taught about the fighters for the grand idea, and it turned out that, in every age, money was stronger than any idea.

My mother's parents lost their civil rights for being part of the "exploiting" classes. Before the revolution, they had owned a small factory on Ordynka

Street (Mother pointed out the building to me later), which was of course nationalized. Grandmother and Grandfather stayed on there, I think as book-keepers. The first few years after the revolution were very hard for them. When Lenin in 1922 instituted NEP, the New Economic Policy, which allowed limited free enterprise to improve the economy devastated by the revolution, the workers voted to make Grandfather the managing director again, and he was reinstated. They liked him. He was a kind and good man. I think he was also too easygoing. Grandmother was the one with a strong personality, and she ran things. During NEP the family got back on its feet, but in 1929 Stalin reversed the policy, and they found themselves deprived again.

Grandmother managed to get orders for sewing brassieres. The whole family depended on her income. There were three children: my mother; her brother Borya, three years older; and her brother Mark, the oldest. Mark died in 1920 of tuberculosis, which he contracted during years of starvation; they couldn't save him. Grandfather helped Grandmother sew brassieres, without complaining. By then he was a broken man and couldn't take a step without her. The revolution had clipped his wings. I never saw him. He was evacuated in 1941 to the Urals along with my uncle Borya, and he died there.

Mother was never able to join the Komsomol (the Communist Youth League) or the Party. I think she really wanted to. She belonged to those who really believed in the Communist idea, a "non-Party Bolshevik." But she couldn't apply. The authorities would have checked her past and found what she was trying to hide.

Mother played piano when she was a little girl. She adored music and wanted to become a pianist. But at the age of fourteen she strained her hands from overplaying and had to give up music. After graduating from high school, she worked during the day as a translator and took evening courses at the Institute of Foreign Languages. Later she took courses at GITIS (the State Institute of Theater Arts) but continued working. The family needed her income; they could barely make ends meet.

Mother, like Father, was a real workaholic; she could not exist without work. I spent my childhood waiting for her to finish writing her doctoral dissertation, "Shakespeare on the English Stage." Mother wrote and rewrote it right up to her defense. She taught theater history in Moscow and in Tashkent, the capital of Uzbekistan. There things were easier—you were farther away from the political bosses in Moscow, which meant that you had a little more freedom. She published several books, her last, *Theater Collections of France,* just before her death.

Before the war, Mother had worked as head of the literary section at Mikhoels's Jewish Theater. She said that in 1940, when Mikhoels returned from a trip to Odessa, he had told her, "Well, Nina, now they've started official state anti-Semitism."

I remember her story of how in 1918, in the very beginning of the Soviet era, when internationalism was one of the main Bolshevik slogans, Grandmother had met a friend, an elderly rabbi on the street.

"You'll see," he said, "a little time will pass, and then they'll blame the Jews for all of Russia's woes."

As befits a rabbi, he was wise. After the war, in 1946, Mother went to Lithuania. She wanted to know how her relatives were doing. It turned out that they had all been killed in the Holocaust.

At the beginning of the war, they were going to draft Father into the people's defense units (not the regular army but ill-equipped "volunteers"). He came home and started packing. The house was in mourning. So many great minds, talents, and unique specialists (for example, Yuri Kondratiuk, after whom the Americans have named a crater on the moon) died stupidly and uselessly in the people's defense of Moscow. The same fate probably awaited my father, but Pavel Vasilyevich Kozlov, the director of NIKFI, came to the rescue.

"Evsei Mikhailovich! We can't manage without you," he said. "I got you an exemption."

Kozlov depended fully on my father, whom he respected and valued. Father was a very active person, a wonderful organizer and manager. Things would have been tough for the institute without him, especially during the expected evacuation of the institute away from the endangered capital. Father got the institute ready to go within a few days and organized the move of staff and equipment to Samarqand, a town in Uzbekistan.

Mother, who was working in the Repertory Committee then, went with me, Grandmother, and my nanny to Tashkent. We were leaving just when Moscow was in a panic, with everyone expecting the Germans to enter the city momentarily. It was a madhouse. The station platforms were overcrowded, making it impossible to get to the trains. The well-known screenwriter Iossif Prut, later told me how he had passed me to my mother through the train window—we didn't have a sleeper reserved but managed to squeeze into the club car.

It took a week to get to Tashkent. Mother later told me that she didn't understand how I survived. It was terribly cold in the train, everyone was sick, and so was I. But she breast-fed me, and that must have saved me.

We lived in a tiny room with one mattress for Mother, Grandmother, and my nanny. I was living and sleeping in a wardrobe that had been pushed to one side of the floor. I actually learned to stand and to walk in that wardrobe.

Throughout my childhood, I had only one doll, a cloth monkey my mother had made for me when I was eighteen months old. I lived with that monkey until I was around ten.

Father visited us rarely, and I almost never saw him. In late 1943 we all returned to Moscow. This is when I really started remembering things.

I remember clearly: the room is dark, the kerosene lamp is lit, and Father holds me close, gives me a kiss, and says, "Well, so long, my little girl." That was February 1945. He was on his way to Germany, to bring back film equipment the Russian army had confiscated. I remember the scratchy warmth of his overcoat—he wore a colonel's uniform then. Later that coat with its insignias hung in the closet of our dacha for a long time. Father wore it when he dug potatoes.

When we returned from Tashkent, we found strangers living in our apartment—they had broken in and were squatting there. There was nothing left of our things. Mother had to battle with the squatters for a long time. At last they were forced to leave and given other housing. Besides us, there were other relatives in our apartment—Father's sister, Rita, whose husband had been executed in 1938, and her daughter, my cousin Innochka.

There was absolutely nothing in the house. Mother didn't take anything with her from our place in Tashkent, because she was sure that everything we needed was back home. Father brought two suitcases from Germany—dresses for mother and, for me, all kinds of trifles. A month after our return, my parents took me for a walk, and when we came back, the apartment was completely ransacked. Even the old furniture they had managed to buy was gone. Only one thing was left: a pair of tiny scissors Father had brought back from Germany. I kept them with me always. When they were stolen with my wallet in 1990 in Vienna, I treated it as a tragedy. It was the only surviving piece from my early childhood.

Father began traveling frequently to work in Leningrad. People could buy beautiful antique furniture there. It was usually damaged, but Father bought it anyway. He loved old furniture, and he either restored it himself or hired specialists to make it look like new. He even restored an old antique clock, a trade he had learned from his father, who had been a watchmaker. Grandfather had died in 1915 of delirium tremens, which was probably the reason why my father never took a single drink throughout his life.

The second day that I remember well was Victory Day. I still can picture the fountains all around and the blinding sunshine. I am jumping up and down at the sink, splashing water and shouting, "Victory! Victory!"

Our House

Our building was special. It looked grim and gray, surrounded by a fence made of metal pipes. It was the prestigious House of Filmmakers, in which all residents were prominent film directors, producers, actors, writers, and cinematographers.

All the interesting activities took place in the courtyard. There were lots of kids, and here I fell in love for the first time—with Fedya Provorov, a boy with clear blue eyes, the son of the cameraman Fiodor Provorov, who lived in the house next door. His mother was a great beauty, also with blue eyes. She often wandered alone in the courtyard; everyone knew that she was mentally unbalanced.

In the evenings, the residents came out. There were many famous documentary and feature filmmakers among them: Dziga Vertov, Alexander Medvedkin, Roman Karmen, Mikhail Romm, Yuli Raizman, Grigori Roshal, Efim Dzigan, Alexander Ptushko, Boris Volchek . . .

As a child, I felt that all our filmmakers were part of one big family. They all loved one another, were such good friends, and enjoyed working together. Later I learned how foolish my illusions had been. For example, Roshal, who directed many films that became "Soviet classics," could not stand Raizman and Romm. Volchek rarely appeared in the courtyard. I guess he didn't want to run into his former wives, Vera and Era, who also lived in the building. He was at the time married to Elena Alexandrovna.

Karmen had an astonishingly beautiful wife, Nina Ivanovna. She was like a statue. We knew that she was his second wife. He had divorced his first, the daughter of Emelyan Yaroslavsky, a Party bigwig. He had a son from his first marriage, and I later met him at VGIK, where he was in a class ahead of me. Nina Ivanovna had a son by Karmen too, called Sasha, who was my age, and we were friends growing up. We are still friends.

Nina Ivanovna created all kinds of problems for Karmen. She was always involved with other men, including a passionate affair with Stalin's son Vassily. That could have ended very badly for Karmen, but he was unsinkable and survived.

The most cheerful person in the building was an esteemed documentary filmmaker, Arsha Ovanesova. You could hear her rollicking laughter every evening, year-round. She was the center of a large group that enjoyed her humor and love of life. It was a great shock for everyone when she had a nervous breakdown.

The Ptushko family lived directly below us. I was friends with Yulya Ptushko, who was a year older and known for her sophistication. When I was six, she invited me to her seventh birthday party. I asked her what she wanted.

"If you're giving me a book, just remember that I read only Schiller and Shakespeare."

I never reached her lofty heights.

Ptushko, a great storyteller in film, strolled around the courtyard, big, fat, and roly-poly. He also laughed very loudly—he and Arsha were the soul of the courtyard party. There was fun every night. It seemed that it would last forever.

Ptushko not only directed fantasy films filled with wonders and special effects but also enjoyed making magical objects. He could turn ordinary seashells into beautiful jewelry, and he gave Mother a brooch he made. Now I own it.

He was known as a model family man. His wife was a voluptuous woman, a singer whose vocalizing could be heard in the mornings: "La-la-la-lalalala." I still hear it in my dreams sometimes. And then, suddenly, after Stalin's death, when everything in the country eased up, including morals, Ptushko left his wife and daughter, moved two alcoholics into their apartment, and moved out to marry our neighbor from the third floor. She was the sound engineer in his film group. What a shock! The domestic idyll cracked.

The same thing soon happened again. Two apartments in our building were given to people from the Ministry of Foreign Affairs. Across the landing from us lived Fyodor Molochkov, head of the protocol department at the ministry, and above us, Alexander Pavlov, the Soviet ambassador to France. I was very good friends with Alyosha Molochkov, Fyodor's son. We were the same age. Every morning his father got into the huge car that came to pick him up, and then he waved to his wife, who was watching from the window. My mother always said to my father, "You just rush out the door. You never look back. That Molochkov is a real family man. Just look at how he says good-bye to his wife."

We later learned that the ideal husband had yet another family. When he was ambassador to Switzerland, he started an affair with his future second wife, Klavdia Romanovna, who worked at the embassy, either in the dining room or in the accounting office. Stories like this are a dime a dozen nowadays, but back then, they were earth-shattering. Until the mid-1950s there was no such word as "lover" in the vocabulary of Soviet film and literature. Such things simply did not happen in Soviet society, and the few straying comrades who violated the moral principles established by the communist ideology were denounced at Party and other public meetings and sometimes even fired. Molochkov was farsighted: he did not leave his first family until he had retired.

As I now think back, all those cheerful pictures of life in our courtyard date to the post-Stalin period. In the Stalin years, people lived more quietly and gathered less frequently. That was the safer course. A wrong word could get you imprisoned.

Every entrance to the building had a concierge. Aunt Klava, as children called her, lived right in the vestibule. She had a couch, a table, and a chair. She knew everything about everyone. She knew where every visitor was going, what they talked about, why they were there. I later learned that all the concierges worked as informers. When my parents were planning a cruise on the Danube in the 1960s, Aunt Klava was called to KGB headquarters, where she had to tell them whether she thought my parents could safely be allowed out of the country together and whether there was any risk they would defect. They also questioned my nanny, Lizochka, as she told us a few years later.

Nothing but gloominess remains in my memory of the Stalin years. The house was a grim gray, and everyone was exhausted by the war, by life, by the deadly fear of being arrested.

I remember the night in 1948 when they took Grigory Irsky, a hunchbacked, kind, and very well-educated little man. He was in charge of the production department at the ministry and the head of a laboratory at NIKFI. Father and he were friends. His wife, Nina, was left behind with two daughters. She earned money by repairing stockings—there even was a market for that craft. The other residents in the building helped her secretly with money. They were afraid to give support openly, and none of the residents ever invited her to their home. But Nina came to our home. Her daughter Irishka was two years younger than me. They all used to visit us in our dacha. Once, Irishka was swinging on a gate and smashed her nose on the latch. She was very pretty and was worried that she would turn ugly. We all kept telling her, "Don't worry! You'll always be as pretty as you are now."

I even remember Dziga Vertov. He used to sit on a bench near our entryway, always leaning on a walking stick, always gloomy and reserved. He seemed hopelessly ancient to me. It was much later that I realized he had died at the young age of fifty-five. Seda Pumpyanskaya, who worked with him, told me that when they found out he had cancer (he wasn't told, although he knew he was very sick), he was given sick leave. He said, "No more than three months. Otherwise, I'll get fired."

Exactly three months later, he came back to work, spent a few days, and went back to bed. But he had to work; otherwise he would starve. His wife, Elizaveta Svilova, was an editor, working for the weekly film magazine *News of the Day*. And Vertov—master filmmaker, pillar of world documentary film, creator of a new language and pathfinder—ended his life editing newsreels, clichéd, monotonous, and official. Well, perhaps he managed to make them less routine, even though he couldn't change their real meaning. But he was not permitted to do what he really wanted to do and what he became famous for— artistic documentaries, such as his masterpiece, *Man with a Movie Camera*, and *Enthusiasm*.

On the other side of the wall of my room lived Alexander Medvedkin, although the entrance to his apartment was on a different stairway. He was a handsome man, tall, and with a military demeanor. He and Father were on very good terms, often laughing and telling stories. He played the mandolin and was full of cheer. I learned later that he had no particular reason to be cheerful. He lived a difficult life. Some of his films had been banned, and he was unable to bring many of his creative projects to fruition—but this did not change him as a human being. He was a legend in documentary film, because in the early 1930s he created a "studio on a train"—the famous "Medvedkin film train" that traveled to factories and collective farms throughout Russia to create documentaries right on the spot.

In the late 1970s he was given the Lenin Prize, the highest state award, for some boring routine film. We were very happy for him, even though the award wasn't for his *Happiness* or *Miracle Worker,* films that had been made at the height of his powers in the 1930s and then had gathered dust on the shelves for decades. Medvedkin and I became friends despite the difference in age.

In 1988, I taped his video memoirs, playing his mandolin and singing Russian Civil War songs. He recounted his service in the Red Calvary and how he met his future wife, Vera Ivanovna, in a village, fell in love at first sight, and took her to the front lines, despite her family's objections. He also explained his daughter's unusual name, Chongara. In 1920, after a victory over the White Army commanded by General Peter Wrangel, he and his best friend swore to name their firstborns in honor of the battle site, the Isthmus of Chongar. After the end of the Civil War, he lost track of his friend but thought of him often.

After Medvedkin's death, I incidentally met a very interesting person who immediately attracted my attention because of his name. He was Chongar Blumenthal, who turned out to be the son of Medvedkin's army buddy. His father had survived the Civil War but died in one of Stalin's camps. A typical Soviet story.

The famous French director Chris Marker made a great film, *The Last Bolshevik* (1993), about Medvedkin and other flaming Lenin revolutionaries like him.

We had a few female cinematographers in our building—the striking Era Savelyeva, with amazing blue-green eyes, who worked in feature films, and Ottilia Reizman, who made newsreels after spending the war in a partisan unit. She went to war with Maria Sukhova, another camerawoman, who was killed while filming. Ottilia was a good-looking woman with a sturdy square build, full of power and life. Era and Ottilia had a great influence on me. I was dreaming of becoming a director of photography. The dream began when I was a little girl. The job seemed so romantic! In those years there were very few cinematographers, not like now. There were probably no more than five hundred in the whole country, and more than a hundred had perished in the war.

Only VGIK trained camera people. You could count the women on your fingers: besides Savelyeva and Reizman, there were Margarita Pilikhina, a brilliant camerawoman in feature film who gave me her blessing; Antonina Egina, who worked at Mosfilm, usually as second camera; and Galina Monglovskaya, a documentarian with the Documentary Film Studio. That was it. It was very hard for women to get into VGIK's cinematography program.

Our building also had many other cinema celebrities. For instance, Ada Voitsik was a movie star of the 1930s, beautiful, thin, tall, and elegant, with a tragic look. Her husband, Ivan Piriev, a famous film director, had abandoned her with their child, Erik, a good-looking boy, but a bit strange. He had played the tsar as a child in Eisenstein's *Ivan the Terrible*. Later he began drinking heavily and led a bohemian life. He eventually married, but that did not change his lifestyle; he still drank a lot. He died young of cirrhosis of the liver, leaving a little daughter, Masha. Ada Voitsik had trouble all her life: First with her son, and then with her granddaughter Masha, a beautiful but wild young woman. Ada was a tragic heroine not only on-screen but also in real life. Everyone in the building was sympathetic.

Our house was like a communal flat that spread over many floors. Everyone in all forty-two apartments knew everything about everyone else, commiserated together, and gossiped.

On the fourth floor on our side of the building lived Mikhail Romm with Elena Kuzmina and their daughter, Natasha. Below us were Irina Venzher and Yakov Poselsky, whose daughter was also called Natasha.

Later, when I was in college, I became friends with Irina Venzher. She told

me many interesting things about the Documentary Film Studio and her life.
I've forgotten almost all of them, but our late-night chats in her kitchen, her
husky, smoky voice, the tea, and her infinite warmth and friendship will stay
with me to the end of my days. I remained friends with her daughter, Natasha,
and her husband, the talented geologist Georgi Reisner, who was the nephew
of the famous writer and army commander Larissa Reisner.

Both Natasha and Galya Volchek—now artistic director of the Sovremennik, one of the best Russian theaters—were seven or eight years older than me,
at that age a huge difference. We were all children of the same house. Now
when I meet Galya, I have the feeling that we come from the same sandbox,
even though we weren't very close as children. But I knew that she was studying theater. We used to wonder, how could she become an actress when she
was not beautiful? But she grew into a handsome woman; married a talented
actor, Yevgeny Evstigneyev; became famous herself; and gave birth to a son,
Denis. We later learned that the couple divorced. All this was grist for the mill
of the house. Natasha Romm married Sasha Alliluev, the nephew of Stalin's
wife. They had a son, Misha, who died very young of blood cancer. All the
surviving children of our House on Polyanka went to the funeral.

We felt we all were part of one family, and that sense of belonging remains.

Bolshevo

Besides our building, which was all about cinema, there was also Bolshevo, thirty kilometers from Moscow, a resort where we spent our vacations. We usually went there in winter. In summer we lived in our country dacha, which Father had built himself. He loved planting tomatoes and potatoes and tending his apple trees.

The filmmakers' house in Bolshevo had been built in 1936 by Shumyatsky, who was the cinema commissar in those days. People went there to write screenplays, and many lived there for extended periods, working or just vacationing. When the country was on the six-day workweek, they usually came on Saturday nights; when the five-day week was instituted, people spent the whole weekend there. In those years Bolshevo was the only resort where cinema workers could go. Later, in the 1960s to the 1980s, the state built similar places not far from Leningrad, in Repino and in Pitsunda on the Black Sea.

The house in Bolshevo was always full. Directors, actors, writers, and cinematographers enjoyed being there. Sergei Gerassimov would come with Tamara Makarova; Roman Karmen, with his wife, the beautiful Maya (who later left him for the writer Vassily Aksyonov—for some reason all wives left Karmen, even though he was handsome and very famous); and also Sergei Yutkevich, Yevgeny Gabrilovich, and Yuli Raizman were often seen there. Sometimes I met Sergei Urusevsky, who had become very famous after making *The Cranes Are Flying,* directed by Mikhail Kalatozov. Urusevsky was a friend of my father's and always responded with some nice joke. But I was very shy and afraid to speak, merely gaping in silent hero worship.

In the late 1950s, our legendary singer Leonid Utesov spent at least six months a year there. The most popular Soviet stand-up comedian, Arkady Raikin, also visited often.

Utesov was a marvelous storyteller, enchanting the entire company. People rolled on the floor, laughing at his jokes. He had stopped singing by then. He would vacation in Bolshevo with his wife and his daughter, Edit. She had a lovely husband, Albert Gendelshtein, a director of popular science films, handsome and masculine. I think he liked me. I liked him too, even though he was a good forty years older. He developed Parkinson's disease, and it was a terrible sight to see that gorgeous man wasting away.

There were all kinds of scandals in Bolshevo. Piriev came with Lusya Marchenko, and everyone gossiped about how he had abandoned his second wife, Marina Ladynina, the star in all his comedies.

Lusya was a pretty and promising actress—her part in Lev Kulidzhanov's *Father's House* was proof of that. She and Piriev's son Andrei Ladynin were schoolmates, and once when Andrei had invited her to his home, his father fell madly in love with her. Piriev was a passionate man who could not live a life of lies. He left his wife, moved in with Lusya, and starred her in some of his films. The story ended when Lusya fell in love with Oleg Strizhenov, a handsome movie star. We witnessed the dramatic scene when Lusya threw Piriev out, yelling from the balcony, "Get out of here! I love Strizhenov, not you!"

After that dramatic interlude, she stopped appearing in films and vanished. I didn't hear about her for many years.

In the late 1970s, while shooting a film about the playwright Mikhail Bulgakov, I needed to interview the screenwriter Sergei Yermolinsky. He lived on the third floor, and we had to pull the cable for our lighting equipment through an apartment on the first floor rather than pull it up the stairs. I rang the doorbell. A slightly shabby woman with faded eyes, an alcohol-swollen face, and a deep scar over her mouth opened the door. There was something familiar about her. Where had I seen her?

"I'm filming Yermolinsky. Could we bring the cable through your place?" I asked.

"Of course, of course . . . I'm in film too."

"Really? Where do you work?"

"I'm an actress. Marina, don't you remember me?"

I was embarrassed. I thought a bit. "Oh, Lusya?"

"Yes."

There stood Lusya Marchenko . . .

Among all its other attractions, Bolshevo arranged screenings of new films, even of some that had not yet appeared at the Dom Kino in Moscow. And there were seminars and meetings with interesting people, first-class experts from various fields.

It was at Bolshevo, as a schoolgirl in the eighth grade, that I began doing simultaneous voice-over translations of films in English and French. The interpreters who came with the film would translate Saturday evenings and leave on Sunday morning. But sometimes there would be an additional daytime showing after tea and cakes (those cakes were so good—the whole house smelled of yeast and vanilla). When they asked me to translate, I was nervous and would first watch the film alone. With time I became more emboldened and started translating "live," sometimes making mistakes but trying to save face and keeping people from noticing. It was a good schooling for me. Until I was thirty, I continued translating films on various occasions, and I always enjoyed it.

Another attraction of Bolshevo was the presence of stores and shops. There were many military industrial enterprises in the neighborhood, and they had their own network for shopping

Of course, now these shops would look pathetic compared with what is available today, but in those days Bolshevo shops were special. You could buy imported goods, which in Moscow were available only under the counter.

Nobody would miss an opportunity to get some nice things. I remember Elena Yutkevich, always elegant and flashy, who would proclaim, "I dress only in Paris and in Bolshevo."

That was one of the great amusements in Bolshevo. Showing off the latest purchases and discussing where they came from and what could still be bought. Much later, around 1975, when the comedian Arkady Raikin lived in Bolshevo and I was making a film about him, we got into my car (he was recuperating from a heart attack) and went to all the hot spots. The minute we entered one of my favorite shops, the salespeople froze with their mouths open, speechless. The few shoppers also forgot why they were there, all of them staring at Raikin.

The manager invited us to see the hidden storerooms, which made my head spin with their abundance. Of course, the selection could not be compared to a supermarket in a remote European town or to today's street markets at the Dynamo Stadium in Moscow. But back then, it was a more impressive sight than Harrods and Marks and Spencer combined.

After Father's death, Mother stopped going to Bolshevo—she couldn't bear being there without him. I went once in a while, but it wasn't as pleasant and cheerful as before; everything was deteriorating. Soon a new oasis appeared in the suburbs of Moscow: the House of Movie Veterans in Matveyevskoe. This was also a warm, friendly, and hospitable place. Retired filmmakers lived in one part of the house, and other rooms were offered to temporary guests. Now the film crowd preferred Matveyevskoe to Bolshevo.

Another place that brought me joy was Dom Kino, a special theater for members of the Union of Filmmakers. My parents went there frequently and usually took me with them.

I remember the premiere of *The Cranes Are Flying,* the first Soviet film to win the Golden Palm at the Cannes Festival (1958). What an event! I was sixteen, and I had just decided to start my studies at the VGIK. The film was about two young, beautiful people who were preparing to get married but whose lives were destroyed by World War II. The story was quite ordinary, but we had never seen a film like that before, with universal human emotions: love, betrayal, fidelity despite betrayal, hope despite shattered dreams. It was alive, burning, and true and would have been impossible in the Soviet cinema of the Stalin era. It was a breakthrough into an unknown world, into the sphere of relations that were taboo for the socialist realism which had been stifling film, literature, painting, and music. We lived in a straitjacket world where every button was buttoned and where you could relax only at home, behind closed doors. And suddenly from the screen, life, passion, and fresh air burst into that world. I wept through the whole movie, staring at the screen, and then clapped with the rest of the audience until my hands were hurting. The standing ovation lasted twenty minutes. It was deafening, an outlet for feelings that could no longer be suppressed.

I experienced something similar only once more in my life: in 1987, watching Tengiz Abuladze's *Repentance,* the first film about Soviet totalitarianism, which was groundbreaking. When I came out of the theater and got into my car, I couldn't get hold of myself for a good half hour. The second time I saw it, I wept in the theater. Today you look at the picture and think, "What's there to cry about?" In order to understand, you have to have lived the way we did—stifling the desire to tell the truth, not believing in the possibility that the truth could ever be told out loud.

I think that because of Bolshevo and Dom Kino I could not imagine going into any profession other than filmmaking. I didn't even notice how the cinema captured me.

Those Times

I lived in a very warm and gentle atmosphere of human relations. I was "Daddy's girl." People loved my father, and therefore they loved me.

In the world of cinema, people treat one another in various ways. One encounters envy, hatred, intrigues, and rumors behind one's back—but Father was spared all that. He stood apart from the creative crowd, and even though there must have been squabbles in the technical field as well, he never mentioned them to me. Perhaps nothing like that ever occurred. I remember going with Mother to a birthday party for Father on January 20, 1953, at his research institute. It was a terrible time, the height of the "Doctors' Plot." A group of doctors were accused of planning to assassinate Stalin and the leadership of the party. It was all an anti-Semitic fabrication intended to kindle attacks on Jews throughout Russia.

Yet the auditorium was packed, there was a sea of flowers, and everyone made wonderful speeches about Father. He had not wanted any celebrations at all, probably to keep a low profile. But they didn't listen to him and held the party anyway. Father was worried, and he later said to Mother (they didn't talk in front of me often, but my ears were tuned in all the time): "Once I complete the project I am currently working on, you can expect that they will come after me like they did in 1938."

I remember those words well. Father was heading a project on aerial photography related to the defense of Moscow. The work was being done on Stalin's orders, and it was planned as a five-year project. It was due to be completed in late 1953.

Father was a gentle and kind man who helped many people. He lent money freely and almost never got it back. That taught him nothing—he kept making loans, unwilling to refuse anyone. His students loved him because he was incapable of giving bad grades. There were all sorts of stories about him at VGIK. Once, he was auditing the oral exam of Vladimir Monakhov, who would later become the cameraman on the magnificent and award-winning *Fate of Man*. Father noticed that the student's wristwatch had stopped.

While Monakhov continued answering questions, Father took his watch, opened it, took a tiny screwdriver, made some adjustments, and repaired the timepiece. Father was good at that profession as well. After all, his father had been a watchmaker.

His wit was always appreciated. Some of his clever remarks were widely quoted. He once said about the institute that a constant struggle was going on: before lunch, with hunger, and after lunch, with sleep. Later, his line was repeated when describing any state institution.

Film technology is not the most fascinating of subjects, but students attending his lectures found his presentations interesting and fun. He told a lot of jokes, some of them quite provocative and crude.

I took his course, and I was amazed that he not only could make a boring subject interesting but also could make people love it.

The supportive and loving atmosphere in which I grew up was, in a certain way, harmful as well. I was accustomed to being liked, to being treated well—I assumed that everyone would always want to be nice to me. I never could adapt to hostility at work, to anger or envy. I did not develop a thick skin, which would have allowed me to go on with my work and ignore the fuss around me. All strange behavior toward me or others upset me.

I don't remember much before 1948. But in 1948, even I became aware of the constant anxiety in the area. It all started when my cousin, Uncle Lyolya's son, a boy of sixteen, was arrested. For some reason, he had tried to visit the American embassy. No one knew why. He later explained that his roommate in his Leningrad school had dared him to go to the embassy and ask for a tourist visa. And then he ratted on him. Misha never made it to the embassy—he was arrested and charged with "planning to apply for political asylum." Uncle Lyolya and Aunt Roza turned to Father and asked him to help. Father tried, went somewhere, and returned very upset: "What have I done? Why did I go? It was horrible."

The anti-cosmopolitan (read: anti-Semitic) campaign was in full swing, and the KGB was arresting people left and right. It was impossible to help. My cousin was given a ten-year sentence. My aunt and uncle sent parcels to his jail, and finally, in 1956, after having served eight years, he was released, but he was banned from living in Moscow. He moved to Bezhitsi near Bryansk, got married, and became chief of a department in a foundry. He and his wife had two wonderful boys, now grown of course, with their own children.

I was often sick as a child—measles, chicken pox, scarlet fever. It seemed as if I was always in bed, and I remember the bedside lamp with the green glass shade. That evening in 1948, I was sick in bed. Grandmother was also sick; she was dying of cancer. I remember the evening because my parents were arguing. Mother wanted to go to the funeral of Solomon Mikhoels, the great Jewish actor. And Father said, "Are you crazy? Out of the question!"

"But why?" Mother demanded. "I have to go! I'd never forgive myself."

Father must have realized that Mikhoels's death was no accident. Once a great favorite appointed by Stalin himself to the presidency of the Jewish Anti-fascist Committee, Mikhoels had not yet been accused of being a bourgeois nationalist and an agent of the world Zionist conspiracy, as it was later claimed during the Doctors' Plot, but there was something in the air, a taste of things to come. Father sensed it, but not Mother. She went to the funeral anyway. She met the coffin at the train station when it arrived from Minsk, and then she went to the services.

In December 1952, when the affair of the Jewish doctors began, we were in Bolshevo. The director of the Bolshevo resort was Konstantin Kuzmin, a sturdy bald man. A businesslike gentleman who kept the entire place running smoothly, he was universally respected. I remember that after a radio report exposing the "murderers in white coats" who were planning to kill the beloved leaders of the Soviet people, Kuzmin came over to Father and said, "Look what your people are doing!"

Father was stunned. The two men had been on excellent terms. Father had never expected to hear something like that from Kuzmin.

I remember Father discussing the incident later with Mother: "Just imagine what people are like! Who can you trust?"

Mother later told a story that seems funny now. She liked shopping in consignment stores, where you usually could find better things than in the regular shops. In January or February 1953 she saw a pair of patent leather pumps, just what she'd always wanted. And they were her size. She was about to buy them when she had second thoughts: "What for? They're going to load us into trains and send us to the camps in Kolyma. What could I do with these shoes there?"

I didn't know it then, but the adults understood that the government was collecting petitions from prominent figures in the country, requesting that, in order to protect Jews from the "just wrath" of the Russian people and from possible pogroms, they should be deported to far-off places. In other words, the government was paving the way for its planned deportation of the Jews.

When Mother told me the story about the shoes, she added laughingly, "I'll never forgive myself! Why didn't I buy them?"

Over the years I heard about the public dressing-down of Dziga Vertov and Esther Shub, both famous documentarians. I didn't know exactly what it meant. Only later did I appreciate how humiliating it must have been for such prominent artists to be forced to confess to nonexistent sins. I was particularly moved by the account of Yuri Karavkin, an editor at a documentary studio, of how Vertov had burst into tears like a child. His heart acted up, and they had to call for the ambulance.

The atmosphere became tenser, and even I, a twelve-year-old girl, felt stifled. Then came the news of Stalin's illness, continuous bulletins about his health. On the morning of March 5, I looked out the window and saw red flags with black borders on the wall of the opposite building. I understood what it meant, burst into tears, and ran to Father. It was very early; he was still in bed.

"Papa! Stalin died! How can we go on living now?"

"One bastard less!" my kind and gentle father replied.

I'll never forget those words, but at the time I didn't fully comprehend them. We were all so brainwashed. I went to school and felt immensely proud: as the best student, I was given the great honor of standing under a portrait of Stalin with my arm raised in a Pioneer salute until it cramped.

Things brightened with time, the doctors were released, the trumped-up charges against them declared false. The Khrushchev Thaw had begun.

I Will Be a Camerawoman

I started school in 1948. In my class of more than forty children, I was the only one who had a father. Most families had lost their men in the war. I think there were two other girls who had fathers, but their fathers did not live with them. I felt almost guilty: I had a mother and a father.

Everyone was very poor. We were given one meal at school. We dressed modestly. The first time I wore synthetic stockings was for my graduation. Sometime in the mid-1950s, after Stalin's death, Father began traveling abroad, and he brought back gifts for me. I remember he once gave me beautiful brown shoes when I was fourteen. I never wore them to school—I didn't want to stand out.

At first I went to School N585 for girls, close to our house. There were forty-four girls in my class. Later we were combined with the boys' classes from N9. But it was still boring. Mother made sure that I took lessons in English and French with a tutor at home. My English wasn't bad. I actually enjoyed reading Dickens in the original version. When I turned fourteen, I learned that there was one school in Moscow that specialized in English—School N1. I told Mother, and she found out that the school was in Sokolniki, a remote district in Moscow.

"No way," she said. "It's a long trip. You wouldn't be able to go there every day."

But I dug in my heels, and in the middle of eighth grade in late 1955, I transferred to the special School No. 1. It was a marvelous place. It was a haven for teachers, many with PhDs, who had been fired from various Moscow colleges during the time when "cosmopolites" were persecuted. The standard of the teachers was immeasurably higher than of those in my former school. Consequently, the students were at a higher level as well. Many came from elite families, including both sons of Georgi Malenkov (prime minister in Stalin's government), the son of Konstantin Simonov (a world-famous writer), and many others.

I spent two and half years there. My parents thought that I should become a historian or a philologist. But I knew: I wanted to be a cinematographer. Of course, my surroundings had a lot to do with that decision. Being acquainted with Margarita Pilikhina, a star among cinematographers, and several other women in this profession meant a lot.

I said, "Papa, please buy me a camera. I want to take up photography."

It turned out we had a camera at home. I began filming, but it wasn't very good. After a while I got the hang of it. I began mastering the theory. But then Father panicked and said that I couldn't major in that field. All the women who chose this profession had miserable personal lives, he said. They were all divorced, without husbands or children. It wasn't suitable for women. The more he said "not for women," the more firmly I stood by my decision.

Once when I ran into Pilikhina in Bolshevo, I asked her whether I should go to VGIK or obey my father.

"Don't listen to him," she said. "Go. There isn't a better profession in the world."

Our conversation took place in my father's presence.

"Fine," he said. "Do what you want. But I'll have nothing to do with your decision."

When I passed the entrance exams, Father was out of Moscow. His work required him to go to Czechoslovakia for two months. I think he arranged that trip deliberately so as not to participate in something he didn't approve. I was later told that Alexander Groshev, then director of VGIK, had inquired in the final admission meeting, "By the way, how many children does Goldovsky have?"

"One daughter."

"If he has only one, then let's admit her."

And that's when I got scared. All the other students in my class were men, and they understood technical matters. I'd always had a problem with technology—and they were older then me. Only two had come straight out of high school.

I had to work very hard. We spent the whole first year on photography. Our teacher was Alexander Levitsky, a master of the old school who had started in film back in 1914. His biography was part of the history of Russian and Soviet film. He taught photocomposition and ran us ragged, criticizing and demanding. He was in his eighties, and I was barely seventeen. I was completely in awe, which made it difficult to work with him.

The mentor of our course was Boris Volchek, also a well-known director of photography. I was more comfortable with him. He lived in our building, had studied with Father, and was a friend; he had known me since I was a child.

Other members of the teaching staff were Eduard Tisse, Eisenstein's director of photography and also a friend of our family's; Anatoli Golovnya, the head of the cinematography department; and Alexander Galperin. I often met these professors in my home as well as in the institute. I had immense respect for them, but they did not overwhelm me. The exception was Levitsky. Tall and thin, gray-haired, and with a mustache, he was stern—I can't recall ever seeing him smile—and squeezed every drop of blood, sweat, and tears out of us. I knocked myself out to do something worthy of his expectations, but I was always dissatisfied with the result. He triggered an inferiority complex about my ability to work as a cameraperson.

I spent every spare minute of my first year taking pictures, developing them in the institute's lab—a marvelous place on the first floor—up to my elbows in developer, trying to improve my photos in the print process. I was not among the best photographers in our class. Some were brilliant, like Sasha Steshanov. He was a professional photographer, but he left after the second year because it became clear to him that being a good photographer and being a good cameraman were not the same. Studying together with people like Sasha Steshanov, Valya Makarov, and my friend Igor Belyakov was not easy but inspiring.

I finished the first year with difficulty, even though I did okay in several fields. I was good in humanities, in many technical courses—like theory of photography, developing film, color theory, equipment, and optics—and also in my father's class, "Introduction to Film Technology." The classes were encompassing and very demanding. During the exams in my father's class, he always invited one or two other teachers to attend. He told me, "Remember, I'm not the only one grading you. I don't want people to say, 'Goldovsky is giving his daughter a free ride.'"

I studied hard. My position required it. I couldn't let my father down. I had been accepted into VGIK, one of the most prestigious institutes in the whole country, so I had to do better than the others. I always encouraged other students, wrote crib sheets, and helped my classmates when they came to me for advice. They knew that I would know the answers for sure. I wouldn't say I was a grind, but I was diligent and persistent. That had started back in my English school.

VGIK had outstanding instructors. The courses in film and theater history, art history, literature, directing, visual arts, and screen writing were obligatory. I worked intensely and not without success. The only B I got was in political economy. Although I managed to figure out the political economy of capitalism, the political economy of socialism was out of my league.

Today I look back on VGIK and see not only the knowledge that we students acquired there but also the unique atmosphere and creative milieu that fostered us. We were surrounded by extraordinary people who became masters and even classic figures of Soviet film. Four years ahead of me was Andrei Tarkovsky; Otar Ioseliani, later a prominent director in the USSR and France, majored at the same time in mathematics at Moscow State University and in directing at VGIK. I can't say that we were bosom buddies, but we were and still are very good friends. Once, my son and I were vacationing in Pitsunda, when we met Otar. There were no rooms, and he asked if he could sleep on our balcony. "Fine, why not," I responded.

During his entire stay on our balcony, we laughed nonstop.

Other fellow students from these days who later became the cream of the crop of the Soviet cinema were Andrei Smirnov, Elem Klimov, Andron Konchalovsky, Kira Muratova, Larisa Shepitko, Gena Shpalikov, Natasha Riazantseva, and many others.

Elem Klimov was very handsome, all the girls had crushes on him, including me. In his first year he made *Fiancé*, a wonderful short film as his class assignment. The title was intentionally misspelled as it appears on the back of the film's hero, working at his school desk. There was so much life, ease, humor, and insight in this picture. The two seven-year-old actors, Romeo and Juliet, from an elementary school, were brilliant. I remember the standing ovation we gave this short piece. We all considered Elem a young genius.

Andron Konchalovsky left no doubts about his brilliant future, especially after he made *The Boy and the Dove*. My schoolmate Misha Kozhin was his cameraman.

Larisa Shepitko was one of Alexander Dovzhenko's students. She was luminous and lovely, and I adored her. Gena Shpalikov, a genius writer, was a good friend. Later, in 1974, he committed suicide.

We found inspiration in one another. And the times were full of hope. The Thaw had begun in the mid-1950s when Khrushchev took over after Stalin. I started at the VGIK in 1958 and graduated in 1963.

On the whole, the atmosphere at the institute was alive, creative, and filled with beautiful, talented, and radiant people. The professionalism I acquired at VGIK came from the climate at the institute, from its very air. The great masters set the tone—Mikhail Romm; Grigory Kozintsev, who lived and worked in Leningrad but came to Moscow to teach his class; and Alexander Dovzhenko. They were real icons. There are no more like them.

The summer after my first year, while the boys were in military camp, I went to work as assistant cinematographer on Andrei Tarkovsky's thesis film, *The*

Steamroller and the Violin, and spent almost six months interning for him. That was real schooling—class work and lectures couldn't give that experience.

Vadim Yusov, the cinematographer on the film, ran me ragged. For the first ten days, my only job was loading magazines for the Mitchell camera. It was huge, and I had to unload the film, load the new stock without scratching it, and then carry the magazines from the darkroom in the main building out to the set, all the way on the other side of Mosfilm Studios. They were so heavy!

Then I was entrusted with the Luxmeter, a new and large exposure meter invented by Mosfilm engineer Mikhail Shcheglov. On the second or third day, I dropped it, and it shattered. I realized my life was over; there was nothing more to live for. The next day, I didn't know whether or not to show up for work. Father pushed me out the door. When I arrived on the set, I was given another Luxmeter, and Yusov acted as if nothing had happened.

I was eighteen and the only female in the camera crew. The technicians were the ones who teased me the most: "Hey, girlie, what are you doing here?" I was very offended then. But time has a way of making things right. Soon they accepted my presence.

For the next ten days, I was the focus puller. Then I supervised the processing of the film in the lab. So I got experience in all the phases of film production.

Yusov was a marvelous cinematographer and a great person. He, and not Tarkovsky, was in charge of the shoot. Nowadays, Yusov is a living icon, but back then he had just graduated from the VGIK. *The Steamroller and the Violin* (1960) was his first Mosfilm film experience.

He was always calm and reasonable. He never made quick decisions, but once he made his final decision, everyone had to obey.

Tarkovsky ran around the set, his hair sticking out in all directions. He was always on the verge of hysteria, his mood changing constantly. His wife, Ira, would come to see him, to bring some food and calm him down, but he remained a bundle of nerves. The only one who kept the group going was Yusov. Watching him work, I learned a lot. I understood how much depends on the way the cinematographer behaves during the shoot. He cannot act nervous or confused. If he shows confidence, everyone around will feel confident. Later, I always tried to follow this rule in my own work.

When I first came to VGIK, I attended all the lectures. After a while, many seemed boring and unnecessary. I began paying less attention to social sciences, especially since I had a good grounding from high school. Throughout my years at the VGIK, I often used the class notes I had made during the lectures of my great high school history teacher, Samuil Levin. This way I managed to avoid most classes on Party history at VGIK. Of course, I did go to the seminars and often spoke. I had my high school notes on Lenin's articles, and I knew everything about the overbearing style of Marxist-Leninist demagoguery. I could talk on practically any subject we were supposed to cover. Moreover, almost my entire class used these notes. Eventually, somebody borrowed that thick notebook to prepare himself for joining the Party, but never returned it.

I spent most of my time at the VGIK going from auditorium to auditorium, watching movies. You can't learn film without watching lots and lots of movies. I spent entire days in the screening rooms, absorbing everything—you never know what will stick and work for you later.

I remember watching Robert Flaherty's *Man of Aran* during my first year. That film is still with me. It's a stunning tale about the unbreakable human spirit.

To this day I can picture the icy sea, the silent cliffs, and the faces of the three protagonists—father, mother, and little boy. I think that viewers will find reflections of Flaherty's idea in most of my films, the idea that people can prevail despite all odds.

There were wonderful evenings at the VGIK. Every Friday night, we had a screening. During the period of the Thaw, a flood of new pictures appeared. Each was a revelation. Lev Kulidzhanov and Yakov Segel's *The House I Live In* (1957), Mikhail Kalik's *Man Follows the Sun* (1962), Georgi Danelia and Igor Talankin's *Seryozha* (1960), and Yuli Raizman's *But What If It's Love?* (1962). We were even shown a few movies still "on the shelf" and not permitted for public viewing.

Volchek often invited former students and colleagues to give guest lectures. I'll never forget the time when cinematographer Sergei Urusevsky came to the institute. He showed us his new picture, *I Am Cuba* (1964) and spent two hours answering questions. I don't remember exactly what he said. But I experienced the scope of a creative personality—what it meant to inspire people and infect them with your passion. None of us ever thought about the commercial side of filmmaking. Even now, and perhaps to my detriment, I still don't think about it. What I would be paid and what benefits I would get have never been among my priorities. The most and only important thing is to make the best picture I can. It doesn't matter if I don't succeed with everything; the significant thing is to aim high. At the institute, we were all focused on art; we wanted to serve art. That is what we were taught at the VGIK.

Our instructors often showed foreign films. There were weeks of French, Italian, American, and British films. Since the movies often were shown during the day in other places, such as the Cinematographers' Union, our screenings

had to start at 7 a.m. That meant getting there at 6:45, unless you wanted to sit
on the floor or stand through the whole movie—or even find the doors locked.
I had to get up at 5 a.m. to make it on time. I had to catch the first subway train
and then walk at least thirty minutes to the institute. I knew that I might never
get another chance to see these films. They were all marvelous! They simply
don't make films like that anymore. What delight we took in Fellini, Bergman,
Godard, Truffaut, Kurosawa, Resnais, Pasolini, Forman, and Kramer. You can
enjoy Stanley Kramer's films today—they're living films—but to us then, they
were a revelation.

The spirit of VGIK will be with me forever. The four years flew by. I am eter-
nally grateful to VGIK and its atmosphere, which we soaked up through our
pores.

Of course that era of the Thaw, the late 1950s and early 1960s, was special.
People attended literary evenings to listen to poets. I fortunately lived near
the Museum of Literature. We always had to stand in endless lines to hear the
poetry readings of Yevgeny Yevtushenko and Bella Akhmadulina.

We had quite a few talented people in our cinematography class, such as the
witty and cheerful Nikita Khubov and Misha Belikov from Kharkov, with his
peculiar Ukrainian accent. Misha was the first to tell me about Vladimir Vysot-
sky; he had tapes of the popular bard, and we all soon learned his songs by
heart. Later I also fell in love with the songs of Alexander Galich, another idol
of those times. He often came to Bolshevo with his wife, Anya, and daughter,
Galya, who was a friend of mine.

Today, especially in America, the very existence of film schools is being
questioned. There are so many, some good, some not so good. The tuition is
high, and there are doubts. Is it important to go to film school to master the
profession? Isn't it better to go directly into production and learn your ABCs
by experience on the job?

I believe that this argument is flawed. Merely knowing how to do things is
not enough. You have to fill your lungs with air before you can take off. You
have to live in the film school atmosphere, breathing the same air with people
of various professions and talents and getting a feel for their different worlds.
That pot, into which each person adds his energy and which becomes charged
with the energy of others, is where future professionals are made—not just
professionals but creative personalities, artists. Their formation is impossible
without contact and exchange of creative ideas.

Documentary makers especially need that nourishment. They get it from
life, from their sense of self in that life and from the considerations and conclusions prompted by life. They get it from the people with whom they interact.

Discussion with other people who are close to them in spirit and outlook is very important.

I teach documentary film now. Some of my students take the class to get a taste of what a documentary is; others are committed to become documentary filmmakers for life. My aim is to create a nurturing environment, a small family of peers in which they can be comfortable and free, a microclimate for a group that share opinions, projects, and creative ideas. Naturally, I show them very good and very diverse films. In fact I am intuitively reproducing my experience from VGIK, remembering how it influenced my whole professional life.

In my second year at VGIK, my classmate Igor Belyakov and I made a ten-minute film, *The Birth of Trains*. He suggested the topic: "I was at a train station. It was interesting to see how they couple the cars, how the fire flies out from under the brake shoes. It could become a beautiful film."

We went to take a look. It really was beautiful: watching the workmen put metal brake shoes over the wheels and seeing the brakes in action, showers of sparks flying in all directions. We had to film at night, but thanks to Father's connections, we managed to get battery-powered lights from the Documentary Film Studio, unique pieces of equipment in those days.

It was my first documentary experience. We filmed the men at work. They were putting the trains together, coupling cars, talking among themselves, sometimes swearing, smoking. They were so involved in their work that they paid no attention to us. They seemed not to notice the blinding lights; they were focused on staying alive and not ending up under a car.

We worked for a month nonstop. We would film at night, go to the institute in the morning for the lectures, and then back to filming in the evening. It was hard work. There were a few breaks, of course, but it was rough going. The material was quite effective, especially for an early effort. Volchek watched our film. He said, "The cinematography's not bad."

He was always stingy with praise, and in this instance he was also upset that we were doing a documentary. After all, we were in the feature film department.

My next work was a short feature. But it gave me no pleasure; the huge synchronous film camera kept me from moving around and improvising. Documentary film seemed much livelier. So I was very pleased when Igor and I were given the opportunity to make our diploma film at the Festival of Youth and Students in Helsinki in 1962. We decided that it could be an interesting film. We began preparing. Everyone told us that we were crazy: "Where are you going? You'll just waste film and won't do anything worthwhile. Don't forget, it's your thesis work!"

We were given five thousand meters of film; two handheld 35 mm cameras, each with five magazines; and a reporter's tape recorder—it broke down right after we got to Helsinki. Our lodgings were in some school. We left early in the morning, came back after midnight, using up all of the ten magazines in one single day. We got around on foot, lugging heavy backpacks with the cameras, film, and spare batteries. We didn't have any Finnish marks, and Russian rubles were not convertible. However, meals were provided by our tourist organization.

From one to four in the morning, we had to reload the magazines in the changing bag. It was hell. I was beginning to think that we wouldn't get anywhere. But the events were interesting, and it was an adventure, being abroad in a strange city with people from all over the world.

I started realizing all the charms of direct observation, of unrehearsed, spontaneous life. Everyone was deeply into the festival, singing, dancing, rallying. Then came some young fascists, attempting to break up the festival. Naturally, no one paid any attention to our camera, especially since there were so many of us filming, and even if someone wanted to "act for the camera," there was no way to know which "side" it was on.

What could possibly be better than a smile that is born before your very eyes? A person is talking about something and then smiles, his face becomes radiant, something wonderful is happening to him, and I manage to capture the moment. It's a fantastic thing! This is the joy a documentary filmmaker experiences when catching authentic feelings. I don't know if I would have gone into documentary film if not for that tiny but euphoric experience. I felt the pleasure of communicating with reality, the thrills of grabbing it, stopping it, as if telling the flow of time, "Stop a moment! You are beautiful."

Despite all our difficulties, the material we brought back from Helsinki was good. Igor Khomsky, a friend from the directing department, put it together. I received my diploma. Too bad that every inch of that documentary has disappeared!

I graduated from VGIK. I thought that I would teach and write articles. I doubted that I would work as a cinematographer—I knew all the difficulties of that work. Volchek invited me to stay on at the institute as his assistant. But after giving it some thought, I decided to work at a studio for a while. I had to experience real filmmaking. How else could I teach students?

Where to Next?

In theory, I could have gone to various studios, but only as an assistant. There was no hope of starting out as a cinematographer. There were only five studios in Moscow, all belonging to the state. Two produced features; one, newsreels and documentaries; one, educational films; and one, animations. Not many films were being made at that time. A beginner could get stuck for several years as an assistant. I didn't want to go into feature films; working on *The Steamroller and the Violin* had left me with a taste of boredom. Tarkovsky was only a student then, and I had no idea that I had been working with a great director. Taking the same shot over and over again, all day long, was simply unbearable to me. Documentary film seemed much more lively and interesting, more suited to my personality. But the Documentary Film Studio, which produced newsreels and propaganda films, was a swamp; the films were boring and full of official clichés. And of course they had plenty of their own assistants, who usually took evening courses at the VGIK. I realized that as an outsider, and a woman in particular, I would not be able to get into that male enclave.

Father said, "Go and work in television. They're just starting up. It is always more exciting to be part of something new."

And so I went. It was 1963. Television was part of a government ministry combining radio and television, the most powerful tools of Communist propaganda.

Documentary production was just starting. When I joined the studio, it had only two camerawomen.

The equality of men and women, which had been proclaimed as a great achievement of socialism, never was accepted in everyday life. Everyone was convinced that camerawork was not for women, and that prejudice was impossible to overcome. The cameramen treated their few female colleagues with mistrust at best.

All of the cameramen had been Father's students, VGIK graduates, which did not keep them from being not only hostile toward me but sometimes even aggressively intimidating.

"Camerawoman? A female? She won't be able to handle it!" they'd say.

Even those who never said a nasty word to me had a message in their eyes: "Why are you pushing your way into our territory? What do you want?"

I began as assistant to Nikolai Minin. He was a good man but a rather mediocre cameraman. The only thing I learned from him was to catch his small 16 mm Arriflex. When he finished shooting, for some reason he simply threw it to me. After four months, I realized that the only way to get out of being an assistant for the rest of my life was to go on location somewhere no one else wanted to cover.

Just about that time, Volodya Azarin, a director, was planning to make a film in the Far North, on the Kola Peninsula, where a lot of mines and pits were located. Not exactly a resort.

I went. I did not try to create anything, only to observe what people did and how they lived. I went 480 meters down, in the elevators with the miners. Of course, the miners had no time for me. Water was gushing from everywhere, and I, dressed in oilskins, filmed them struggling with the dark, the cold, the pouring water, and the coal they had to hack out of the face of the mountain.

I worked with an East German, 16 mm nonsynchronous, semiprofessional, semi-amateur Pentaflex camera, which had a strange round motor attached. I used the motor as a handle. The technique did not differ much from the familiar 35 mm Soviet-produced Konvas, but this camera was lighter, allowed us to travel with a smaller crew, and, most important, was less obtrusive to the people we were filming.

I shot the picture. Volodya edited it, and, strangely enough, *Literaturnaya Gazeta,* one of the most prominent newspapers, reviewed it. The reviewer even commented kindly on the cinematography. Some of my colleagues just couldn't forgive that. My first job, and it was being praised by the press!

Fortunately, I went on maternity leave soon afterward and gave birth to my son, Seryozha. When he was five months old, I went back to work. By then, I had been given an operator's rating, which gave me the legal right to work as a cinematographer.

In looking back on my life in television, I see how varied it was. Not everything was great. I was a cinematographer and had to film what I was assigned. Selecting material, especially in the beginning, was impossible. With time, I learned how to find acceptable compromises. I understood that one can easily combine the pleasant with the useful. The useful was the daily newsreel; the pleasant was making films. And thus, combining both, I spent twenty-five years in television.

The first television studio in the USSR was on Shabolovka Street, not far from my house. It was very much like a film studio, but on a lower standard. Not many professionals had graduated from VGIK. A lot of people were just passing through. Nevertheless, I recall those days as lively and creative. That is probably the case for anyone starting out. When we later moved to Ostankino, a huge thirteen-story complex that to me looked like a palace—everything spanking new and with all the latest equipment—work became even more interesting. We knew, of course, that there were some problems. The building had not passed the health code. There were rumors that the levels of radiation were too high, with no explanation of what type of radiation it might be. But in good Soviet tradition nobody paid any attention. People worked day in and day out. Life was very interesting and intense.

At first, practically the only story I had to cover was the opening of yet another cafeteria.

The television chiefs were not about to give a novice cameraperson, and especially a woman, anything more responsible to film. I also covered endless openings of art shows, each one worse than the next, all filled with socialist realist optimism. I also did conferences and meetings of representatives of the fraternal socialist states at the House of Friendship, dealing with the people's struggle against reactionaries and the forces of imperialism.

Every story was shot the same way: establishing wide shots, medium shots, and close-ups of the room, the speakers, and the audience. There wasn't much creativity in that, but I did get to arrange the lights to give depth to the space and illuminate the objects.

Our colleagues from documentary film laughed at us, for they were certain that they were doing real documentary work and we were merely degrading their lofty profession. But it soon became evident that it was just the other way around. The weekly show *News of the Day*, produced by the Documentary Film Studio, was useless and unwanted. We gave the real news every night on *The Latest News*, while the movie newsreels shot on 35 mm for theatrical distribution were a couple of weeks out of date. They had to rename their product to *Chronicle of Our Days*, but the audiences didn't want to watch it; they had become used to getting the news on television the day it happened. The 1960s saw the start of a new documentary coverage of news and opinions. I was lucky. I started my career in the beginning of the TV era, and in the Soviet Union my professional growth coincided with the development of television. I was in the right place at the right time.

Eventually I was given more responsibility to cover official stories. We used to call them "parquet floor" stories. I filmed meetings in high offices, the arrival of VIPs from foreign lands, government delegations, and Kremlin receptions. Once, when we filmed Brezhnev, he graciously shook my hand. Sometimes Galina Monglovskaya was filming events for the Documentary Film Studio. She was a beautiful woman, and Brezhnev always kissed her hand.

Doing a story on big official events, say, a session of the Supreme Soviet or a Party congress, had special quirks. All general shots had to be done in the first fifteen to twenty minutes. After that, participants would doze peacefully, which our millions of viewers were not supposed to see. The delegates slept because their average age was way over sixty, and the sessions were extremely boring. I had to get all the close-ups in the first few minutes—interesting faces, eyes filled with wisdom and sparkle. It was very hard to make such shots. If you didn't get them right away, you had to wait until after the lunch break when the delegates returned cheerful and ready to stay awake for at least the next quarter of an hour.

I filmed four Party congresses. We were always given pep talks by some official, telling us what important work we were doing and how to do it on an even higher ideological and artistic level. In response, we were filled with a sense of importance and responsibility.

When we covered the arrivals of VIP guests at the airport, we had to get there two hours early or else we wouldn't be able to get in at all. The police set up roadblocks, and police cars buzzed around with sirens and blinking lights, escorting official cars with banners fluttering. We took up our positions. Three camera operators would be assigned, each in a predetermined location. We were not allowed to move around on the tarmac or in the arrivals area. We were supervised by the head of the Ninth Department of the KGB, which was responsible for the press. He was a rather amusing-looking but dangerous man named Comrade Kurnosov. Anyone who broke the rules would not be allowed to film official occasions and subsequently was demoted for an unspecified time.

The State Committee for Television and Radio treated its employees ruthlessly. It was a microcosm of the totalitarian system, with an exact copy of its hierarchy. The ordinary cameraman was subordinated to the chief cameraman, the chief cameraman to the department chief, the department chief to the studio director, and so on. At the top of the pyramid was a minister who reported to the big bosses from the ideological department of the Central Committee of the Communist Party. They in turn, reported to Mikhail Suslov, the never-changing ideology secretary of the Party, the dreaded enforcer of the will of the Party and of the government. The most insignificant "mistake" was punished swiftly and cruelly. I remember when, due to an assistant's error, one of our leading cameramen used the same film cassette for two stories: once for a dog show, and the second time for the arrival of Premier Alexei Kosygin at the airport. The two events were superimposed. The cameraman was immediately charged with anti-Soviet activity.

There's another event I still recall with horror. I was filming Semyon Tsvigun, deputy to KGB chief Yuri Andropov. I was using color film. My assistant had loaded the cassette with daylight film without telling me, and I set the exposure for artificial light. Since the color temperature is different, Tsvigun came out blue like a corpse. The national *Vremya* newscast began at 9 p.m. Five minutes before the show, I got a call. Screams and shouts: "Are you nuts? Why is your Tsvigun blue? This is anti-Soviet behavior!"

I spent a sleepless night, expecting terrible repercussions. I could be fired. I rushed to the studio at nine in the morning. I was expecting to be chewed out by Deputy Minister Georgi Mamedov. I wasn't called in. There were more important issues at hand. That day our troops invaded Afghanistan.

Another time, we were covering the arrival of French president Valéry Giscard D'Estaing. I was again filming for *Vremya,* the main national news show, and two of my colleagues from the Foreign Service were supposed to put together footage for the foreign television companies. I got back to Ostankino and left my camera, certain that my assistant would unload it. The assistant did not. I got a call at 8:45 that evening.

"Where is the material?"

"It should be in the lab."

"There's no material in the lab."

I quickly came up with a solution: "Use the footage they have prepared for the foreign newscasts, and replace it with my material tomorrow. No one needs their stuff tonight."

They followed my advice. Meanwhile I rushed to the studio and found the material in my camera. I got off the hook that time as well, but I was afraid that my luck wouldn't hold forever. We were in constant fear—and with some good reason. Several of our colleagues were always in trouble, stepping on hidden mines.

For all that, and in spite of all that hustle, it was rewarding to work in the news; it was an excellent training ground, a form of exercise. The story I had to film daily required mastery of the profession. We had to get the highlights of an event, cover it in real time, and usually tell the story within forty to ninety seconds. This challenge was interesting from a creative point of view, and it called for speed and good reactions; we had to build each shot neatly, so that it included all the main elements. A shot is like a word in a sentence; you can't use the wrong word.

We worked diligently. We made tests, which no one working with video does anymore. Even when we covered a very simple story, we went beforehand to check the location to see if lights would be needed, how much cable would be required, whether a generator would be necessary. The most ordinary gallery opening could take five or six hours to cover. The lights for each shot had to be carefully arranged. Shadows in the background had to be avoided—the skill of a cameraperson can be judged from the number of shadows behind the subject. If a sculpture was inappropriately placed, we did not hesitate to turn it. Some shots were staged. We would ask people to walk up to the paintings, look at them, and pretend to be talking about them.

In those days, the cameraperson had to be creative, as we had been taught at the VGIK. People don't have that sense of creativity anymore—only documentarians from the old school exercise their craft the way it was taught in those days. Today's newsreel camera people run around with their Betacams as if they were using a watering can. The actual process of filming has become so simple that only the most elementary technical knowledge is necessary.

Today the cameraperson shoots the story and rushes to the next assignment, in order to make more money. In our time we would go back to the studio after each filming. A screening room would be waiting, and we would review, discuss, and evaluate our work. This, of course, was part of our responsibility and obligation.

For me, it was very important to work on daily stories because it allowed me to keep a camera with me at all times. All the equipment, as well as the material and facilities, belonged to the studio. A private citizen simply could not buy anything like it on the open market.

In the system of total state control, there was one positive aspect: we never worried about financing. Not only did we receive a monthly salary, quite respectable for the times, but we were also provided with all the material we needed in our work. The government was always generous in supporting its ideological machine. Back then, we considered this to be normal. This was the Soviet system, and we did not know any other.

Such things have changed in Russia now and have started to resemble what has almost always been the practice in the West. Today's Russian filmmakers have to spend more time on finding the funding for a film than on making it. Many interesting ideas never see the light of day.

Lessons of Television

Pre-television documentary films consisted of images, music, and narrative text (titles in silent film). Reenactments and staging were just about the only way to film people. The 35 mm technology was too bulky, heavy, and immobile. By the mid-1960s we started using 16 mm cameras. I remember my pleasure when I held the small Arriflex for the first time. It was like a toy, weighing only 2.2 kilograms (about 5 pounds). It was easy to work with—we could run with it, climb the highest spots, and film without a tripod in a moving car. The very first day I got my hands on the camera, I climbed onto the hood of a Volga sedan and made a marvelous traveling shot through the neighborhood. I watched that sequence many times on the editing table and was always impressed by the smoothness of motion. It looked as it had been made with a dolly.

But even more important, we could film and record synchronous sound with that camera. The camera itself was noisy. That wasn't an obstacle outdoors, but indoors the camera had to be muffled. We would use a big cassette for ten minutes of filming, then put the camera in a blimp, then put it on a tripod and connect a battery; another cable joined the camera with the tape recorder. This complex construction weighed around 70 kilograms (about 150 pounds), but at least we could do an interview with sync sound.

It seems ridiculous now when I recall how long it took to make the necessary preparations, getting the lights ready and setting up the camera on the tripod. We would place the subject in front of the camera and say, "Please pay no attention to us. Make believe we're not here and speak calmly. Just say what you want to say."

Then we would clap our hands in front of the subject's face (instead of a clapper), to synchronize film and audio in editing, and the person would start speaking, pretending not to know we were filming. The interview was usually shot three times: once in a close-up, another in a medium shot, and the third in a wide shot. This was done to allow smooth editing. These interviews would seem horrible today, forced, stiff, lacking natural expression. Of course, in those days it was an achievement when a person could speak his or her own words and not read a prepared text, as it was done before.

With the appearance of portable synchronous film cameras, the entire world turned into a set. The need for live reporting grew organically from the very nature of television. As a consequence the documentary genres started to develop swiftly in the mid-1960s. This was happening in the United States, in Europe, and in the Soviet Union.

In 1968 a new studio called Ekran emerged as a special division within the State Committee for Television and Radio. Ekran included four separate units —for narrative, musical, animation, and documentary films. The documentary unit very quickly became the largest producer of documentary films in the Soviet Union. Ekran Studio hired young, talented directors, scriptwriters, and cinematographers, all graduates of VGIK. Several outstanding directors from the provinces were also invited to join Ekran. This invitation was something special in itself. In those days it was almost impossible to get permission to live and work in Moscow if you didn't already live in the city, but Ekran was able to get permits for its employees. The studio hired the cream of the crop; rapid enhancement of documentary films was the most important goal of Ekran.

Thirty-year-old Viktor Lisakovich became the artistic director of the studio. The wonderful cinematographer Sergei Medynsky became chief cameraman. He and a few of his colleagues came from the Documentary Film Studio, realizing that television was going to be the place of the future. All the camera people who had worked on television before 1968 were automatically transferred to Ekran. And so I ended up there as well.

Father was right: it's great to be in at the beginning of any undertaking. That was the case in television when I started there; it was the first day of creation. There was a lot of work, everybody was enthused, and the atmosphere was friendly and creative.

But those days were not without clouds. The period of the Thaw was coming to an end, heralding a long time of stagnation. Russian tanks rolled into Czechoslovakia in September 1968, the war started in Afghanistan, we had problems with Poland, and other bleak events clouded the sky. However, everyone lives his or her own life, and everyone tries to find something good in it. I'm not idealizing Soviet television, but I had a great time working there.

Being a cinematographer, I had many opportunities and could make documentaries, as well as news reports and television programs for various departments, such as literary drama, youth, and popular science.

No other profession would have allowed me to travel as much as I did when I was working as a cameraperson. I was in the North of Russia, in the Far East, in all fifteen republics of the USSR, and even in Antarctica. I was in villages and tiny towns—I filmed everywhere. I met the most diverse people, which gave me a good sense of the country and an understanding of the real problems of real life.

At school and even at the institute I was painfully shy. It was hard for me to talk to people, to start a conversation. I spent months going over what I had said to people and always had doubts afterward. I was overly sensitive and self-critical. However, my professional life changed my personality. Working in television meant dealing with all kinds of people, from farmworkers to academicians and government officials.

I became more sociable. I forced myself to change my personality as my work demanded. It wasn't easy, and it wasn't instantaneous. But gradually, step by step and year after year, I grew different, and even I could see the difference. Calling someone, introducing myself, making contact, talking to strangers and getting them to respond with sincerity and frankness—everything that had been a problem was now so easy that I marveled at the change in me. And if I did have misgivings, they would not be over trifles but to the point: Is the film working or not? Am I headed in the right direction?

The rhythm of my life changed too. I can't say that I was sluggish as a teenager, but I preferred to sit and read and take care of my own things rather than work too hard on the job. But as I became more involved professionally, my obligations started to take over. In the beginning I was a little lazy. Who wants to be out in the freezing cold? I had to protect the camera from snow when the car got stuck in snowdrifts, and I had to drag all the stuff two kilometers through the woods. It was hard even with an assistant. Sometimes, stuck in the mud and the slush, I'd think, "God! Am I going to be doing this all my life?" But gradually there came a sense of satisfaction from the smallest trifles of work—a nicely framed shot, an interesting moment captured, a ray of light falling just as I wanted it. Not to mention the rare joy that came from filming details that I couldn't even notice without a camera. The camera is a sensitive organ that sees and captures many things. It makes me more observant.

In the end the profession turned me into an absolute workaholic, a person totally consumed by her work, unable to find comparable satisfaction anywhere else. I've been like that my whole life. I sometimes think, "Well, isn't it time to stop? Why do I keep filming? How much can one do? It's time to live . . ." But then it turns out that I am truly alive when I'm with my camera. Without it, I'm bored.

Teaching

One day I was in Leningrad, filming for the literary-drama department. We were at some factory, and a man came in. My editor saw him and got very agitated. "Oh, that's my chief!" he said.

Since the man wasn't my chief, I was a lot less worried. He watched us work and then came over and introduced himself. That's how I met Enver Bagirov, a meeting that had a profound influence on my life.

He called soon afterward. "I have an idea," he said. "Would you like to work with me on a picture?"

Working with a smart person is always a gift—and a rare one during my early years in television.

"Of course I would. What's the picture?" I asked.

"I think it would be interesting to do a movie about Smirnov."

The writer Sergei Smirnov was one of the most famous television personalities of the time. Not only was he a talented writer, but his stories on-screen about World War II revealed its horrible truth to millions of viewers. He spoke about heroic things in a very unheroic manner. He talked about ordinary human lives, the unrecognized heroes of the war, many of whom became known thanks to him and belatedly received their just rewards.

The marvelous film *Katyusha,* directed by Viktor Lisakovich, my VGIK classmate, had put Smirnov on the map. The idea of doing a film about him was intriguing.

I met with Bagirov. He suggested an approach that our television had not yet mastered: "Let's build the whole picture on interviews. Smirnov will not speak; others will talk about him. During the next anniversary celebration of the defense of the fortress in Brest, we'll go and talk to veterans and record their accounts."

As an example, he showed me an Italian movie about Fellini. It was an attempt to create a portrait of the great director through interviews of people who knew him well. The movie had not yet been shown in the Soviet Union, but Bagirov had seen a copy and wanted to do something like it.

I don't remember the details of our work back in 1966. But I remember my constant state of euphoria. Everything we filmed was living, immediate reality. We selected people by carefully looking for exceptional character, facial expression, and manner of speech. We wanted not only to give the viewers information but also to introduce them to unusual people who could relate the extraordinary personality of the writer. We knew where we were heading, but we did not know what each person would say, nor did we want to. We preferred spontaneity and sincerity. In addition to the defenders of Brest, we interviewed others who knew Smirnov—writers, close friends, his wife. The mosaic of interviews created the portrait of Smirnov.

We worked enthusiastically, completed the full-length film quickly, and watched its broadcast. Unfortunately, no copy remains. It simply vanished like so many other TV programs. I was pleased with this work, not so much with the finished film but more with having participated in the creation of a then-new genre of documentary film portrait.

The meeting with Bagirov turned out to be more significant then merely a working relation. He was put in charge of the Department of Television Journalism at Moscow State University. He decided to bring in new teachers, to add some fresh ideas. He knew of course that I was a graduate of VGIK and interested in the theory and history of documentary film. Consequently, he offered me a position in his department, which I accepted. At that time I already had had some experience from teaching at the VGIK extension program.

I must confess that my teaching experience at VGIK had been neither pleasant nor successful. I didn't really fit in with the staff. They treated me as a child, and, after all, I was only twenty-two! Most of them were my former teachers, who had been very kind to me when I was a student but later had trouble considering me an equal. They kept telling me how to behave, what to do and what not to do, what to say to the students and what not to say. What they said wasn't in the form of advice but more as directives. Then there was the exhausting system of administrative paperwork, endless and unnecessary—that was a drag. I had pictured teaching differently.

My experience at Moscow State University was much more rewarding. When I started, most of my students were older than I. Many were working part-time in television, and some knew me from there.

I tried to explain to my students the essence and importance of my profession. I showed them film clips, brought in my colleagues from Mosfilm and Ekran to lecture, told them amusing stories from my work. I wrote lecture outlines and created several courses. I really got into teaching and convinced Bagirov—which wasn't very hard, because he was always open to new ideas—that students of journalism should know not only how to write but also how to make films. They had to understand what could be done with a camera and lights, how to film people, and how to put a story together.

"What do you need for that?" he asked.

"We need to buy four or five of the cheapest, simplest cameras."

It was 1968. There were no video cameras then, of course. We bought a few Krasnogorsk amateur cameras and Soviet-made reversal film, first black-and-white and then color. The cameras were primitive, without synchronous sound, and we didn't have lights. The selection of suitable topics was therefore limited. But that did not keep the students from discovering their talent. They always came in with something new. Every class brought me joy.

I remember when Tanya Alexandrova (with whom I would make a film about Anastasia Tsvetayeva some fifteen years later) created a story about a friend's pet monkey. It was filmed so well! Fresh, radiant, human, tender. That monkey jumped around the apartment in such an amusing way. Zhenya Khmelev did a film about Mikhail Bulgakov. Sasha Politkovsky, who was interested in karate, made a beautiful movie, *Landscape under Snow*. I think it was one of the best works he has ever done. Kolya Tarasov went to Borovsk and brought back a nice and gentle fifteen-minute film about the town and its inhabitants.

Some students chose to make thesis films, acting not only as writers but also as directors and cinematographers. This sort of undertaking was always met with resistance by the department, even though the instructors were experienced and well-meaning. They simply believed that filmmaking should be taught at the VGIK and not at Moscow State University. To them, a journalist's job was writing. But many students wanted to expand their knowledge and learn how to work as filming journalists. Their desire to create films as part of their thesis was very strong. Every year at least four students out of maybe eighteen made a film for their graduation. It was difficult for me to prove that filmmaking was just as important as preparing a theoretical paper on "The Role of Interviews in Television Journalism" or "Television Reporting: Theory and Practice." Bagirov, however, supported me and permitted me to teach several courses that interested me.

Even though teaching was never my main and only occupation, I did not consider it secondary. I gave it all the energy and attention I could, and I spent a lot of time with students. But I could teach only part-time, no more than two or three times a week, either in the evening or early in the morning. The rest of the time I worked at the studio. And that's how I spent my whole life, combining filmmaking with teaching. They were like connected vessels. Making films fed my teaching, and the work with students was a stimulus to my filmmaking.

When I started at Moscow State, I had no idea that I would stay there almost thirty years. I left in 1995, when I was offered a professorship at the School of Theater, Film, and Television at UCLA—the University of California in Los Angeles.

The Weavers

When I started out, documentary film could hardly be called "documentary." Almost all of it was staged. It was practically impossible to work differently with the existing equipment. But in the mid-1960s, things started to change.

Pavel Kogan and Petr Mostovoy made *Look at the Face,* in which a hidden camera was placed in a cardboard structure to watch the real emotions of people as they were looking at the *Litta Madonna* in the Hermitage. Borya Galanter, whose *Shagovik* was primarily staged, did some direct observations with his camera. The film *Katyusha,* by Lisakovich, made us realize how impressive an ordinary human face can be when everything is real—not staged, not set up, not rehearsed.

But in spite of a few successful attempts, documentary film, limited by the awkwardness of 35 mm technology, did not overcome the use of staging. It was the introduction of the 16 mm equipment in television that provided the opportunity to change all that.

For filming *The Weavers,* the first feature-length film I made for Ekran, I used a new 16 mm French Éclair synchronous camera, one of the first to arrive at the studio. The camera weighed only about twelve kilograms or so (about twenty-five pounds), which allowed us to work without a tripod when so required. It had a 12—120 mm zoom lens, so we could shoot close-ups from a long distance, thus not distracting people during their conversations. This method was already popular in America, where they called it "direct cinema"; in Russia we referred to it as "observational style."

The screenplay, with the working title *Calico Town,* was by a young writer, Venya Gorokhov. It described the fast turnover of labor in small textile towns in central Russia. In these places the whole workforce often moves from place to place without settling down. Girls come from villages and then try to leave the smaller towns for bigger cities. The topic was purely social—about labor —but it gave us the opportunity to reveal life as it was lived in the Russian heartland.

I spent six months in the factory dormitory, sharing a room with two workers, the central characters of our film. The food was bad. The cafeteria served only boiled potatoes, garlic, and potato salad—nothing more. On the entire floor, we only had one toilet and one shower. There was no place to go to in town. Moscow was an eight-hour bus ride away. My little son and my husband were in Moscow, and of course I wanted to be with them, but that was impossible; I had to stay on location the whole time. And I was sick a lot during that period. Yet those six months were joyous and creative for me. I was following my characters in their everyday life, capturing events and happenings in their relationships. I felt euphoric when watching real life, being in the thick of things; therein lies the pleasure of shooting a documentary with the observational method.

I am very grateful to Nikita Khubov, who had asked me to work on the film. We had studied together in the cinematography department at VGIK. Later he made his directorial debut in Belorussia with *Frank Discussion,* a story about young people. The film was considered too revealing in those days, and he went through a lot of hassles before he got it done. He returned to Moscow just when Ekran was being formed. For his first film there, he chose a screenplay by Gorokhov. Khubov asked me to participate because the movie needed a female cinematographer who could live in the dorms and be with the characters all the time. We also got Zhanna Gistseva, a female sound technician, and Alla Zaitseva, one of my students from the journalism school, as location scout. We sent her to Furmanov, a town in Ivanovskaya Oblast, three hundred kilometers from Moscow, where a small textile factory was operating. Her cover story for making inquiries without revealing that we were going to film in that place was that she had to gather material for writing her thesis. In fact, she later used her story about the making of this film in her thesis. She went there two months ahead of us, met the girls in the dorms and the factory directors, and identified everyone who could be of interest for our film. By the time we arrived, we had all the information we needed.

Alla found twelve girls, from whom we selected the seven most striking ones, each very different from the others. We had to find out where they came from, what their families were like, what had brought them to Furmanov, what dreams and aspirations they had, what they thought of their co-workers, how they looked at their life now, and what they were expecting of the future.

I filmed a fabulous sequence with a girl named Luba while she cooked *lobio,* a Georgian bean dish, in the dorm and talked about her trip to Georgia, where she had a boyfriend.

He had told her, "Stay with me here! Marry me! I will love you forever—we will have children. I'll teach you to cook real Georgian dishes."

"No, no!" she had replied. "I have to go home, I can't live away from my place."

But he kept repeating, "Stay here! Look at our delicious fruits. You just go out in the garden and pick an orange or a peach. It's all yours."

Of course, these were fantasies. She had never been to Georgia, and she didn't have a boyfriend. Unexpected questions confused her, but she continued making up her stories. She didn't want to give up her illusions.

Another girl had a boyfriend in the army. She had waited for his return, and when he came back, she realized that she didn't love him anymore.

Each girl had her own story, and all of the stories were very sad. The dorm had stupid supervisors, and the factory had indifferent bosses and Komsomol leaders who made sure that no one got out of line.

The most colorful girl was Zoya Frolova, known throughout Furmanov as a talented and extraordinary person who stood out from her surroundings. She had grown up in an uneducated family, she had had no opportunities to continue her education after high school, and she certainly didn't fit into her limited provincial world. She expressed her fiery personality by getting involved in big scandals; she was the leader of the local hooligans and spread panic in this quiet town. Then she married Sasha, a bus driver. They had a whirlwind romance, and she got pregnant. Sasha's family was old-fashioned, and so was he. If there was a baby on the way, they had to get married. He forced Zoya, who hadn't wanted to get married.

Zoya kept leaving Sasha, and again and again she went back to him. She didn't want to live in a family where the in-laws hated her and life was dull and dreary, with the same routine day in and day out—eating, drinking, taking care of the baby.

We filmed Zoya and Sasha together at the registry office. Then we filmed Sasha alone, when he told us that he had married Zoya only because of the baby. Then we had an interview with Zoya, who said that she had married Sasha for the same reason—the baby. We also interviewed the chief clerk of the registry. She had been smiling when she put the ring on Zoya's finger, congratulating the couple and wishing them a wonderful future. Fifteen minutes later, she spoke angrily into the camera: "A fine bride! She's got a belly, in her eighth month. Everyone knows what she is. The poor boy! From such a good family, an honest Soviet worker. How did he ever get trapped like that? It's not going to last long."

Nikita edited all these scenes into a single, rather horrifying episode. Every little detail that came under the camera's gaze gave evidence of the gray, repulsive life of the town. We didn't emphasize the grayness; it was evident by itself. We showed the traditions of the town and the face of Soviet provincial life.

In those years, we were not allowed to show any negative side of life in the USSR. That scene alone would have shelved any film. But I was also bothered by an ethical issue: all those girls who told us about their problems usually had no idea that they were being filmed. And they talked about very intimate things. I must say that the euphoria of filming "life unawares," to use Vertov's term, was so powerful and the joy at being able to pick up the camera and record the very birth of a feeling, thought, or action was so great that I tried to stifle my frequent doubts and the embarrassment of invading people's privacy.

Once, Alla informed us that Zoya had come to her very depressed and anxious and said that something terrible had happened that she wanted to share. Alla thought that this could be of interest for our film. She pretended to be busy so that we would have time to prepare. After some hard discussions we decided to film the conversation between the two girls with a hidden camera.

Through new acquaintances in Furmanov, we had found an apartment with a window between the kitchen and the living room. The owner allowed us to use her place for filming. We put the camera in the kitchen and disguised it as much as possible. At first I had planned to film through the glass window, but then I changed my mind. I needed a clear opening to get a sharp image. And had someone looked very carefully through the window, the reflection of the lens could have been detected. We disguised the microphone in an ashtray, draped the windows, and put bright bulbs in the room lamps to get a decent exposure. The next morning, Alla and Zoya showed up. (Alla had told her the apartment belonged to relatives.) They munched on sandwiches and cheap wine, while I was in the kitchen filming, wearing earphones. We got about forty minutes of an astonishing conversation. Zoya opened up completely and explained why she couldn't stand being with Sasha.

"I can't stand this boring life anymore." She was looking for great passion and exciting adventures. Neither Sasha nor the town could offer that. It was too bleak. She had decided to leave him. She was rebelling against the boredom of her life.

When Zoya had told Sasha that she would be leaving him, he had replied, "You can get out, but I won't give you the child."

Zoya told all this to Alla, weeping into her wine. I filmed from the kitchen.

It seemed like the usual collection of marital woes. But Zoya was really desperate. She had already bought acetic acid to poison herself. (Looking back at this extraordinary shoot, I see at least one positive aspect: Alla managed to talk Zoya out of committing suicide.)

As they were talking, Zoya glanced at the window and yelled. "Oh, what's that? Is that a camera?"

My hair practically turned white. If Zoya realized we were filming her, she could easily have asked her friends to harass us. But Alla stayed calm. "You mean that? That's my grandfather's camera. He enjoys photography. Don't pay attention."

I remember returning from this adventure. I was very worried. Nikita was waiting for us in the hotel, pacing nervously.

"How did it go?" he asked.

"You know, I think we went too far," I replied.

When we watched the material, we realized that we had. To make public that kind of spiritual nakedness was ethically unacceptable.

When I had first read Gorokhov's screenplay, I had said, "This is going to be very depressing."

Nikita had replied, "You have to get used to the idea that the film might be banned or you might be fired. Always consider first what you may be getting into. Give it a lot of thought beforehand."

"Come on. What do you mean?"

"I'm serious," he said.

Nikita knew from the start that this was a risky project. He was five years older than me and had much more experience, having faced problems with the film authorities in Belorussia. I was young and lighthearted and, thank God, blissfully unaware of what could happen. Now I'm grateful that I had this experience early in my career.

This was still the time of the Thaw, and we were inexperienced fools. We really had to wise up quickly.

Our *Weavers* was destined to remain on the shelf, precisely because we showed too much of real life and presented too many true stories. Our bosses wanted us to show high ideals on the screen, the glorification of the Komsomol, and instead our heroes wanted to get married and complained that they had no friends, nothing to eat, and nothing to do. Life in that town appeared boring, hard, and lonely.

We began shooting the picture in June 1968 and finished in December. By then, Soviet tanks had invaded Prague. The atmosphere in the country and, of course, in television changed. A new ideological clampdown began. This back-and-forth, the freeze and the thaw, came in waves during the Soviet period. The leadership would ease up on the reins and then pull back again.

Nikita had planned to finish editing by June 1969. Ekran didn't let him. The bosses at Ekran were scared, and they put the film on the shelf. A few months later, they destroyed it. Fortunately, Nikita and I had made a copy, so thirty minutes of fascinating material has been saved. But Nikita Khubov was fired.

Our aim had not been to humiliate our protagonists. On the contrary! We tried to show that each of our heroines, despite her surroundings, had something radiant inside, that despite the filth and nastiness a person could and should live with dignity. I feel a special tenderness for *Weavers,* for it was a great milestone in my professional life. It taught me love for real life. I still think that this was the most interesting material I have ever filmed. I think that if Ekran had allowed us to complete the picture, it would have been outstanding. I felt very bitter then and still feel bitter about this film. But in any negative experience one can find something positive. For me it confirmed that nothing interests me more than filming ordinary people. They usually live their normal lives and pay no attention to the camera. They are sincere and down-to-earth. And as a cinematographer, I can live with them the way I am accustomed to live, making the kind of films that satisfy my heart and soul.

I learned one more very important thing from working on *Weavers.* Formally, I was the cameraperson. But in fact the observational style changed the very nature of documentary work and the interrelationships among professions as they had developed over many years. As the cameraperson, I was now responsible for more than creating the visual image. Often I had to make independent decisions, without the director, following the development of the live action. I had to resolve problems that were usually within the competence of the screenwriter and the editor. They started to become mine.

Working on *Weavers,* I sensed that I could be more than a cameraperson. Honestly, that thought scared me at first. I hadn't formally studied directing or editing. Second, I realized how much more serious the level of responsibility was. The best evidence of that was that the director of *Weavers* was fired, while the cinematographer had been chewed out but kept on. Third, even though I had enjoyed the sweetness of the observational style, I saw that it was much harder working that way than in the usual staged filmmaking. Screenplays became pointless, because it was impossible to carry out what the screenplays called for. Life unfolds unpredictably, following its own spontaneous logic, and if you follow it, you have to depart from the scenario. It is as enchanting as it is risky, because the finale cannot be predicted.

I was not prepared for that kind of turn in my life then. All I wanted was to continue doing what I was doing. Filming life as it is. Remaining a cameraperson.

My First Film Portrait

In the late 1960s the whole world was excited by Dr. Christiaan Barnard's heart transplant surgery. A new era had begun, and it looked as if humankind had conquered death. In the USSR, similar experiments were headed by Professor Alexander Vishnevsky. So when my old VGIK classmate Igor Khomsky suggested making a film with him about a heart transplant that was to take place soon at the Military Medical Academy in Leningrad, I agreed instantly. One of my reasons was that my father had grave cardiac problems. What if the incurable could be cured?

The next day, Igor and I showed up at the A. V. Vishnevsky Institute of Surgery to meet its director, Vishnevsky himself. From the start, our conversation was not hopeful. Vishnevsky refused our request to film a heart transplant. He didn't consider the operation to be perfected, and he doubted it would be successful. Such an operation had to be prepared and tested before it could be made public, he said. We did our best to persuade him; we begged and pleaded. He was immovable.

"Come back in the fall. We'll talk again," he said, standing up to indicate the audience was over.

We left, saddened and depressed, and tried to figure out what killer arguments we could have made to change his mind. We went over the conversation, recalling the surgeon's responses, his humor, liveliness, expressions, and gestures.

We gradually switched our focus from the heart transplant to Vishnevsky himself. What an extraordinary man! Just a few minutes of conversation had been enough to see his brilliant mind, uniqueness, and breadth of vision. We realized that his personality, which revealed his character so plainly, was perfect for film.

"Why don't we do a film portrait about Vishnevsky?" Igor said.

"An excellent idea," I replied.

Now all we had to do was convince Vishnevsky.

We returned to see him the next day and told him our idea. We promised that we would not get in his way, that our equipment was "invisible and inaudible." He listened wearily, indifferently, his hand shading his eyes.

"Why don't we do it after my vacation?" he suggested. "I'll rest up, play some tennis, drop a few kilos so that I'm young and handsome again, and I'll be in a better mood too. Come back in September."

It was May 1969. We couldn't delay that long for production reasons, so we started pressuring him some more. He finally gave in. He probably was too weak to resist; he was tired, and for a moment he was indifferent to it all. A few days later we showed up at the institute with our camera and sound equipment, to film a meeting of the staff with French surgeon and professor Charles Dubost. At that moment, Vishnevsky actually realized just what he had agreed to, but as an intelligent and responsible person, he couldn't go back on his word. He submitted.

We were a bit too pushy perhaps, but I don't regret it. Otherwise there would be no film portrait of that amazing man. You rarely see such a noble appearance — animated face and hands, expressive movements, gestures, and intonations. Vishnevsky had an actor's gifts, and he never hesitated for a second. He had lively eyes, which mirrored his mood and every passing emotion. Keeping my eye on the viewfinder for hours was a real pleasure; watching him was infinitely interesting.

Our film was unusual for the period, using the direct cinema technique, as in *Weavers* (1968). I was in Vishnevsky's office with my camera, filming him as he dealt with colleagues, patients, operations, talking on the telephone, joking with some people, berating others. Emotional and easily aroused, he spoke with heat and temperament, not hiding his attitude toward people or the matter at hand. He reacted with great emotion to everything. He was a striking, cheerful, explosive man, filled with life. He was totally photogenic.

Vishnevsky's extraordinary character energized us. Throughout the filming, I was afraid to miss a single event — meetings, operations, conversations. The film flowed like a river; we spared nothing. I didn't even think about how to structure the film — I was doing a character sketch. I filmed a lot of material. Igor edited it.

When I was filming the *Weavers,* I was trying to capture the texture, atmosphere, nuances, and charm of real life. In *Surgeon Vishnevsky,* we had something else — the human dimension. It was when I was making this film that I first truly understood that a documentary film cannot be made about just anyone, even though, as the classic Italian neorealist screenwriter Cesare Zavattini once put it: "Every human being on earth is of interest." The content and the subject of our film were Vishnevsky himself: the person, the personality.

After this film, I was looking for special kinds of people—out of the ordinary. They didn't have to be academicians or "heroes of labor." But they had to be unique.

From today's viewpoint, there is nothing special about *Vishnevsky*. But for those days, the picture was a revelation, shot entirely in the observational method. There was not a single word of narration, and all the necessary information came from Vishnevsky himself and the characters. At the 1969 Leningrad Festival of Television Film, *Vishnevsky* won the prize for best camerawork.

Richard Leacock once said, "Cameramen are treated with respect, but they are not the ones who are invited for dinner. What a strange profession."

Unfortunately, the situation in film is that even though being a cameraperson is considered both creative and respectable, when directors need to blame someone for a picture's failure, they pick the cinematographer. The first time I experienced this was with *Vishnevsky*. Igor, the director, had expressed dissatisfaction with my camerawork during editing. He was also upset that I, and not he, had been awarded the top prize of the film festival.

Not long after *Vishnevsky,* I told Alyosha Gabrilovich, another director in our studio, "I would like to shoot a movie for you."

He replied laughingly, "Your place is in the kitchen."

"That's nonsense!"

"Just kidding. But I never work with camerawomen."

That's what pushed me into directing. My thanks to Gabrilovich. He wasn't the only one; other good directors didn't want to work with me either. So I thought, "Fine! I'll manage without you. I'll make my own movies." This minor incident changed the course of my life. But I wouldn't have gotten far without the help of good people. Valentina Nikitkina, then head of the Ekran Studio script-writing department, supported my directorial debut. My thanks to her!

Since then, I have made more than thirty documentaries that I directed and filmed. I was probably the first woman in Russia who combined these two professions. It has been always easier for me to do both than to explain to a cinematographer what I wanted. In making documentaries, the most important decisions usually come during the shoot.

Professional Infatuations

Sometimes the most ordinary events become extremely important and determine the development of the rest of your life. For me, such an event was meeting Raissa Nemchinskaya, the circus gymnast, in 1970.

I met her at her son's house. He was my good friend, Max Nemchinsky, a theater director. Raissa was lively, witty, and charming and spent the evening enchanting us with tales of her circus life. She was the center of attention, and it was obvious that she was used to it and expected it. She looked around thirty-five or thirty-eight, but simple math showed that she was older than that—Max was almost thirty.

That evening stayed in my mind. When I ran into Max some time later, I hinted that I would like to be invited again. He told me that his mother was performing abroad and wouldn't be back for two months.

"Does she still perform?"

"Of course. And she's in Moscow for only a few days at a time, moving from one city to another."

I learned that Raissa was fifty-nine, an unheard-of age for a circus aerialist. She was unique in circus history. Despite advice from friends and colleagues, she didn't want to hear about retirement. The circus was her only passion, the meaning of her life. Moreover, it was her home, the only place she felt comfortable. Later, when I was making my film about her and spending hours in her trailer, I came to feel the power and depth of her feelings for the circus arena. She needed the daily performances, the audiences, everything that made up the atmosphere of her profession. Her old friend, Tanti the clown, said, "She can't live without the circus."

Raissa's artistic life had been a hard one, filled with tragedy. While learning from the famous Corelli aerialists, she had an accident that kept her bedridden for several years. No one believed that she would ever walk again. Her inhuman stubbornness got her on her feet; two years later, she was back in the ring. She was at her peak in the 1930s–1940s. She performed the most complex numbers with her partner and husband, Izyaslav Nemchinsky. Then she suffered another accident. But she never lost her certainty that she would return to the circus sooner or later. Every day, through horrible pain, she trained at home on a homemade trapeze, until she got back into shape and returned to the show.

Work was sacred to her, and everything about it had to be perfect. She would not tolerate the slightest indifference toward her work from anyone: circus hands, performers, or director. The sweet-smiling woman turned into a fury, attacking the hapless victim with all the heat of her temperament. But I can't remember a single time that she did not get what she wanted—not for herself but for her act. Colleagues varied in their opinion of her—there was no pious uniformity. But that was about her personality—her professional mastery and discipline elicited only awe and respect.

This amazing woman, Raissa Nemchinskaya, became the heroine of my directorial debut in 1970. Kornei Chukovsky, in his book on the painter Ilya Repin, comments on how an artist subconsciously falls in love with his subject. This is the main characteristic of the relationship between portraitist and model—the sincere, unfeigned, and irrational infatuation with your subject. The first "protagonist" I fell in love with was Raissa Nemchinskaya.

At the time, she was performing in the big tent in Gorky Park. We often sat in her trailer. There were always three of us: she and I and my camera, which had become an integral part of me. One day Nemchinskaya was in a strangely meditative mood, following her success in the matinee; the young audience had applauded long and loud and called her out for several bows. After that intoxicating moment of success, she suddenly fell into depression.

My "hunting instinct" was paying off when I filmed this change of mood from success to despair. This was the very moment a documentarian is always looking for.

And we continued our conversation, which had begun long before that. It wasn't so much a conversation as a confession—a confession pushed by my provoking questions.

That confession went on for six weeks, the duration of my filming. Raissa told me about her first performance with the Corelli circus, also under a tent in the same spot in Gorky Park, almost forty years earlier. She recalled the details of that day, her anxiety and fear of the audience and her vow never to go out into the ring again. And suddenly, without any connection to the present, she burst out with something that must have been festering a long time: "The circus is my whole life; the meaning of my life. Once I leave, I will never come back. My heart would break if I saw people working and I wasn't one of them."

She never did leave the circus. She worked right up to the last day, actually the last minute, the last second of her life, to her last breath. She had finished her act under the top, and while she was taking her bows, she fell facedown. Her heart had given up. That was August 3, 1975, at the Dnepropetrovsk Circus—brand-new, shiny and festive, where she loved to perform. She was sixty-four.

"My heart would break if I knew that people were working and I wasn't one of them." Those words, spoken in a moment of frankness, precisely expressed the essence of my heroine's character and the main theme of my film about her. Nemchinskaya was the perfect interpreter of the human qualities I had considered most lofty, pure, and valuable ever since I saw Flaherty's *Man of Aran*— obsession and infinite fidelity toward one's work.

More than thirty years have passed since then. In that time I've filmed many people from various walks of life and of different ages and personalities. But all of them were obsessive like Nemchinskaya. Clearly, these are people who interest me the most.

The memory of Raissa has become part of me.

Five or six times I tried to get *Raissa Nemchinskaya, the Circus Actress* approved for broadcast by the studio executives responsible for ideological and artistic concepts. They found several aspects bothersome: the sad atmosphere, reminiscent of Fellini's *La Strada,* the middle-aged heroine, surrounded by miserable, lonely women who lived in circus vans and applied heavy makeup to hide their weary eyes. And they didn't even perform in the spectacular ring of the country's main circus in Moscow, but somewhere in a small tent. But what most irritated the studio bosses was the heroine herself. She did not belong in the context of television reality then. They insisted on making changes that I felt would destroy the picture itself.

This was my first time as a director. I hadn't learned the tricks of getting a film past the artistic board and the bosses' offices, but my sixth sense told me that if I went on making corrections, the movie would be ruined, and this film would be gone and there wouldn't be a next one. I decided to leave the studio, even though I knew it would be very hard to find another job.

So I turned in my resignation, and it came as a big surprise. All my filmmaker colleagues had liked the film a lot when I first showed it. They found it unusual and applauded it. They told me that I had made a marvelous film. And now I was resigning.

Three hours later I was told that Boris Khessin, the director of Ekran, wanted to see me. I arrived at his office all upset.

"Marina, now why were you so hasty? You always have to say, 'One, two, three . . . ten . . . fifteen,' and only then make a decision. Did you count to three?"

"No, I didn't have time."

"There, you see! But I've counted to three, and I'm prepared to apologize."

"One, two, three," I said. "I'm sorry, Boris Mikhailovich."

"Fine," he said. "Soviet television does not need films like this. They may possibly show it once or twice. If that is what you want, go ahead and finish the postproduction."

His intuition had been correct. The film was aired only once. Since then it has been placed in the television archives and presented to students and professionals as an achievement of Russian documentary film.

My next picture was *Yuri Zavadsky* (1971), about our legendary actor and theater director. Zavadsky started out in 1915 with the famous Vakhtangov Studio and later worked in the Moscow Art Theater with Konstantin Stanislavsky. In 1924 he created his own theater and went on to become a renowned director, one of the icons of the Soviet theater.

I don't consider this film one of my best works, but the television bosses loved it. Ideologically, it was ideal. Zavadsky had never been in conflict with the authorities and had always been a conformist. Sergei Lapin, the minister of the State Committee for Television and Radio, loved and idolized him. Lapin was a well-educated man—I'm not sure that many of the executives of television today would have heard of Zavadsky.

Zavadsky was seventy-five when I made the picture. He came to see it on his birthday, July 12. Stella Zhdanova, Ekran's editor in chief, came in to the screening room in the middle. She wanted to meet the celebrity. But he was so moved by the film that he paid no attention to her. The old man sat there watching himself and wept. He later told me, "It felt as if I were at my own funeral."

Zavadsky invited me to his birthday party. His apartment was filled with roses, white and red. I had come with an enormous bouquet. "Yuri Alexandrovich, you have so many flowers, it's incredible!"

"This is nothing. Let's go to the bathroom."

He opened the door, and I saw that the tub was filled with roses, floating in the water; this is when I learned the trick of making roses last.

The guests were interesting. Among them were Vera Maretskaya and Rostislav Plyatt, stars of Soviet theater. They were masters of telling jokes, and everybody in the room laughed nonstop, Zavadsky included.

My picture glorified Zavadsky—and he deserved it. He was a good actor, a decent and dignified artistic theater director, and a good person. He never hurt anyone. However, I think the movie was a bit boring. Zavadsky was not at his best when we did the filming. He had jaundice, and he seemed depressed because the play he was directing then, *Petersburg Dreams* (based on a Dostoevsky novel), was monotonous. There was no conflict in my film. Everyone I interviewed was complimentary about the master. I realized it even when I was shooting, but there was nothing I could do about it.

The person who was most pleased by the film was my mother. As a theater specialist, she had idolized Zavadsky since she was young, when he was an incredibly handsome and talented actor. Later she became very good friends with him. I was also glad to have made the film—it was only my second work as a director, and I learned a lot during the filming and editing. And, of course, I appreciated the priceless material I was preserving for history.

The greatest actors of the Russian theater of the twentieth century, Tsetsilia Mansurova, Vera Maretskaya, Rostislav Plyatt, and Serafima Birman—were all in my film and contributed by telling the story of their time. I also filmed the poet Pavel Antokolsky, a friend of Zavadsky from their youth. Antokolsky recalled Marina Tsvetayeva's lines, which she had dedicated to Zavadsky: "You are as unforgettable as you are forgetful." I suspect that Marina had had flings with both men. I think the very fact that these people were captured on film made the effort worthwhile. Zavadsky passed away soon afterward, and so did many of the others I had filmed. The last time I saw Zavadsky was at his birthday party.

Every new film teaches me something. This one awakened my interest in preserving history through people who had left their mark on Russian culture. Today this film is more valuable than when it was made. To this day, it's shown at least once a year on television in Russia.

Them

Television was a state within a state, just as totalitarian as the big state. The atmosphere and mind-set was probably even harsher than within the political system as a whole. The TV screen was the system's bastion—the main mechanism for influencing the masses, a powerful brainwashing tool. The executives in charge in the 1960s–1980s had been brought up by the ideological school of the 1920s–1940s.

This included the ministers of the State Committee for Television and Radio, Nikolai Mesyatsev (1959–1967) and Sergei Lapin (1968–1985); their deputies; and the heads of all the departments and associations. They were all quietly hated, despised for their servility and readiness to serve the incurably ill, rotting system, to be its "watchdogs" (Lapin's term), but you had to give them credit for their brains and management skills.

The television bosses were buttoned-up; they tried not to smile or show that they were still human. The only exception was Yuri Letunov, a vivid, talented, handsome, and unusual man. He was the head of the Department of Television Information, which was considered the most politically important. He had created *Vremya*, the most popular nationwide news magazine televised every evening at nine. He knew he was in a strong position.

He was very kind to me. He liked my *Raissa Nemchinskaya*. It was only thanks to him that, in 1975, I could make my film about Arkady Raikin, the great Soviet comedian. Letunov gave me unlimited film stock, the precious, hard-to-get Kodak, and told me, "Go and film!"—even though there was no screenplay nor a convincing proposal. Raikin was performing in Moscow and making a big television series at Ostankino. It would have been a shame to let the opportunity slip, and Letunov realized it. Alas, Letunov died young, at around fifty.

The television bosses were real professionals and smart. We knew what to expect from them, what was allowed, and what wasn't. I say this without nostalgia: Our relations were clear-cut and rigid. It was practically impossible to circumnavigate the system. The structure of the system had been built brick by brick over the years—solid and blocking any other path. As a rule, the bosses could sense an unwanted breeze a mile away.

In the early 1980s, I was making the film *Before the Harvest* about the life of Nina Pereverzeva, Party member, role model, famous combine operator, and member of a kolkhoz (collective farm). But I wanted to make a human picture, without fanfare and drum rolls. My heroine was a smiling, kind, and pleasant woman. Her fellow villagers liked her for her friendly personality and for her hard life.

And I liked her a lot but realized that she was not a happy woman. Her husband drank hard, her son had problems with his wife, and there was something wrong with their daughter as well, while Nina herself worked at full steam from morning till night. I felt that the facade was colored nicely, but behind it was a hard and somewhat depressing reality. I wanted to retain just a small inkling of the heartrending sadness—let the viewer see that this seemingly successful heroine was not quite that happy.

No one would have allowed me to say anything openly about her complicated and rather dual life, but to give the viewers at least a hint of it, I created a sequence in which I shot her exhausted after a full day of work, walking under an umbrella in the rain, down a puddle-filled wet road leading who knows where. It was a sad shot and very emotional.

The picture was accepted, and no one made a single remark. But when I saw it aired, I was speechless. The entire sequence, so important for me, had been deleted. I hurried to find out what had happened.

"Mamedov ordered it cut."

The bosses could catch a whiff instantly of the slightest deviation from the official ideological line. My first independent picture, about the circus performer Raissa Nemchinskaya, had scenes that I was forced to cut. In some of them, the heroine was agitated, upset, almost hysterically expressing her opinion to the circus director; in others, her hairdo askew, she sat curled up in the corner of a couch, dog on her lap. These scenes added up to a sense of moral discomfort. I left them in, although our editor in chief, Leonid Dmitriev, and the picture's editor, Ludmila Lopato, told me that the scenes would definitely be noticed. "You don't need them," they said. "Why don't you take them out before you're forced to do it?"

Others had a different advice: "Leave them in to be 'white dogs.' You can always cut them later."

"White dogs" was a professional term, meaning something like a red herring. These were things we left in that weren't essential for the meaning (that perhaps created confusion or ambivalence) and that would upset the authorities, so that they would demand the cuts, which we would do gladly, hoping that it kept them from noticing other, more important things that we would therefore get to keep.

I really wanted those scenes in this film—they weren't "white dogs" at all—but I had to cut them. They sensed an alien spirit.

One of my films, *This Is Our Profession* (1973), was as clear as a glass of water. Its point was that being an artist was not a profession but a human quality. The film shows Slava Zaprudnov, a glassblower, not only as a productive worker making lamps at the factory but also as an artist creating amusing and curious figures out of glass in his spare time. I had thought that the very idea of creative work as a part of any activity would interest the viewer. But to my surprise, no one in the leadership of our studio wanted this film.

Stella Zhdanova saw the picture and said, "Brilliant, but it'll never get through."

"Why not?"

"He's an individualist. Where's the collective? He's not a worker. He's a craftsman."

What the bosses wanted to see in a movie was the pulse of a big factory, the collective's daily life as it struggled to meet and exceed the plan, and the Party's leading role. There was nothing of that in my film. Moreover, I hadn't bothered to bring in as a consultant someone whose authority would be enough to cover up my ideological immaturity and to prove that there were no errors in the film. That required not only great demagogic skills but also a good résumé, with a long list of honors and high positions in the Communist Party hierarchy.

They couldn't stand independence, no matter whose, but especially of artists and filmmakers. We were all their vassals and slaves. They in turn were, of course, the slaves of their masters, and all of us were the slaves of the system.

There is an ancient curse, perhaps the most horrible one for Jews: "May you be the slave of slaves!" We all suffered that fate. We were slaves of slaves: our bosses, however democratic or autocratic they chose to be with us, were the slaves of their superiors, who were the slaves of the system. That system knew no other form of relationship.

I never wanted to make films about politics. I wanted to make films about interesting people—preferably the ordinary ones. A circus performer, a three-year-old boy from a family of workers, a seven-year-old future composer, a glassblower, a textile worker. I loved making films in the countryside. Simple people open up in a very interesting way when you spend a lot of time observing them. Getting these topics approved was hard. Films like these were not the ones that created a good reputation for our studio in the eyes of the authorities; they were not the ones that got reviewed in the official press. Our bosses couldn't make political capital from them. But I kept trying to get authorization for things that I believed in. Sometimes I succeeded, sometimes not.

The director of Ekran was Boris Khessin, a well-educated and intelligent man with a wide network. He would hire as screenwriters moderately liberal and sometimes even very liberal writers who couldn't get a job elsewhere. Leonid Likhodeyev wrote for us, and Khessin allowed me to bring in Anatoly Strelyany and Gennady Lisichkin, whose reputations were almost scandalous in official circles. Khessin hired the brilliant Boris Galanter to make films that were subtle, far from politics and blatant propaganda. But these were exceptions rather than the rule. Most of the films were made, as the popular term put it, by tested masters of the ideological front, like the international journalists Seiful-Mulyukov, Zorin, Dunaev, and Kaverznev. Khessin also brought in Brezhnev's aides, leading lights of the Party's Central Committee—Blatov, Alexandrov, Shishlin, and Ignatenko. An experienced and cautious man, he intentionally and wisely balanced "right" and "left," if those designations could be used during those stagnant Soviet years.

My colleagues—and I too—would get very upset over Khessin's critical remarks and would scream, "Khessin is a coward!" Now, of course, when the passions have calmed and are half-forgotten, I realize that he was no coward. He was experienced, having learned a lot at the State Committee for Television and Radio, and he knew how the system worked and how to work the system. He knew that if he got fired, it wouldn't make things any easier for us.

Naturally, he was concerned about his own career. But he also cared about the work. In the years he headed Ekran, it became the best television studio in the country, with a powerful collective of workers, professionals with good cultural background and decency too. Khessin knew how to pick people and deal with them. He was never rude to his subordinates; he always behaved impeccably and diplomatically. He built up the studio carefully and achieved the best results that could be expected. My almost twenty years of work in advantageous surroundings was due mostly to him (he was in charge of Ekran from 1968 to 1988).

In that period, television cinema became very significant and started to play a much more important role than before. TV documentary grew to a level unmatched in the country. Technically we were the best equipped of all studios in the whole Soviet Union. Only Ekran worked with modern and foreign (mostly German and French) 16 mm technology. Khessin's attention to the technical side came not only from his understanding of its importance but also from his being on friendly terms with Genrikh Yushkyavichus, the very wise deputy minister responsible for technology. Yushkyavichus had worked abroad as a USSR media representative for many years, had a European education, was a good organizer, and knew the field well—everything new being done in the world. He knew how to select people, real professionals. All of us who worked in television in those years owe him a debt of gratitude.

Let me tell you a typical story, which I witnessed myself. It explained a lot to me then. In 1976, Khessin had to approve my film *Deniska-Denis,* about a three-year-old named Denis Galkin who showed that even at that tender age a person is already a personality. The film turned out well, and everybody in Ekran was pleased. I had spent two months living with the Galkin family and made a touching living portrait of the boy and his parents. Naturally, it had nothing to do with politics. Everything was fine, except that instead of the budgeted twenty minutes, it ran thirty; the top television executives had to approve this change. Khessin, who was delighted with the picture, said, "You know, I'm tired of fighting the battles for all of you. Let's go see Mamedov together. You're a woman—maybe he'll go easier on you."

I went with him, and I'll never forget that screening. I wore a pants suit that Mother had bought for me in Switzerland. It was very becoming, making me look slim and even elegant. But we weren't supposed to wear pants suits at the studio. This wasn't written down somewhere, but many unwritten rules were strictly enforced. It may seem silly now, but women were expected to wear only skirts at work. We could wear slacks out on a shoot—if it was cold. Women weren't allowed inside the Kremlin in slacks. Naturally, I had considered whether or not to wear my pants suit to see Mamedov. But I looked so good in it, I decided it would help my feminine charm. And then I thought, "What am I afraid of anyway? What nonsense!"

Khessin and I were waiting outside the screening room when Mamedov appeared. He shook hands with Khessin but merely nodded at me, appraising me with the eye of a traditional Central Asian man (he was from Azerbaijan) and clearly not liking what he saw. He sat down and asked us to sit too. We watched the film. The narration was written by the famous actor Zinovy Gerdt, who did the voice-over. The text was wonderful, and he read it beautifully. He was Jewish, born in Odessa, and his accent revealed his background.

Then came the discussion. Mamedov crossed his legs. So did I (it was a low armchair, it was more comfortable, and I felt less at a disadvantage that way).

Without looking in my direction, as if I wasn't there at all, Mamedov berated the film to Khessin in the coarsest terms. It was a public flogging.

"What kind of film is that! Who needs the scene where the child bites his mother? A child should love his mother! And how can anything like this film be shown on television? What are you teaching the children? And that voice of Gerdt's—everyone's sick of it. It's disgusting, with that provincial talk . . ."

His tone was lethal, and every word was filled with venom. Khessin's face turned blotchy, and he mopped his brow. Mamedov did not deign to speak a single word to me or look at me, but at the end, just before leaving, he said, "Well, what do you have there? Thirty minutes instead of twenty? Fine, I approve it."

And he left. Without a "thank you" or a "good-bye." That was his style, and not only his; as far as I know, most people in the Communist elite were like that. Often, they were much cruder.

Khessin sat in stunned silence for a few seconds—they seemed like minutes to me. I was completely destroyed. And then he looked up at me and said, "See, I told you so."

I felt desperately sorry for him. I realized that this wasn't the first time he had to put up with such treatment, nor would it be the last. He had to meet with Mamedov every day, and any meeting could be like this. I never forgot that. How could those people squelch everything human and decent in them to be able to treat others that way! However, Mamedov was not stupid at all. On the contrary, he was a very bright man, and the television machine rolled very smoothly under his management.

"Why did you wear a pants suit?" Khessin asked me.

"What's the problem?"

"You know he doesn't like it."

"I don't know. I wanted to look nice."

"Well, never mind," he said.

Khessin was a kind man. He never hurt others for his own amusement.

I rarely saw Mamedov after that, fortunately. The directors with whom he dealt were either the ones who made political films and got direct instructions from him or those who got into trouble—they got the full menu of abuse from him. God spared me from being in either position. But I did have two more memorable meetings with him.

One was in 1980, before the Moscow Olympics. Twenty cinematographers, considered the best in the studio, were entrusted with filming the historic event. I was among them and extremely happy, especially since we were given brand-new Arriflex cameras, with a very good zoom, and the most modern system of synchronization. I knew I would never return that camera. It would be wonderful for making my films, and of course I was fascinated by the Olympic games.

I was assigned to equestrian sports; I was responsible for all the filming in that section. You'd think it was only sports, but we were given training for a whole month—called in, instructed, advised on what to wear, and warned to watch the activities to the very end, to help with the editing. One hundred 16 mm copies of a twenty-minute summary of everyday sport events had to be distributed every day around the world. The main thrust of the instructions concerned our behavior, especially around foreigners. We were to shun long conversations with them, speak only about work issues, discuss nothing, and avoid politics at all costs. Mamedov came to almost every such meeting and gave us instructions for two hours. He told us to be vigilant and avoid any incidents, to be businesslike always, to keep everything at the highest level, to put our country's best foot forward, and to keep our foreign colleagues from filming any drunkards or other dubious subjects.

The day before the Olympics started, Mamedov gave us another warning about the danger of enemy provocation—he had filled us with anxiety already. The United States was skipping the games, boycotting us because of the help we were giving to the people of Afghanistan, so Western journalists would try to present the Olympics in the darkest colors. At the end, he said, "And I wish you good work. This is the first and probably last Olympics in your life. I doubt this will be repeated in Moscow in our lifetime. So be sure to enjoy your work."

We were stunned. Despite our reporting experience and ability to work in any situation, we were so constrained by the system that normal human words seemed like a breath of fresh air.

My other meeting with Mamedov came in 1982, before my trip to the Antarctic. My friend, the journalist Ella Vlasova, wanted to make a film in the Antarctic. We were going to be the first Soviet women to go to this part of the world. Ella had pushed for this trip for two years. Yevgenij Tolstikov, the deputy chairman of the Hydro-Meteorological Committee, blocked it: "Over my dead body. The South Pole is no place for women." He meant he didn't want women bringing passions and temptations into the calm equilibrium of the men's collective there. If you want to send journalists, send men—there are plenty who want to go there.

For a long time, Ella had known Yuri Izrael, Tolstikov's direct superior, and had made films for him. So she managed to persuade him.

"All right, go," he said. "This is an interesting project, in fact."

We prepared for a long time, so long that it seemed we would never actually go, but just continue preparing. And then, suddenly, we were told we would take off the next morning. Although the news was unexpected, we were practically ready: cameras, lights, film—all were packed.

"Mamedov wants to see us," Ella announced.

And we both rushed over to the State Committee of Television and Radio. We entered his office, and Mamedov was sitting there, looking grim as usual, without a welcoming smile. At least he stood up, shook hands, and invited us to sit down. It was a brief conversation. He didn't ramble. He formulated our goals and instructed us on our behavior.

"You must be disciplined," he said. "You must bring back good material. Do you realize the responsibility, how much money we're spending on this? This isn't a jaunt to Odessa. Go. Make your film. And one more thing: by New Year's we must have material on how the people celebrate New Year's Eve on our station at the pole."

"How can we film New Year's when we will be back here a month before the celebration?"

"Organize the party. Take everything with you. We want to show it here on December 31."

We didn't argue—that would be like spitting into the wind. In parting, he added, "And of course, film on a high level. If you do a bad job, you'll never again go any further than the suburbs of Moscow."

Those were his final words. But they didn't upset us—we had so much to get done that day.

To say that my trip to Antarctica was an incredibly vivid part of my life is to say nothing. I still dream about it: the landscapes, icebergs, ice caves, bare cliffs, flocks of penguins, and huge gulls. A description of our filming there and our adventures, some quite dramatic, would take too much time—that's another book. But I do want to reminisce about a few things.

When we boarded the plane, I took the camera equipment with me into the cabin as usual (I never trusted anyone else with it), but the cans of film had to go as luggage. When we got to Mozambique, from where we would fly to the South Pole three days later, we found that the plane had been overloaded and the film had been left in Moscow.

I confess that Ella was stronger than me in this situation. She said, "Don't worry. We'll figure something out." Salvation was quick in coming. We were met at the airport by Gena Kurinnoy, a cameraman who worked as the correspondent for Soviet television in southern Africa. I barely knew him; he had recently moved to Moscow from Belorussia with his young actress wife, who had just graduated from theater school. Gena simply asked how much film we needed. We were expecting 5,000 meters. He said he could give us 4,500 meters, which was his annual limit. When our film finally arrived from Moscow, he would take it. And in the meantime, he would borrow from other foreign correspondents. He made the offer before we could even ask for his help. He was astonishingly kind and generous. We became close friends when he returned to the USSR in the late 1980s. But he didn't stay long in Moscow. He was sent on another long assignment—this time to Yugoslavia, where the war was starting in Bosnia and Serbia. He was the first Soviet journalist to go on that assignment, but he never returned. His wife and their two children waited for him in Belgrade for six months, and then they were sent home. No one ever learned how and where he died.

When our plane landed on the ice fields of the Soviet Antarctic station Molodezhnaya, all 158 people came out to meet it. They had been on the South Pole for nine months without a single guest from the mainland. All they had was the radio and the radiotelephone. Of course, the new arrivals, including us, were bombarded with questions. What was new at home? It was the fall of 1982, and we all sensed that change had to come. Suslov, the chief ideologist of the Communist Party, had just died. Brezhnev was hopelessly old and impotent, he could barely walk, and he slurred the few words he said (giving rise to innumerable jokes). But it wasn't funny. The situation was ripening, and we all knew that there was a major power struggle behind the scenes.

Even in the Antarctic, at the very end of the earth, people tried to follow events. Anxious rumors traveled through the station on November 10. Radio communications were interrupted by a magnetic storm, but through the hiss came strange sounds that resembled funeral music. This continued for twenty-four hours. The tension increased. Late that evening, Nikolai Rybkin, the station chief, managed to call the closest station on the pole, the American one. The Americans said, "We think your head of state died," but they couldn't catch the name. To be on the safe side, Rybkin announced a day of mourning.

The next day, the radio was working, and we learned that Brezhnev had passed away. A meeting was organized hastily, and everything was official and proper: speeches, a minute of silence, a gun salute. Just like on the mainland. Even though everyone had expected it, people were still both saddened and anxious. Being so far away from home and not knowing what was going on was very strange. We felt totally helpless, even though we realized that we wouldn't have been able to do anything at home either.

Despite the strict orders from the directors not to drink, everyone got pretty stoned that day. The totalitarian regime was undermined even at the South Pole.

By the time we got back to Moscow, Yuri Andropov was the country's new leader. Vilen Egorov, the editor in chief of the Educational Department, said to Ella and me: "Drop in on Lapin—report to him. He wants to see you."

We brought Lapin a little piece of Antarctica—a stone. Lapin, a strange-looking man and very short, almost a dwarf, was unusually gentle. We shook hands, and I had the impression that he had no bones in his hands. They were tiny and very soft. I remember thinking, "How can somebody with such soft hands be so ruthless?"

The last time I saw Mamedov was in 1991. My mother was in the Kuntsevo Hospital, and I visited her frequently. Once as I came down the hallway, I saw Mamedov in a patient seating area, watching television. Uncombed, wearing slippers, and seemingly hung over, he certainly didn't look like the big boss he had been. He was no longer working for television. I don't know why he was hospitalized. He paid no attention to me. He hadn't recognized me; his eyes were clouded over.

Today, as I look back on those days, aware of what we lost and what we gained, I can conclude that despite all the difficulty of working under police control, totally dependent on the whims of the bosses, I recall those men without rancor. After all, they were confined by the system too. They were obeying instructions honestly in their own way. They didn't have much choice—none of us did. They were risking their jobs, and we were risking our reputations and professional conscience.

Television then was just what television in totalitarian times had to be. It could not have been otherwise.

The Ordeal

It was so hard to get every picture accepted by the studio executives — even the most harmless films. I had so much trouble with the simple one about the glassblower. *Arkady Raikin* also barely squeaked by, even though the comedian was celebrated and universally respected. But the film lacked aggressive social optimism. And how Mamedov mocked *Deniska-Denis,* an unassuming film about a three-year-old boy. He didn't like my pictures because they could not be used politically.

My films were often praised in the press. Many publications had journalists of a somewhat liberal bent who always wanted to support fresh, human movies. My films differed from the ones the authorities admired. And therefore the authorities never considered me one of their own. I don't mean that they persecuted me or hated me. I'm a peaceful person by nature, and I didn't muscle in where I wasn't needed. And my direct superiors, I repeat, were professional, decent people who understood what I was trying to do and that they couldn't expect anything different from me. If they could, they let me make my films and didn't expect to profit from them. Incidentally, what didn't thrill the bosses back then is a plus now: the films haven't aged, and they can be shown without embarrassment today.

After Mamedov's criticism of *Deniska-Denis,* I tried, as usual, to propose some new projects, but I was refused every time. The bosses suggested I select one of the topics that were part of the studio's annual work plan preapproved by the minister. These stories were usually about the heroes of socialist labor and prominent personalities.

"I made a film about a glassblower," I said. "You didn't like it."

"Right. Because your point of view was wrong."

"Well, that just means I'll do something wrong this time too."

I always wanted to make films only about things I understood and felt. And if my heart wasn't in it, no point in doing it. No compromises there.

I got tired of beating my head against the wall, unable to find a topic I really wanted to do. I began thinking about going away, to work in some other city. And then opportunity arose.

At a seminar for documentarians at the Cinematographers' House in Repino, a resort twenty-five miles outside Leningrad (now St. Petersburg), I met Gadilbek Shalakhmetov, a young journalist from Kazakhstan who had just graduated from a screen-writing program. I made a suggestion: "Let's create something together."

Gadilbek was just starting out and seemed pleased. "What do you want to film?" he asked.

"I want something with tension, a life-and-death struggle. Passions that are strong, real ones, not made up. Heroics without fanfare and padding. It would be great to film a person who went through a life crisis but did not break, who retained the life force and continues working."

That was, in fact, the main theme of most of my previous films—obsession. My heroes were people in love with their work, their professions. A film requires conflict, and it was part of my favorite theme—life on the edge of the possible. Obsession gave life a meaning. That was the only way to live—putting your all into your work and trying not to notice what was going on around you.

"I know of a man," Gadilbek said. "He's a famous Kazakh oilman who had an accident a few years ago. His name is Rakhmet Utesinov."

He told me the man's story. It was just what I was searching for. A few years before that, I had wanted to do something like a documentary version of *Nine Days of a Year,* a film by the great Mikhail Romm. Made in 1962, during the Thaw, it had made a tremendous impact on our society. It was a thoughtful film about a physicist who suffered a fatal dose of radiation during testing but continued to work, hoping to complete his experiment before dying. The film was extremely sad and yet filled with heroic optimism. It was "my" theme. At that time I had almost found an appropriate subject for a documentary: a theoretical physicist who continued working even though he knew his death was near. But the editor with whom I worked cooled my enthusiasm.

"This is unlikely to pass," he said.

"Why not?"

"It's too grim. Don't do a film about death. Give me something more optimistic."

The television screen showed no conflicts: we were not supposed to tell the viewer about the real dramas going on in life or about anything upsetting. The social optimism demanded by the executives did not permit anyone to die on-screen or even grieve for the dead. It was as if no one ever died in the Soviet Union. The Leningrad Party boss Tolstikov was well known for his reply to foreigners who asked about the death rate in the USSR: "We've already solved that problem."

And yet the idea of a hero with such a dramatic life would not leave me.

"All right then," I said to myself. "So no one dies of leukemia here. But we do have car accidents and other catastrophes. They can happen to anyone."

Utesinov, the subject proposed by Gadilbek, had been head of the oil industry on the Mangyshlak Peninsula. While driving across the Karagiye Depression in Kazakhstan, he had an accident, the car flipped over, and his spine was broken. Confined to a wheelchair, he continued to work—he was writing a book and still proposing new ideas to improve oil drilling and fighting with the conservatives. In other words, he was still in the action. My intuition told me this man could be my next hero.

I decided to fly out to see him in Novy Uzen, also in Kazakhstan, about ninety miles from Shevchenko (now Aktau), so that I could meet him and his family and see the locations. Gadilbek came out there too. I liked what I saw: the desert, camels, sand, rocks, cactus, the Karagiye Depression, 433 feet below sea level, wind, and a city in the middle of the desert. It was exotic! I had never filmed anything like it. And I liked Rakhmet Utesinov and his wife, Sakish. And the man who replaced Utesinov as head of the oil industry seemed good too. He was a boring clerk, without any scope or vision, a former Komsomol worker who ended up in that job by accident. His name was Yuri Korchagin, and it was funny because he was the very opposite of the character Pavel Korchagin, a mythological revolutionary hero from the popular Soviet propaganda novel *How the Steel Was Tempered*.

I was fired up by the prospect of making this film as an independent and the possibility of getting away from Ekran, where there was no hope of decent work. Just then I was in another low in the cycle of ups and downs that characterized my relations with the authorities. And it was not only about the authorities. It was a gender issue as well.

Being very sensitive to the atmosphere at my work, I always felt that as a female filmmaker I wouldn't get strong support from my male colleagues. It's not that they were hostile toward me, no. They just believed that it is not a profession fit for females. In addition, they were skeptical because I was one of the few professionals who worked on films not only as a writer-director but as a camerawoman as well.

I can't say that this upset me very much or that I fought it desperately, but every now and then some remark would be very painful. But I continued my way the best I could. I wanted to show them: you wouldn't let me make my film at Ekran, so I'll do it with another studio.

So, in 1977, I went to a television studio in Kazakhstan to make *The Ordeal*. For Kazakhstan's documentary film world, I was a big shot—from Moscow, from Ekran, with a good reputation, with six films to my credit, all well received by the studio's artistic council and the press. And I was the only woman in the country who was both director and cinematographer. This was very unusual, and thus I was known and respected in professional circles. So I was greeted with open arms in Kazakhstan. They gave me everything I needed. I had never had such pleasant and generous conditions, where I didn't have to fight for every trifle.

I worked with delight. I liked my hero, the exotic beauty of Mangyshlak, and the industrial landscapes of the oil rigs.

The film was quite good. Gadilbek and I received the prestigious Lenin Komsomol Prize, awarded by the USSR Young Communist League, for best documentary of 1978. If I had made the film at Ekran in Moscow, I wouldn't have gotten any awards.

But here we had Kazakhstan, the screenwriter was a Kazakh, the film was about a Kazakh and had a heroic plot, a success in the emerging Kazakh film industry, the close cooperation of Moscow and Kazakh filmmakers—everything the Party liked. I can't judge whether they gave the prize for the film itself or because it matched their expectations. But having the Lenin Komsomol Prize came in very handy in the future.

After this experiment, I was looking for an opportunity to work on my own again and made an unpretentious twenty-minute film called *The Beginning* (1979), about children again, this time future composers. Seven-year-old kids under the guidance of their teacher, Tatiana Kaluzhskaya, composed music. She had a magical system for developing children's creativity. Again Ekran could not make political hay from it, and so I again had to face the same problem: to find someplace where I could make my kind of film. Ekran's preapproved list was still the same boring exaltation of socialism. The stagnation era of Brezhnev was at its peak. So I decided to run away from Ekran again— this time to the Literary and Drama Department of Central Television (Litdrama, for short). I didn't have to run far—it was in the same Ostankino building as Ekran.

It was a great help to me in life that I started out as a cinematographer. I could work without getting into politics. I could earn a living without making serious compromises with my conscience and at the same time getting pleasure from my work. The Litdrama Department was a wonderful place to work. It produced cultural programs and attracted the cream of the Soviet intelligentsia: writers, directors, artists, and so on.

At Litdrama, I made several good films with director Dima Chukovsky of which I am still proud. Konstantin Simonov wrote the screenplays and narrated three of them. The first, *What an Interesting Personality* (1974), was about the artist Vladimir Tatlin, a master of the Russian avant-garde of the early twentieth century. The next film was *Alexander Tvardovsky* (1976), about the recently deceased poet and editor of the liberal journal *Novy Mir (New World)*. It was very simple. Simonov talked about the poet, and the great actor Mikhail Ulyanov read Tvardovsky's poetry. We filmed it at Simonov's dacha in Peredelkino, a writer's colony outside Moscow, in front of a huge window that opened onto the vista of snow-covered birches. But for all the simplicity, Simonov's restrained manner and profound narration, as well as Ulyanov's totally unpretentious reading, made it quite moving and very powerful. The film turned out to be a big success. It was highly appreciated by the press and got great responses from the audience.

Simonov was a special person during the Soviet years. Talented and smart, he wrote good poetry and serious, profound prose. He was accepted in Party and government circles and among writers. He had managed to preserve his human decency and yet serve the authorities. Simonov got away with many things that the Party leaders would not have permitted to anyone else. In 1980 we were working on another film; this one about Mikhail Bulgakov (1891–1940), a writer who was semi-banned; his works were printed in tiny editions, and writing about him was not exactly encouraged. Simonov and literary scholar Marietta Chudakova prepared the screenplay for *Mikhail Bulgakov*, which told Bulgakov's story through letters written by him and his wife, Elena Sergeyevna. The few people who remembered Bulgakov added to Simonov's story with their reminiscences.

Simonov wanted to continue this series of films with the writer Alexander Serafimovich (1863–1949), whose life and work were very little known, and the two great Russian female poets of the twentieth century, Anna Akhmatova (1889–1966) and Marina Tsvetayeva (1892–1941), who were semi-banned then too. Alas, Simonov did not live long enough to make the films.

Among the other films I made at Litdrama were *At Pushkin's Home* (1982) and *Russian Legends* (1983), in collaboration with Dmitri Likhachev, another outstanding personality, literary scholar, and writer. We filmed the piece on Alexander Pushkin in Leningrad just when the poet's apartment-turned-museum was under reconstruction. It was a mess, with empty rooms and torn-up walls. Likhachev walked through the miserable interior, talking about the life and tragic death of the great poet. Nina Popova, the museum's director, also participated in the film; she too was a brilliant storyteller. The film created a sad and strange, but powerful, effect.

Together with Dima Chukovsky, Likhachev and I also made *You're a Fiery Man* (1979), about Dima's grandfather Kornei Chukovsky, the classic writer of children's literature, and *Tvardovsky's Home* (1982), with the talented liberal critic Vladimir Lakshin.

I think back on all those films with great love. It was such a pleasure to work as a cameraperson and not to do the work I didn't want to do at Ekran. I participated in exploring new history-related topics with the most respected and knowledgeable writers and scholars in the country. At the same time it gave me a profound professional experience as a cinematographer. It was very satisfying and serious, really creative work.

At Litdrama, I also directed one of my most favorite documentaries, *Pushkin and Pushchin* (1981), written by historian Natan Eidelman. His fame was at its zenith in the 1970s and 1980s, when everyone was reading his books on Pushkin and eighteenth- and nineteenth-century history. For a long time, Eidelman, the son of an "enemy of the people" (his father had been arrested in the 1940s during Stalin's purges), was not being published and was suspected of being a dissident. Then suddenly his books started to be printed, and they became instant best sellers.

I met Eidelman at a party, and it struck me that he was a born television personality. He was a great raconteur, enchanting me not only with his knowledge of the material, facts, and details but also with his extraordinary energy. I was dying to make a film with him. We discussed several themes and chose the least offensive to the authorities—the theme of the friendship of two lyceum students, the poet Alexander Pushkin and Ivan Pushchin, a Decembrist (member of the anti-tsarist rebellion of December 1812). Thanks to the support of the editor in chief at Litdrama, Konstantin Kuzakov, the topic was approved, and we started filming.

Let me tell you about Kuzakov. He was rumored to be Stalin's illegitimate son. (When Stalin had been exiled to Siberia in 1912, he lived in the house of a Cossack woman named Kuzakova.) Kuzakov was very well educated, incredibly smart, farseeing, and cautious. He of course appreciated Eidelman's talent. He also liked my films and wanted me to work for Litdrama.

I was euphoric throughout the whole period of filming *Pushkin and Pushchin*. While preparing for the film, I read everything possible about the lives of Pushkin and Pushchin and the history of the Decembrist uprising—I couldn't work with a coauthor of Eidelman's stature without serious preparation. It took almost six months. But what a half year it was—so much joy and satisfaction! Eidelman, I think, felt more comfortable in the nineteenth century than in the twentieth. He told me a lot of fascinating things that were extremely helpful.

When I was ready, we started to work on the screenplay, discussing every detail. Then we started filming, which went very quickly, because everything had been planned. We used the antiquated Soviet synchronous Moskva camera, which with all the bells and whistles weighed around 250 pounds, and the equally ancient nonsynchronous Soviet camera Konvas for outdoor scenes. I decided to film in 35 mm rather than 16 mm, as in my previous films, because I wanted to achieve a richly colorful picture. I wanted to complement the textual information with an emotional visual and musical atmosphere. We filmed in many places. Besides Moscow and Leningrad, we went to the Pushkin estate in Mikhailovskoe; to the Vyra train station, home of the hero of Pushkin's tale *The Station Master;* and to the tiny town of Petrovsky Zavod in Siberia, where the tsar exiled the Decembrist rebels after the uprising.

My friend, the artist Yura Ivanov, created marvelous paintings for title cards to introduce each chapter of the film. The actress Alla Demidova recited Pushkin's poetry. Marina Krutoyarskaya wrote beautiful music. And of course there were Eidelman's brilliant, dramatic, humorous, and touching stories. For the first time in my life, I was completely satisfied with my work.

Kuzakov liked the film too. He was melting with pleasure when he screened it. He loved Leningrad passionately, and I had captured the city in an emotional way. Powdered with wet white snow, vast empty vistas, the Fortress of Peter and Paul, the horses on Anichkov Bridge, the heavy cast-iron chains . . . I had a high fever when I was filming, which apparently added to the mood (I always catch a cold in Leningrad—its climate is not for me!), Kuzakov even shed a tear while watching the scenes in Siberia, where Pushchin had been exiled. This I shot when it was forty degrees below zero, with the izbas—little log houses—covered in ice and glistening in the sun. Kuzakov approved the film without requiring a single change and thanked us for our excellent work.

The next executive who needed to approve the film for a broadcast was Stella Zhdanova, who had been promoted to deputy minister in the culture area. She had always been well disposed toward me. I asked her if I needed to be at the screening. "No, no," she said. "I'll watch it when I have time."

Well, the bosses may have their tricks, but directors had their own. There was no difficulty finding out when the screening would be. I dropped into the projection booth and looked through the window into the screening room. Stella Zhdanova was nervously pacing in the darkened room.

A few days of silence followed. I didn't call her; she didn't call me. Finally, I asked Kuzakov, "Well, did the bosses like it?"

"To tell you the truth, Eidelman's Jewishness won't allow us to air the film in prime time—there will be too much mail from people asking why we couldn't find anyone else to do a show about the great Russian poet."

The film was shown at ten in the morning, on June 6, Pushkin's birthday. It was shown once and never repeated. Who lost? Everyone—including those people whose angry letters and telephone calls the television bosses feared so much. We had no better raconteur and expert on the nineteenth century than Eidelman.

That ended the euphoric experience of my "escape" from Ekran. But there had been so much pleasure in the work! I still recall it as a gift from fate. Working on *Pushkin and Pushchin,* Eidelman and I became good friends. I saw a lot of him and his wife, Yulya, and we dreamed of filming Pushkin's *History of Peter the Great.* We never made it. Natan Eidelman died of a heart attack before he was sixty.

Nikolai Sivkov and Anatoly Strelyany
(*Arkhangelsk Muzhik*, 1986)

Nikolai Semionovitch Sivkov

kov's house

Sivkov's family

ВЛАСТЬ СОЛОВЕЦКАЯ

Dmitri Sergeevitch Likhachev, academician

Oleg Vasilievitch Volkov, writer

Solovki monastery (view from outside)

Solovki monastery (view from inside)

An old cemetery in the woods

Dmitry Uspensky, general

Efim Dmitrievitch Lagutin, worker

Zoya Dmitrievna Marchenko, stenographer

The church on Sekirnaya Hill, Solovki

Shooting *Solovki Power*

Anastasia Tsvetayeva with our crew in her home after the shoot (1986)

Elena Obraztsova and Vazha Chachava (*More Than Love*, 1989)

Anastasia Ivanovna Tsvetayeva (*I Am Ninety, My Steps Are Light*, 1989)

Oleg Efremov, actor and director (*For the Theater to Be*, 1987)

Compromises

I joined the Communist Party in 1966. This is how it happened. About a year after I started working in television, I was told, "You are invited to be a guest of honor for the May Day celebration at the State Committee for Television and Radio on Pyatnitskaya Street."

That was unimaginable. I did pretty good work, but an honor like that? I later learned the ulterior motive. Orders from higher up called for a young woman to represent the cinematographers who worked for television. There were three of us, and I was the youngest. I was selected.

I sat next to Georgy Ivanov, then deputy minister of television. He was a tough man and knew his work—he had worked in the Ministry of Culture before that. Everyone feared him. They knew that if he called them on the carpet, nothing but a few bones would be left. And there I was, sitting next to him.

There were speeches, people droning on and on. Suddenly he turned to me and said, "Did you hear that Baskakov broke a leg?"

"Really?"

"The better question is whose."

That joke swiftly made the rounds. Baskakov was the deputy chairman of Goskino, the state film committee and was known for his grim and harsh management style.

My time in the presidium with the big shots that day was the first—and, thank God, the last—involvement with these rarefied circles. But a few months later, the secretary of the Party approached me. He said, "We've been given three spaces for new members in the Party. We want to propose your candidacy."

"The Party? But I'm too young. I'm only twenty-five."

"That's fine. They're trying to bring down the median age. They need young people. We've checked. You were always active in the Komsomol." That was true. At vgik, I was the secretary for the Komsomol (Communist Youth League) in the cinematography department.

"Think about it," he went on. "It's a serious step and a great honor."

"Would they take me?"

"They will. I've discussed your candidacy with the chairman of our Communist Party Committee. You're in graduate school. We need people like you."

I came home and said, "Papa, they asked me to join the Party."

"Well, and what did you say?"

"I said that I'd consider it, but that, in general, I agreed."

"Are you crazy? Why do you need to get involved in that shit?" And he told me a joke, which works on a pun on the word *vstupat,* which means "to join" but literally "to step in": "Rabinovich, did you step in the Party?" "Where?" he replies, looking at the bottom of his shoe.

Father's reaction worried me a lot. He probably knew much more than me. At that time we knew little about the crimes of the Stalin regime, committed with the Party's participation. And we still had sweet hopes that Khrushchev's Thaw would build socialism with a human face.

"What do I do now? I sort of indicated that I accepted."

To tell the truth, I myself sensed deep down that I was doing something wrong, but I didn't have the strength to say no. I knew that my refusal would have repercussions at work.

Father did not stand up for his opinion, and after a while he said, "You know, maybe you're right. If you don't join, you won't get anywhere in television."

At that time, I didn't know exactly what awaited me after I joined. I had always been a social animal and lived with the sense of belonging to the collective, to a common cause.

I was given the application form to fill out. They began preparing me. (Later they told me about an acquaintance who worked at a scientific institute. When he was told, "We've decided to prepare you for the Party," he replied without a second's hesitation, "Am I a pig that needs to be prepared?" No one ever brought up the subject with him again.)

God, I had to get the approval from twelve levels of authority. I had to know all about dialectical and historical materialism, about the principles of democratic centralism, about the Communist Party leaders of other socialist countries, and other things I can't even remember now. After the eleventh test, I was accepted as a candidate for membership. That took a year. In late 1967, I was made a member. And in 1968, our tanks rolled into Czechoslovakia. I felt terrible.

I was a member of the Communist Party for twenty years. Should I have been? Or would it have been more honest not to join? Perhaps. I do know that

otherwise I would not have gotten ahead in television. In an ideological organization like television, a camera operator who was not a Party member could
never be promoted.

Joining the Party did not change me and did not keep me from understanding and evaluating what was going on or prevent me from acting on my own
in the most important moments of life. I did not get muck on my shoes or anywhere else. Yes, of course, I watched the growing senility of the system, and
I did not try to counter it or fight for it. In my wildest dreams, I could never
have expected it to collapse on its own. We all felt that it would last forever or
at least for our lifetime. I just tried to do my work well.

My job gave me a certain freedom. But freedom always has a price. My Party
membership was my payment. Without it I would not have been able to work
as a director. I probably would not have been allowed to defend my doctor-
ate dissertation, and certainly I would not have been permitted to combine my
television work with teaching at the Moscow State University School of Journalism for almost twenty years. That permission had to be renewed annually,
and it was done grudgingly and had to be signed by the minister of television
himself.

I was kept worrying that I would lose my Party card. The Party rules were
stringent, especially in television. One of the cameramen was expelled from
the Party for losing his card. Another one, however, was only chewed out for
leaving his card behind on a beer barrel—he was the secretary of our Party
organization. I couldn't understand why he was treated so leniently, but later I
learned that he worked for the KGB. By then, I knew that practically every third
person in the cinematography group worked for the secret police. In order to
work for television, you had to have various clearances. I ended up having a
clearance as well. I don't think I ever filmed anything that actually was secret
or that I had information that might be of interest to potential spies. But I did
often work in Star City, home of the cosmonauts; in the Kremlin; and in Bai-
konur, where the Russian spaceships were launched. A person needed clearance
just to set foot in those places. I wouldn't have gotten that clearance without
my Party membership.

Party meetings were routine, duller and more boring with every year. We
treated them as inevitable events—medicine may taste bad, but if you want to
live, you take it. If you want to work in TV, you go to the meetings. Almost
everyone in the documentary studio was a member of the Communist Party.

The most difficult time in my Party life was the expulsion of Arkady
Edidovich.

In 1981, Maxim Shostakovich, chief conductor of the Radio and Television

Symphony Orchestra and son of the great composer, stayed abroad instead of coming home to the USSR. News of his defection roared through the corridors of Ostankino like a bomb blast. In a totalitarian state, this kind of event had enormous ramifications. If a relative of a television staffer left the homeland (which was becoming more frequent in the 1970s), the person became a pariah—forced to accept a demotion or leave altogether. The person's coworkers also suffered: they had to demonstrate their moral condemnation in order to keep their own jobs. The Maxim Shostakovich incident made things much worse. From then on, if your relatives applied for immigration, you were in danger of being fired at any time—some people quit, some were dismissed. Natasha Dovgalyuk, whose daughter married the son of a Russian Orthodox priest in the United States, had to quit as department head and continue to work as an ordinary staffer.

And then lightning struck. Cameraman Arkady Edidovich's daughter was marrying an American. Arkady was deputy secretary of ideology of our local Party organization. What a nightmare! Everyone was whispering about it. I almost fainted when I heard, and I started imagining what would happen.

Misfortune rarely comes alone. Larissa, Arkady's wife, fell seriously ill. She also worked in TV and was a highly respected and creative editor in young people's programming. And Arkady himself had to go in for difficult surgery at the same time. They prepared almost three months for the Party meeting that would decide his fate. Party secretary Lev Dovgvillo spoke privately with all of us: "Do you understand what this means! We have to fight back! This shames our entire studio!"

I knew that the question of expulsion would be raised at the meeting, and I was very worried about what to do. I couldn't vote against my comrade. My son, Seryozha, who was seventeen then, said, "Just don't go! Get sick! You shouldn't be there."

But I couldn't not go. At the meeting, I started to understand Stalin's Terror of the 1930s. Before, I used to think, "How lucky I am! I was born when people no longer had to fear arrest, lie all the time, and betray their friends— all the horrors that my parents' generation had faced." And suddenly I myself had to experience pretty much the same thing, without threat of arrest or torture, of course.

I was flabbergasted to hear people who had worked with Arkady and me for twenty-five years demand him to condemn and denounce his daughter.

"American missiles are aimed at the Soviet Union and your daughter marries an American? How could you allow that?"

"How can I renounce my daughter?" Arkady said. "Her life worked out that way." (Incidentally, his daughter, Lena, and her husband, Carl, have a lovely family, now with two grown daughters. Lena is a lawyer, and they live in Los Angeles.)

There were four abstentions—I was one of them. The rest voted for expulsion. Dovgvillo, his eyes yellow with hatred, demanded, "Let the ones who abstained explain their reasons."

A representative of the Party Bureau of the State Committee for Television and Radio was present at the meeting. He had been my student in journalism school. He never worked as a journalist; he became a Party functionary instead. But there are all kinds of functionaries. "No. That's their private business," this envoy of the higher-ups unexpectedly ruled.

When the meeting was over, no one came over to me. No one said a word, even though generally I was on very good terms with most of them and they had elected me chairman of the Cinematographers' Council.

I showed up at work the next day, and people avoided me, waiting to see how things would turn out. I expected a serious reprimand.

Natasha Yudina, a friend I could talk to, came up to me the next day and said, "What have you done! Why did you do it? You didn't save him anyway. He was expelled—you knew that would happen. And now you won't be able to work here. You'll be fired."

"Well, it's too late now."

"You're crazy."

Why were we all so afraid? That fear must be contagious. We lived with it every single day, and there was no way to get rid of it.

For a while, my first husband and I lived in a communal flat. I was given a samizdat book—a manuscript of a banned book. I think it was Alexander Solzhenitsyn's *Cancer Ward*. I read all night, went on location in the morning, and forgot to lock the door. I was in a panic all day: what if one of the neighbors walked in and saw the banned literature? My mother always worried when we read samizdat (or *tamizdat*), which had been published abroad and then smuggled into the USSR.

Once one of Seryozha's friends made some silly amateur film joking about Lenin and Felix Dzerzhinsky, the founder of the KGB. A fine topic indeed. His apartment was searched. Fortunately, he had managed to hide the film and then came to hide it in our place. I knew that the KGB could come at any time to search our place as well. So I took the film to a friend, and we flushed it down the toilet. It turns out there was a legal term, *unitazirovanie,* for our action. It meant "destroying evidence by flushing it down the *unitaz.*"

Sharp Angles

Most Soviet television documentaries portrayed people in an official way, creating only role models. That's why it was so hard to work on them. A film is interesting only when there's conflict, edginess, something unusual, and those were the very things that were hard to get past our bosses. The editors feared conflict the way devils fear church incense.

Even though the subjects of my films were positive characters, I still tried to show other aspects, such as their ability to take action and readiness to stand up against, if not the regime and system, then at least the circumstances. I was always looking for such people to become characters in my films. At the same time, I was trying to find scriptwriters and journalists of the same kind to help me create controversial stories. I wasn't interested in working with conformists like Tatiana Tess or Yevgeny Revenko, journalists who were loved by the bosses. They always glorified the heroes of the communal farms and recounted their great triumphs.

I wanted to say something significant, without pretentious words and emotions. I wanted to tell about worthy heroes who lived for their work, who fought for it, and whose fight could be shown on-screen.

Damir Belov, an honest and talented journalist who knew how to write proposals that would not scare the higher-ups, suggested that I film *The Eighth Director*. Our subject was Viktor Litvinenko, the director of the Tutaev Automobile Plant. He was a young, energetic, and straight-thinking man who had a critical view of the country's situation and wasn't afraid to get into conflict with his bosses. He was trying to do his job—to modernize the factory after it had been neglected for so many years. He was a "new Russian"—a person with entrepreneurial energy, with no reference to nouveau riche vulgarity. He had a vivid chiseled face and a life history filled with unusual incidents—he was all sharp angles.

This was a new experience for me: making a film that was polemical and critical of our stagnating Soviet life. I moved to Tutaev, formerly known as Romanovo-Borisoglebsk, an ancient Russian town some three hundred kilometers northeast of Moscow and about forty kilometers from Yaroslavl, where the factory was located. Every day I took my camera, went to the plant, sat in Litvinenko's office, followed him around on the factory floor, and filmed his daily life as a manager. He spoke harshly about the state of his industry and about what was happening in the region; his relations with the Regional Party Committee, who represented the real power in this area, were very tense. We made the film without self-censorship. We had decided to make a candid film without considering the wishes of our bosses. I remember the profound horror I felt during the filming, always anxious about how things would work out. Damir Belov then smoothed the edges with a soft, moderately compromising text, but left it sufficiently pointed.

Back then, in 1981, preparations were under way for the next Party congress, and slightly critical commentaries were encouraged by the chief executives of the Communist Party. There were glimmers of a turn toward a struggle with shortcomings (inadequacies), especially in the work of the ministries.

We invited Yevgeny Veltistov to be our consultant for *The Eighth Director*. Veltistov at that time was in charge of the television section of the Party's Central Committee, and we needed his support. He was also known as a writer, a creative person who was easy to work with. Since he was behind us, we felt we could keep some of the sharper points in the film.

When the film was ready for postproduction, Veltistov decided to screen it in the Kremlin during the coming Party conference. He felt that at that political moment the picture suited the needs of the Central Committee. When Khessin, the director of Ekran, learned of Veltistov's intentions, he panicked. He clearly didn't want to show the high Party executives a controversial film that openly criticized the Party organization of Yaroslavl and the Ministry of the Automobile Industry. He organized a studio discussion in which the participants tore the picture apart, not from an ideological point of view but from an artistic one. It was ugly. Khessin set the tone, and the artistic board—the leading directors of the studio—followed, one after another criticizing the picture's alleged flaws. The film needed more work, said my own colleagues, my fellow thinkers and friends who worked with me in the Ekran zoo. I don't want to name names here.

The relationships inside Ekran were always complex. Everyone was talented, but who is without envy? As I already mentioned, I'm certain that there was a male complex at work as well. The male directors believed that issue films were a men's field and that men had a monopoly on them—and not all men at that, just a few special ones. All that phony criticism upset me, and it complicated the release of the film. This was the first time I had furious verbal exchanges with my colleagues. It took a long time for me to get over it—the hurt, the injustice, the insults I had to listen to.

They didn't pass the film and instead asked me to make some changes. The changes were trifles that took only a few hours of editing. But Khessin achieved his goal: the film wasn't shown at the Party conference. Later it was broadcast on prime time. As expected, *The Eighth Director* caused an uproar.

The most hostile reaction came from the Party leaders in Yaroslavl. In those years, the Yaroslavl correspondent of *Pravda,* the national Party newspaper, was Galina Bystrova, and she hated Litvinenko. But Pravda's film critic, Andrei Plakhov, praised the film. Bystrova attacked the press who had applauded Litvinenko and my film. She suspected a Zionist conspiracy. Goldovskaya had made a film about him, she said, and even Plakhov took the bait, giving the film a good review and thus supporting Litvinenko, who was a suspicious person from who knows where. She hinted broadly that he was a foreign agent serving Zionists, even though Litvinenko was a pure-blooded Ukrainian and served only his work and, through his work, the country. It was a full-fledged public denunciation.

Immediately after the article appeared, Polyakov, the automobile industry minister, visited Ekran. His assistant had called, informing us that the minister had missed the broadcast and wanted to see the film. Our chief editor, Valentina Murazova, set up a screening for Sunday and asked me to join her. Polyakov arrived in a Chaika limousine, accompanied by a retinue of other cars. He entered with great self-importance, intended to impress upon us his stature as a government official. Our staff loaded the projector and ran the film. Polyakov kept making sarcastic comments, reacting to almost every statement Litvinenko made, clearly showing his displeasure.

Murazova held her own. I want to give her credit here, because it was not always easy to work with her. She was moody, saying yes today and no tomorrow. She didn't like me very much; at least, I used to think that. I always had trouble understanding whether she wanted me to make a film or not, whether she'd let me do it or not. After all, I wasn't a staff director. I was considered a cinematographer at Ekran. But she was a professional, and a principled one. If she let you work and she had approved the film, she backed it all the way.

"Why didn't you come to me?" Polyakov asked. "I would have suggested the right director of an automobile plant to film."

"You know," Murazova replied, "we make documentary films here, not commercials."

The film never aired again. Litvinenko was fired. He fell ill and was hospitalized for a long time. The Party authorities continued to badger him, but a few years later he was back once again, as the director of a plant in the defense industry. Unfortunately, I've lost track of him and don't know what he's doing now.

The Eighth Director sparked my taste for strong issue films, the knowledge that I was doing something needed, and the intoxicating spirit of fighting the good fight. I wanted to work on films that could make a splash in the swamp, even if it brought pain and problems for me personally.

I am used to thinking of myself as a serious filmmaker, and I hope that I have earned the right to do so. I've always treated the profession seriously and respectfully. It is for others to judge how good a director I am, but everything I did, I did with sincerity, without selling out. Being envied by men hurt, but it taught me to keep up appearances. Being attacked (of course, not by everyone and, of course, not all the time) just made me stronger. I tried to find a kernel of truth even in unjust criticism, so that I could grow creatively and professionally. At the time of the criticism, naturally it hurt a lot.

Those years were filled with absurdity and stupidity, fear, bureaucracy, and censorship. And yet through the distance of time, I can definitely state that the good outweighed the bad. And many of the things we considered obstacles no longer exist—those artistic boards, for one thing.

Yes, we used to call our Ekran collective "the zoo of the like-minded." Yes, like any collective where the tone is set by creative people, we had envy, jealousy, and hostility—as in any group. But life in this creative milieu offered ideas and experiences. The opportunity to see the works of colleagues, to discuss them, to be in the process of developing projects (we watched one another's works in all the stages—first draft, rough cut, and final result) taught us the profession and how to get the maximum from the material. We watched films in every genre; we had about twenty directors, and each of them had his or her own style and point of view. Even painful criticism, sometimes fair and sometimes not very, was beneficial. It helped me acquire professional qualities as well as the necessary defense mechanisms to deal with criticism.

When I worked in Soviet television, I was part of a professional circle of colleagues, and some of them became lifelong friends. These were people with the same blood group, so to speak, who shared the passion for our profession. We trusted each other's taste and gave each other priceless support.

On the Threshold of Change

After making *The Eighth Director,* I realized that my interests had shifted toward issue films, which put new problems on my agenda. I had to find bold and fearless journalists who knew contemporary issues. Liberal journalists, who were few in those days, were mostly writing for such Soviet newspapers and magazines as *Novy Mir, Literaturnaya Gazeta,* and *Moskovskie Novosti.* One of them was Gennady Lisichkin, an economist and journalist. He wrote pointed articles touching on the very foundation of the socialist system. Naturally, the bosses in television did not want to see him among their writers—he was too controversial. But I managed to get him past their watchdogs.

In those days, there was a lot of talk about expanding the production in collective and state farms to other, nonagricultural areas such as electronics and textiles, and Lisichkin slipped in as a specialist in that area. He had a degree in economics, was about to defend his doctoral dissertation, and was a highly respected professional. His chief at the Institute of the Economy of Socialist Countries was Oleg Bogomolov. We decided that he would be a priceless addition as consultant on our next film—a member of the Academy of Sciences, a member of the Party's Central Committee, a man with access to the highest spheres. People had to take his opinion seriously, and that included our television executives.

Bogomolov also understood that whenever we tried to get a film approved, we would have to resort to the standard Soviet demagoguery, stressing a topic's relevance and political significance.

We started making *The Center of Gravity* (1984), a film exploring new and more modern ways to improve the economics of agriculture. I hadn't worked on such issues before. I had been more interested in people and their inner worlds. I was terrified throughout the filming because the theme seemed so complex, dry, and "inartistic." It wasn't clear how I could make something human of this not very attractive and unemotional material. I understood almost nothing about the economy, and I had to rely totally on Lisichkin. In his turn, he had no film experience. So I taught him a few things about filmmaking, and he taught me about agriculture, economics, and politics. This was the first time I had worked so closely with a journalist. Before this film, my screenwriters usually showed up when we had finished editing. Working with Lisichkin was enlightening and allowed me to plunge into new areas. Not only did we complete the film, but we also made a decent one.

Our heroes were manufacturing various products completely unrelated to agriculture. That way there was work in the winter, creating supplemental income and keeping the young people on the farms. Mikhail Vagin, chairman of large collective farm in Voronezh, initiated the production of souvenirs in the Khokhloma style. Vassily Starodubtsev (who later became notorious for his part in the failed coup attempt against Gorbachev) organized a dress factory on his collective farm (kolkhoz) that employed a good part of its female members. We also filmed a kolkhoz in Estonia that manufactured electronics as well as working in agriculture. The radios produced brought in more money than the farming did.

From the artistic point of view, this film was not a big achievement. But it definitely was not conventional. It carried a hot contemporary message that favored one side of an ongoing struggle within the government, in which the liberals supported the idea of decision making on local levels and the conservatives favored decision making coming only from the Central Committee of the Party. The film hit a nerve.

Our studio executives didn't want to get involved in this fight and decided to shelve the film. And here came Bogomolov, our consultant. He immediately understood the core of the problem and decided to take the matter to one of the liberals—Nikolai Baibakov, chairman of Gosplan, the State Planning Commission for the economy.

"You know, there's a documentary just made for television that I think is very important for the policy you are planning to promote," Bogomolov told Baibakov.

Baibakov requested a screening. We brought him the film, and it was shown to his top people. He was very pleased. "This is just what we need now!" he said. "Thank you for the film."

He called Lapin, the minister of television. It was 7:30 in the evening, but Lapin was still in his office. "I just saw a film made at your Ekran Studio," Baibakov said. "It should be shown as soon as possible in prime time. I think this film is very timely."

Lapin gave orders to broadcast *Center of Gravity* at 8 p.m. the following Friday, when everyone watched television. After it aired, a friend called me. He knew how things worked behind the scenes in the Soviet system. "What's happening?" he asked. "Is the policy being changed?"

There was nothing shocking in the film. But apparently we as a society had learned to read between the lines and were able to sense the drift even in an ideologically "safe" film.

Nowadays, I miss the feeling that the films I am making are important for society and can make a difference. My old friends, documentary filmmakers joke, "We are completely independent—nothing depends on us anymore." Back then it was different. When I was making films in the 1980s, I knew I was doing something that could end very badly for me. My knees were weak with fear: Would the film be all right? Would I be fired? Is this the end to my career? Or not yet? There was a constant sense of risk. But at the same time, it gave me an intoxicating, addictive high that came from knowing that my film was needed, that it was helping society move forward.

Lisichkin and I became friends while working on *Center of Gravity*. Through him, I met his journalist colleagues Zhenya Budinas and Anatoly Strelyany. With them, I made my next two films.

First came a film about Vladimir Byadulya, the chairman of a Belarussian collective farm, a Hero of Socialist Labor. It was Budinas who suggested making a film about him. Budinas was considered a controversial journalist then, a troublemaker who was unafraid of criticizing the Soviet regime or speaking out against the Communist Party. He wrote a book about Byadulya, in which he described him as an amusing and interesting character.

Budinas and I decided to make a film about Byadulya, who was clearly extraordinary: witty, coarse, stingy, petty, charming, generous, and sly—a great mix. He got away with a lot of things by playing the fool and the eccentric. He had a foxy, sharp-nosed face, not handsome but expressive. No one could ever predict what he would say. And that was so interesting! He was unlike the faceless types who filled the screen, reading prepared texts and clearly showing their one-track minds. Byadulya was a live person and, most important, a strong leader, not afraid of making decisions and taking responsibility.

This was my third film in a row about peasant life. I liked things better in the country: nature, small villages, the faces of the peasants, their natural behavior. I preferred this to city life and urban landscapes. And our hero's personality permitted a more intensive debate about the dilemma of agriculture, a subject that always attracted the interest of the Party and its leaders. Agriculture always was a problem for the Soviet regime.

I knew I was taking on difficult material again. I was counting on Byadulya's extraordinary personality and natural sense of humor and of course on my screenwriter, who knew our hero well. Budinas's screenplay was yet another piece of flummery. It was intended only to please the bosses and get us into production. I decided to follow the flow of life and trust my ability to capture what was most characteristic, vivid, and interesting, sometimes provoking events and situations myself. Then, in the editing room, I would try to build the film on the logic of the material. Lord, how wrong I was that time!

The first week went well. Our crew, which I had selected carefully, worked smoothly. We were surrounded by lovely scenery and pleasant people. I was getting a feel for Byadulya and letting him get used to me while we waited for the screenwriter to arrive.

When Budinas came, I realized that he and Byadulya had no rapport. I even got the feeling that Byadulya and others treated Budinas with irony. Budinas was a first-timer in documentary film, and all his suggestions were useless. He came up with situations that would never have occurred in reality. I had never scripted or staged situations for the people I was filming, and Budinas's ideas were absolutely unacceptable.

I can usually find a compromise in any hopeless situation. My many years in TV news had been a good schooling: so many events, so many trips, so many people with whom I had to find a common language. I also knew how important it was for me as the head of the film crew to stay calm and never show confusion or nervousness. But this time it was impossible to compromise with Budinas. He had no self-control. He shouted and insulted me in front of others —Byadulya, the farmworkers, the crew.

I lost it: "Zhenya, get the hell out of here."

That evening, my gaffers approached him and said, "Either you walk out now, or you'll need an ambulance to leave. Get lost!"

He left, thank goodness. I stayed alone with my crew and made the film without the scriptwriter. He came to Moscow later, when we were finished, acting as if nothing had happened, and said that he liked the film. By the way, its title was *Hello, Byadulya Speaking*. That's the whole story. Even today, twenty years later, I get upset when I think about it. But I learned a lot from that experience.

Before *Hello, Byadulya Speaking* (1985), I had always tried to keep my presence out of the picture. I didn't want to interfere with the life unfolding in front of my camera. "Fly-on-the-wall style" best describes this way of shooting.

My main goal was to avoid ready solutions and to let the viewers experience the situations together with my characters. Then the viewers can draw their own conclusions. For *Hello, Byadulya Speaking,* I had originally planned to have Budinas ask all the pertinent questions of Byadulya, thus opening a two-way conversation that would reveal the subject's character. Budinas's departure put me in an extraordinary situation. I had to communicate with Byadulya myself.

The result was unexpectedly good. He spoke naturally with me, and not even the glassy eye of the lens seemed to bother him. I don't think anything concerned him but his work. In the course of the conversation, we came upon some unexpected twists that forced me to irritate him intentionally to get him to talk more. And it worked.

In the editing phase, I discovered that my off-screen presence, the conversational style of conducting an interview, allowed me to build narrative into the fabric of the film more organically than when I cut my questions out of the sound track.

All in all, this film gave me more than I expected. It taught me that the method of interactive communication with the characters brings interesting results, and I have used it ever since.

In spring 1985, I received an unexpected offer—to film the Jewish Musical Theater on their tour throughout America. I would have to work as director, camerawoman, sound person, and, obviously, interpreter. I was told that the top Party officials who planned this tour had chosen me, a woman, for a reason. Our authorities had always scared us with the idea that, because of the cold war, we could become the targets of provocations, assassinations, and bombs. They thought a woman was a less likely target.

The KGB agent who was assigned to the group as an actor turned out to be a nice guy. He hinted that my usual minus (that I was Jewish) was a plus in this case. In every way, I suited those who had planned this trip.

I refused the trip, though, knowing that this wasn't just a theater tour but a tour with a political message, and I didn't want to play that game. Once you get dirty, it's impossible to get clean.

The political message was that Jews were happy in the Soviet Union. They even had their own theater, and they could travel freely to America. Of course, no one would have dared to organize a tour like this during Brezhnev's days. The bosses would have feared that half the theater would defect. And that might have happened—many ballet stars did just that.

The work would have been tough. I was supposed to use video. That was a new technology for me. I hadn't used it much, and I was worried that I would not be able to handle it well.

Finally, they forced me to go, and I'm glad they did. In preparation for this trip, I daily exercised my skills on the new video camera, and a week before we were supposed to depart, I was pretty proficient on the Betacam. My fear was gone.

I had to take about three hundred pounds of equipment along: camera, video player, monitor, portable lighting, microphones. Of course, I had help dragging all that stuff around, but I was supposed to use it all by myself. These are the situations that make you a pro, though. You learn the way some people learn to swim—by jumping in and flailing to keep from drowning.

The end result was a pretty good film: *Tumbalalaika in America*. Back in Moscow, my editors were sure that the film would never get through the censor's scrutiny. Already Jews were bad enough. But America! I showed it as a beautiful, free country, where people were happy.

The film was shown to Alexander Yakovlev, the chairman of the Ideology Department of the Communist Party. Surprisingly, he gave his approval for broadcast. Ekran's bosses, however, cut one scene out. I had filmed people sitting in a park, drinking, chatting, and listening to music. They were free. What was so provocative about that? For Soviet television at that time this was an unusual picture of America. Soviet viewers were used to seeing only trash and slums. Our correspondents seemed to interview only the homeless and the unemployed, with garbage dumps in the background. Those stereotypes were so ingrained in us that I always thought American films were exaggerating the well-being of normal life in the USA.

We had seen the changes coming in the Soviet Union long before they began. Everything was rotten and collapsing. I remember my conversation with Lisichkin in 1984 during the filming of *Center of Gravity*. We were discussing the Soviet economy, wondering when it all would collapse.

"It's inevitable," he said. "A country can't function with this economy. Something has to give."

Anybody who understood the situation had to come to the same conclusion. I had traveled the country a lot and had met many people from different walks of life, and all of them felt the same way. The country was moving toward the abyss. Many newspaper articles described the situation with an unprecedented measure of truth, yet the government's propaganda machine proceeded at full blast. Dissidents were imprisoned or locked up in mental institutions. The regime was in no hurry to yield.

As a member of the Party, I had to attend seminars and lectures on the state of the union. In the mid-1980s the leaders of these events openly told us that we were on the eve of witnessing great changes in how information would be disseminated: the Americans would be launching satellites, and the Soviet government would no longer be able to jam Western radio. The coming information explosion worried the leadership of the country. How could they retain a monopoly on information?

It was no secret that production was falling, the economy was collapsing, warehouses were filled with domestic consumer goods that people wouldn't take even for free, and the war in Afghanistan had turned into a trap that we had set for ourselves. The rulers were trying to figure out how to avoid the coming catastrophe. Was there a way out? The joke said there were two, through the Spassky Gates and the Borovitsky Gates—the only open entrances and exits of the Kremlin.

But no one was counting on that.

Arkhangelsk Muzhik

Back in the Brezhnev days a popular joke went like this: "Is a two-party system possible in the USSR?" "No. We couldn't afford to feed two parties."

Throughout the Soviet period, no one dared mention a multiparty system. There was only one party, whose leading role was defined by the Constitution. Now it all seems like a bad dream—did it happen? But in those days, when a second party was still impossible but was needed to move the nation forward, journalists performed the role. Gorbachev, many felt, used journalism—press, radio, and television—as a kind of opposition party. I was fortunate to work during the years when documentary film was needed as never before.

Every year we had to turn in a plan outlining what we would want to produce during the following twelve-month period. Usually I prepared ten to fifteen projects in the hope of getting one approved. As mentioned, I always tried to have vivid, unusual-thinking journalists to work with me. One was Anatoly Strelyany. I loved his book *Visiting Mother,* about his native village and its people, his mother, their neighbors, and daily life in the village. He wrote in a lively and entertaining way. The picture that emerged was sad but undoubtedly truthful and also funny.

For many years "village prose"—literature on peasant life—was very popular. The powerful novels of Valentin Rasputin, Viktor Astafyev, Fedor Abramov, and Vassily Belov were devoured (that interest has died out completely now), for it showed a glimmer of truth about the system. My interest in country life had a reason: I believed that documentary film could explore the plight of villagers in a visually descriptive way.

I suggested to Anatoly that he write a proposal based on his book—and strangely enough, despite his dubious political reputation, the proposal was accepted. The plan was made a year in advance, which is ridiculous for documentary film. So much could change in a year!

At the end of 1985, when the time came to start working on this film, Anatoly and I met to figure out how to go about it.

"What if we don't do this film?" I asked. "Why don't we do something different? If we film in your village, how do we deal with the fact that everyone speaks Ukrainian, which Russian viewers won't understand. Russian television won't accept a film in Ukrainian. Are we going to do it with subtitles? Or ask everyone to speak Russian?"

"They can speak Russian," Anatoly responded, "but not very well. It won't look natural—they're used to speaking Ukrainian. And it would be silly for me to speak Russian with them."

That wasn't the only thing that worried me. "If we make a film based on the book, we'll touch on some problems that are current today," I pointed out. "But shouldn't we look for something even more relevant? Let's not rush this. Maybe we'll come up with something else."

"Do you know, I think a very relevant theme is individual farming," Anatoly suggested, "a return to what Stalin's forced collectivization ended. I'm reading a lot in the papers that private farming has been revived in various areas. They don't call it that, to avoid again being branded as kulaks. What do you think of that?" Kulaks were farmers who had been characterized as being excessively wealthy.

"That seems more like investigative journalism," I said. "and I am not a great fan of that genre. I would prefer to make something more artistic."

"Let's not do just one farm, but several. Different places, different textures. That will give artistic and visual variety. I know an excellent place in Estonia. There's a family that left the collective farm and started a private farm, producing milk, cheese, and kefir, which they sell to a store. Another example is a private restaurant in Georgia. The owners breed sheep and make *shashlyk* [kebab]. And I read about a peasant in the north, in Arkhangelsk. He owns a herd of sixty bulls, and he wants to revive his village. And in Bendery, in Moldavia, there is a place where the city folk were given large plots of land, and on weekends they grow tomatoes, vegetables, and fruit that they sell to the state—a form of private entrepreneurship."

"You're right," I agreed. "That's interesting."

Anatoly quickly wrote a new proposal for the film *His Own Boss,* and I took it to Murazova. "Our studio plan included a project entitled *Visiting Mother,*" I told her, "but we determined that we might be better off changing the subject and making a picture about individual enterprise."

"It's a good idea. But let's not change the title yet. It will cause loads of problems—we'll have to go to Lapin, get permission. It will take lots of time, and it's not certain that permission will be given. Let's keep the working title and see what happens. We'll always be able to change it later."

We planned to shoot in six different places. First, I went to Bendery and spent ten days preparing for Anatoly's arrival, shooting landscapes, the people in the city, and the people working the fields. They lived in tents and picked tomatoes. I filmed their life and their work and interviewed them; they told me what they liked about their enterprise. I got to know Alexander Novozhilov, the director of the local production unit, with whom we discussed all the pluses and minuses of the situation. Anatoly arrived, and I filmed their long conversation. I filmed a lot, but there was nothing striking in the footage. I came back to Moscow and watched the material.

The landscape was very flat, not eye-catching, and the tomato plantations were inexpressive, as were the fruit orchards. Novozhilov was very buttoned-up. Anatoly was wearing a suit, which didn't seem right on the farm, making him look like a visiting Moscow journalist. This was his first time as a documentary character. He and the director didn't manage to have a simple and natural conversation. The material was boring. It was nothing better than a piece for *Vremya,* the national TV news.

"It's not working," I said to Strelyany.

Disappointed, I got ready for the next site. Before I left Moscow, I met with Sasha Bekker, a journalist who had written for *Izvestiya* about Nikolai Sivkov, our next hero. I asked him a lot of questions. It turned out that Sasha had interviewed Sivkov after he sent a letter to the paper. Sivkov wrote that he wanted to revive the village where his father had lived and where there was only one house left. He wanted to start up a big farm, but the collective farm, where he used to work and which had originally promised to help him with equipment, wouldn't let him do it.

"He is a striking man. You'll find him very interesting," Sasha said.

I set out to Arkhangelsk, taking along both film and video cameras; I had decided to use both. I had used up most of the film stock of precious American Kodak film allotted to the project and realized that I would quickly run out of film—I had five more places to cover. And I wanted to try a new technology, mixing film and video.

It was a three-and-a-half-hour flight to Arkhangelsk. Then we took a ship along the Northern Dvina River, disembarked in a village near Sivkov's village, and continued from there by boat to his place.

There I found an amazing piece of land with fir trees and a broad river—pristine countryside. In the forest, on the banks of the Dvina, stood a wooden house, where our new hero lived with his wife, Galina, and their son and daughter. When we arrived, the question arose instantly: where would we live? Rooms had been booked for us in a tiny hotel, actually the guest house for kolkhoz workers in the village of Ust-Vaenga, six kilometers from Sivkov's private farm. The kolkhoz chairman sent a four-wheel-drive truck to take us to the house. There were no roads, and no other vehicle could have covered the way there.

We had five people in my crew—sound man, assistant, video engineer, production manager, and me. The first moment I saw Sivkov, I knew right away that he would be a perfect protagonist of the film. Moreover, he could carry the entire film with the power of his personality. He was sly, very smart, and quick to speak and make decisions. His precise and laconic language was full of images, quips, and humor. As I later learned, he had only two grades of formal schooling, but life had taught him all he needed.

He had been a seaman and a kolkhoz worker, he had worked in timber and bred pigs. He was an electrician and a mechanic, and he could repair engines and put in telephone lines. He had tried his hand at everything and had mastered a thousand professions. Self-taught, he had achieved everything through hard work, which did not diminish his energy in the least—he did everything with enthusiasm. We quickly developed rapport; I knew I had to stay in his house. That would help me to figure things out faster, as we had only seven days to do all the filming. I asked if I could do that.

"Please do stay with us," he offered. "But you'll have to sleep in the kitchen. If that suits you, you're welcome."

There was a kitchen and a big room where the whole family lived. I sent the crew to the guest house in the village and asked them to come back in the morning. I moved into the kitchen, which had a small cot. I kept the cameras with me.

After the crew left for the village, Sivkov went to feed the cattle, and I took a walk in the woods around his house. The sun was setting, with red rays slanting into the forest. There were huge blackberries dotted with dew, enormous mushrooms, the fragrance of hay in the air, and a mist over the river—God, it was beautiful! I was so lucky to be there filming. What a wonderful profession I had!

The next morning, I started following Sivkov around. There was a problem with the electricity. He climbed up the pole to do a repair and kept up a running commentary on his battles with the kolkhoz administration, who offered him neither understanding nor support. Hanging upside down on the pole and waving his tool in the air, he ranted angrily over the useless bureaucrats. He didn't sit down for a minute the entire day, going from chore to chore. I followed him with the camera, and we talked nonstop.

In three or four days he gave me a clear picture of the reasons for the problems in our economy, as he saw it. He did it simply, using examples that everyone could understand, and by referring to his own personal problems, not the entire country's. For example, why did he have such tense relations with the kolkhoz bookkeeper? She was envious and wanted to count what was in his pockets instead of her own. Why was there a salary ceiling at the kolkhoz? If there was a ceiling, you couldn't jump over it, and if you couldn't, then you didn't feel like jumping at all. Why didn't the kolkhoz chairman help Sivkov, rather than creating a lot of problems for him? Because it made life simpler for the chairman. To do nothing was easier than to do something. And the whole system was not prepared to readjust to the new economic endeavors. Sivkov talked about himself, but what he was saying was an explanation of why the Soviet economy was at a dead end.

What's the most important thing in a documentary? The character. The person. One whose life epitomizes the sore spots of today. Sivkov was such a person; his problems illuminated the flaws of the society. You could feel the enormous power of his desire to overcome them. He had conflicts. His whole life was a challenge to the swamp surrounding him. His conflicts weren't only with the local authorities but with the degenerating Soviet system. There was no place for an island of real life that he was trying to create for himself. He was beating his head against a wall, but he had no intention of retreating. He wanted to run his life his own way. His story was dramatic and fascinating.

I wrote down the main points of our conversations, selecting what most vividly covered the situation, both his personal one and the country's, so that when Anatoly arrived, I could point out for him the best subjects to discuss with Sivkov.

I also told Anatoly, "They're going to put us away for this film. Everything the man says goes to the root of the problem. I know they'll kick me out of the Party for this."

Back then, there wasn't even a glimmer of a hope to ever achieve the freedom that television enjoys today. Nothing Sivkov said was appropriate for airing. He spoke openly, which was new and, as I thought then, totally unacceptable for television. If we managed to get something onto the screen, it had to be surrounded, camouflaged by hints that people had to figure out for themselves.

"So we'll suffer once for an idea," Anatoly replied.

"I'm afraid."

"So we're not making the film?"

"Yes, we are."

With a sense of doom paradoxically mixed with a sense of happiness, I made the film. We filmed everything we needed on the farm, and then we called the kolkhoz chairman. He came with his deputy, both typical products of the system. All the characters were so vivid we couldn't have picked any better from central casting and run them through auditions. The kolkhoz chairman, a smart peasant but slightly confused and cowardly, had his own logic, and he expressed his position convincingly. His deputy, in a huge blue cap, held an enormous file folder to his belly (I'd pan over to it from time to time, which looked both funny and metaphorical), creating a living symbol of bureaucracy.

These characters could have been specially created for my film. They were all perfect. Sivkov was like fire. Full of energy and killer sarcasm, he attacked the chairman as if he were a bull attacking a red flag. The chairman fought back reluctantly, for it was not easy holding up to Sivkov's pressure. Galina, Sivkov's wife, was a weary middle-aged woman, like a squeezed-out lemon, looked worn out by the daily grind of work from morning till night.

"I don't need anything," she said. "He keeps trying to achieve something, but I don't need it."

Anyone could see that she didn't. Everything was a great effort for her. It seemed that their family had its internal conflicts too.

The son was energetic and young, also full of desire to work and follow in his father's footsteps. They had another worker on the farm, a young fellow whose wife had left him because of his drinking, and work was like a cure for him. Sivkov hired him, saying, "Watch it. If you start drinking, you're out of here." The man worked honestly and hard.

There was also the wonderful daughter. At thirteen, she traveled six kilometers alone to the school, either by boat or, in the winter, on horseback over the frozen lake. She was like her father. She was interested in the farm's economy and felt free and confident in their farm life.

The Sivkovs had a greenhouse, where they grew tomatoes, cucumbers, and green onions. The girl was in charge of the vegetables. It was so impressive. This was the Far North. No one else tried planting anything other than potatoes. But they were growing fresh vegetables. This was perfect for the idea of the film too. It gave evidence of how much can be done if a person really wants something to happen.

The house itself looked more like a henhouse and was also photogenic. It had once belonged to Sivkov's father, and Sivkov managed to preserve it. It was in the middle of a forest that created an aura of austere nature. We traveled by boat a small distance from the farm and found the remains of a large village that had been full of life before the revolution. Now the houses were uninhabitable, dilapidated. We filmed this abandoned village, with birds squawking in the distance. It reminded me of the village burned by the fascists from Andrei Tarkovsky's *Ivan's Childhood*, a film I love.

My anxiety vanished during the filming and was replaced by happiness that remained to the very end. There was so much beauty and power in nature! It was so wonderful being with these people and filming them. The material was delicious and juicy. The characters were vivid, unusual, and imbued with a deep sense of inner dignity and freedom.

The Northern Dvina River was wide and gorgeous, with forests on both banks. In the middle, not far from the Sivkov's farm, was a narrow island covered with grass and brush. Sivkov had moved his bulls there. He didn't need to take them pasture, they couldn't run off, and no one could attack them. He could sit on his porch and watch them through his binoculars to make sure everything was fine.

Everything came out all right for the theme, the personalities, and the situation. On the very last day, the helicopter I had requested arrived and allowed me to film the farm from above. I was lucky to get a shot of Sivkov in his boat, rowing right into the picture. For a feature film, we would have had to look long and hard to find a suitable landscape. Here it just fell into our lap as part of this film. We couldn't have hoped for better.

In seven days we filmed four hours on video, mostly interviews and conversations and around eight hours of film. When I looked at the footage in Moscow, I realized that we had succeeded. But my anxiety came back and settled deep inside me. There were many reasons for that. First of all, our script contained six sequences. Deviating from the script always brings complications when you turn in the film, and here we not only had changed the topic but also had reduced the number of sequences from six to one. As the director, I had to take full responsibility.

I had cooked the porridge, and now I had to eat it. If the film was a success, it would be a major victory for our studio. If it failed, that would be blamed on the professional incompetence of director Goldovskaya.

I knew I had taken a huge risk, but deep in my heart I felt that the film would be something special. How the authorities would view it was a different issue, but as the creator of the film, I did not need to feel ashamed.

When you start a film, you always think about what its fabric will be like. I had a clear sense of the concept. The story would be about the conflict between one man and the establishment. It would be a microcosm of the situation in the country. But what about the style?

The style depends on the material. Making it up, creating it artificially, is working in vain. You can't impose it on the material, because the audience will feel its artificiality. I wanted to show the routine of the family's life—it had a poetry of its own. As I filmed Sivkov, I observed his life very closely. The life of a man who wants to set up a farm is not known to any of us. We don't know the details and routines that it entails. It was interesting to observe, to convey the aroma of that life, which I had witnessed. Let the viewer discover what had astounded and enthralled me.

It took me roughly a month to edit the film. We named it *His Own Boss,* as Anatoly had proposed. First I had to digest the filmed material, then make a paper cut, then a rough draft on my home VCR, and finally complete the film in the editing room. Anatoly sat down to write the narration. His style of writing perfectly fit the film. It was easy to work with him. He kept telling me, "I'm like a tube of paint in your hands. Squeeze wherever you want."

I was delighted and impressed by his generosity. The work was what mattered to him, and he also understood that the main creator of a film is the director. In my opinion, that did not diminish him as the author—on the contrary. He was the brain of the film. It doesn't really matter who does what in a film. It's the teamwork that counts. The main thing is for the director and the screenwriter to have a common understanding of what they're doing, so that they work in close contact without undermining each other. That is how we worked with Anatoly. He had a healthy streak of pragmatism, and he did not hide his desire to make money. At the same time, since he was a scrupulously honest, serious, and professional man, he gave his all to the work. He helped me find my orientation and made me understand where to place the accents. The topic of the film dealt with essential economical and political issues. Anatoly was an expert in both. He told me that as a college student he had tried to understand the wrongs of the socialist system by reading everything Lenin had written.

From the very beginning, Anatoly said, "Make the film the way you want it." I must confess that I had never put together any of my other films with such ease. It just flowed. It's probably the only one where I had no doubts about its structure. It came together just the way I felt it that first day on Sivkov's farm.

We showed the film to Anatoly's friend, a prominent economist. "I'm afraid for you," he said. "The picture's wonderful, but it has so much truth that it can cause you a lot of trouble. Bring in a consultant from the Party's Central Committee."

We brought in Lev Stepanov, from the ideology sector of the Communist Party.

"It's a wonderful film," he said, and as I remember, he added a few more compliments. "I have only one recommendation, and you have to comply with it if you want me to take part in this venture. You understand, of course, that as the official consultant I take a much bigger risk than you. You're taking a risk too, but what are you risking? At worst you'll be reprimanded, possibly fired, but I will certainly lose my job. But still I believe this film must be shown. Give the film a different title. 'His Own Boss' reeks too much of kulaks and so on. You don't need that. We're not ready to see the truth about the forced collectivization. Call the film *Arkhangelsk Muzhik*."

I was thrilled. That was a perfect title. As children, we had all learned the poem by Nekrasov with the lines:

> Soon you'll learn in school
> How the Arkhangelsk muzhik
> By his own and God's will
> Became wise and great.

The poet used the "Arkhangelsk muzhik" to describe Mikhail Lomonosov, who, born an ordinary Russian muzhik, or peasant, in a northern village of Arkhangelsky region in the eighteenth century, became a great scholar and scientist and founded Moscow State University. By calling Sivkov an Arkhangelsk muzhik, we raised him in stature, making him a figure of national significance.

The first screening of the film was received with deafening silence. The artistic director of our studio asked, "Who is the cinematographer?"

"Me."

He looked bewildered. "Really? You?"

He had never liked me much.

There was more silence, and then the head of the studio said, "The film is wonderful. But I cannot take the responsibility to approve it."

"Let's show it to Kravchenko."

Leonid Kravchenko, the deputy minister of television, watched it and said, "We will broadcast it."

A few days earlier my friend Alexei Guerman, a film director from Leningrad, had dropped by my home. I showed him the film. "Well, if they air that," he said, "I'll believe that things are changing in our country."

Kravchenko was close to the higher spheres, and he must have sensed that the film was needed now because it would allow television to herald the substantive changes that were about to happen.

Before I had presented the film to the studio, I had been bombarded with phone calls from Vladimir Dolgikh, the secretary of the Arkhangelsk Regional Party Committee. He threatened me and made demands. "Before you show that film to anyone, you have to show it to us," he insisted.

"I'm in the process of editing it," I would reply. "The film isn't ready yet."

"When will it be ready?"

"I don't know. The work is going slow. I can't promise you anything."

I was in a panic. All my work might be in vain.

I went to Kravchenko to tell him about the threatening calls. He replied, "Don't worry. We will air the film anyway."

I think that Kravchenko had something more important in mind. He wanted to use this occasion to implement Gorbachev's policy of reducing the power of the local party organizations, which were opposed to any changes in the country. So he ignored the threats of the Arkhangelsk Party committee and set the time for the first broadcast.

The film was aired on a Thursday at 8 p.m. — prime time, just before the network news program *Vremya*. It was a bombshell. The next day, everyone was talking about it. I had that many phone calls only one other time in my life — after *Solovki Power*. I know that instructors canceled their lectures and held discussions of the film. It was discussed in the factories and plants, at the KGB, in colleges, and in trolleys and the metro. About a dozen articles appeared in the newspapers, including *Pravda*. The reviews were all positive. I'd never had press like that before.

Everyone sensed that change was coming, wanted change to come, and they all supported the film. I'm sure that there were other people on each newspaper who preferred staying in the stagnant swamp, but they kept quiet.

Everything seemed to be going amazingly well. There were no signs of storms ahead. I was highly praised by the studio executives, since I had completed the film well ahead of schedule and at considerably lower cost then budgeted. It was the first time in my life that I got such great appreciation. In the past my films received only moderate response even when they had been praised in the press, since they were apolitical. But with this film, I had hit the bull's-eye by covering an important political issue that had been taboo for decades.

On Monday at the usual briefing, Kravchenko pronounced *Arkhangelsk Muzhik* the best program of the week. He also reported that the Central Committee of the Communist Party had requested a copy on Friday, and on the following day, Saturday, the copy had been sent to Gorbachev's dacha. On Sunday, Yegor Ligachev, the ideology secretary, saw it, and on Monday the Secretariat of the Central Committee met to watch and discuss the film. We don't know what they discussed, but the reaction was positive. Naturally, all that pleased me very much.

Two weeks later (it was in December 1986), the program was scheduled for a repeat at 1 p.m. on Sunday. When I turned on my television set, I saw figure skating instead of the *Arkhangelsk Muzhik*. There were people who had missed the show and wanted to see it, and there were those who wanted to see it again. And instead, they found the usual nonsense of the stagnation era. It was the typical practice of totalitarian television to replace anything controversial with figure skating or *Swan Lake,* performed by the Bolshoi Ballet.

But what had happened to *Arkhangelsk Muzhik?* I was in the dark all day Sunday. Monday at 9 a.m., I had a call from Kravchenko's secretary. He wanted to see Anatoly Strelyany and me immediately.

We were there in thirty minutes.

"What on earth have you done?" he asked harshly.

"What have we done?" We were surprised.

"Do you know about the terrible trouble you've caused? We received a horrible letter. You can read it at the committee offices in the personnel department. Don't tell anyone what you've read. Bear in mind that storm clouds are gathering over you. You didn't check things out. It turns out that your Sivkov is practically a traitor to the homeland."

"What?"

"He had applied to the Chinese embassy for political asylum. And during the elections to the Supreme Soviet of the USSR he did not vote, and often he has spoken out unfavorably about the Soviet regime."

"We never heard of anything like that."

"Well, just go read the letter."

Strelyany didn't go, but I did. The staff showed me a letter signed by Comrade Dolgikh, the secretary of the Arkhangelsk Regional Party Committee, the man who had threatened me on the phone. I quote from memory:

Despite our repeated warnings, the staff of Central Television made numerous political mistakes in the film *Arkhangelsk Muzhik.* They turned N. S. Sivkov into a hero, although he is a politically unreliable person who has been caught in anti-Soviet activity many times. In 1974 Sivkov applied by letter to the Chinese embassy, requesting political asylum. Despite requests and persuasion from the chairman of the village council, he refused to go and vote, claiming that elections in our country are pro forma. Besides that, he has openly criticized the Soviet regime and was in constant confrontation with the workers of the Regional Party Committee and with his fellow villagers, the chairman and the bookkeeper of the kolkhoz. He always made impossible demands. We had warned the film director that we should be shown the film before it was broadcast, but our warnings and requests were in vain. We feel it necessary to call this to your attention and to hold the filmmakers responsible.

The letter carried notes from Ligachev, the ideology secretary of the Communist Party—an opponent of Gorbachev's—and from Chairman Aksyonov of the Ministry of Television, requesting an immediate investigation and stringent measures.

My mood plunged. We were grist for the mill. Somebody was showing somebody else what's what, and we were the pawns who paid for it.

Later it became clear that Ligachev wanted the film stopped and that we were caught in the middle of a political fight between Gorbachev and Ligachev.

I immediately called Sivkov at his farm. Thank goodness he had a telephone. I didn't want to talk about all that by telephone, but there was no choice.

"What happened? What is this they're writing about you? What's with the Chinese embassy?"

He laughed loudly. "Hah, I caught them out!"

I didn't understand a thing. Later, when the passions cooled, we invited him to Moscow and taped yet another interview, which unfortunately didn't survive. In it, he explained that he had always had confrontations with the authorities.

"I don't give a damn about them! I've hated them always," Sivkov said. "They couldn't put me away. I could always find work without them—if not as a telephone man, then as an engine repairman on a ship; if not that, then cleaning out manure from the cowshed. I wanted to get proof that they were keeping me under surveillance. Me, a simple peasant who never did anyone any harm. The party organs can't stand me. So I tried to get proof of the Party's direct ties to the KGB. In 1974, at the height of the Cultural Revolution, when only an idiot could think about moving to China, I jokingly sent a letter to the Chinese embassy asking for political asylum, since I was planning to take up farming and the Chinese had suitable fields. Of course, I knew that no one would ever let me out and I had no intention of going anywhere, but I wanted to see what would happen to that letter. I've been wondering for a long time where that letter was. And it turned out that our authorities had kept it in my file. It obviously never reached the embassy—it was returned to our region. And now I've caught them, those idiots! And as for the elections, I didn't go to vote. Voting is when you have a choice between at least two people. How can you choose when there's only one? What would change whether I went or not?"

He was clever and smart, that simple muzhik. I remember when I returned from the Far North, I picked up *Literaturnaya Gazeta* and found an article by Alexander Gelman, our famous playwright, about the problems of the Soviet economy. I read it with amazement. The article was well written, as was usual for Gelman, but almost everything in it mirrored what I had just heard from Sivkov in much simpler terms and with greater clarity. Living in the sticks, on his farm, he had understood the system as well as any man from the intellectual elite. Here you had the wisdom of a simple citizen.

The rumors about the brewing conflict over the film spread like wildfire. Many of my colleagues stopped greeting me, just in case. It really hurt. I took sick leave and stayed away from the studio for almost three weeks. It was disgusting and devastating.

Relationships were always very complicated in the television industry. Even the people whose decency you did not doubt tried to keep a low profile when things got tough, and if they did say anything supportive, they made sure that no informers, of whom there were many, could hear them.

The clouds continued to gather. Yevgeny Veltistov, head of television in the propaganda section of the Central Committee, called. He was named chairman of an ad hoc commission (of three people) to investigate the case of *Arkhangelsk Muzhik*. Before leaving for the Far North, the committee members spent a lot of time getting directions to Sivkov's farm. I explained, they left, and they were gone for a long time. Around ten days later, another call came from Veltistov.

"Come and see me," he said.

I went to Staraya Square, where Party headquarters were located. "Everything's fine," he said. "Your Sivkov hasn't done anything terrible. He is a cunning fellow, not without sin, but your film isn't about that. It's about something else, the phenomenon. There is no question that Sivkov is a phenomenon. You made a good film, so don't worry—we'll show it again."

The film was repeated. And two years later, Anatoly Strelyany and I received the top State Prize of the USSR for the best documentary. I think that the press helped bring about a beneficial resolution. Glasnost, Gorbachev's policy of openness, had begun. The press did not know the full story, but the fact that the film was taken off the air and replaced with figure skating was fodder for very sarcastic articles. *Moskovskie Novosti* and *Ogonek,* the two main publications of perestroika, had a lot of fun mocking the television bosses. So did *Izvestiya* and *Literaturnaya Gazeta.* Each article was a slap in the face of the bosses. Kravchenko had taken a big risk broadcasting *Arkhangelsk Muzhik,* and now he was getting slapped for being afraid to do it a second time.

There's nothing better than a banned film. The director becomes famous very quickly. The whole story with the ban and then the second broadcast brought me a lot of celebrity. It was a political film and yet not about politics— it was about a man with all his human qualities. But perhaps the return to the individual was the most important aspect of the changes that were coming. I don't know if it was an anti-Soviet film, but it was definitely an anti-stagnation film.

I was forty-four when I made *Arkhangelsk Muzhik*. Not long before that, I had traveled to India as a tourist. Galya Maklakova, an artist, was on the same tour. She was also very interested in palm reading. One day she took my hand, studied the lines for a long time, and said, "You will have many turns of events in your life, good and bad. But you know, fame awaits you. You will become very famous."

"Come on," I said. "Fame? That's unlikely."

"You'll see."

"And when will all this happen?" I asked.

"When you're forty-four."

She was right. *Arkhangelsk Muzhik* made me famous—maybe not really famous but at least very well known.

I was completely euphoric when all the hassles with the film were over. But the perception I gained has not left me since: Films do matter. And they can make a difference.

Oleg Efremov

In February 1987, when all the troubles around *Arkhangelsk Muzhik* were over, I felt like a squeezed lemon. I needed a serious rest. And the very same day that I decided to take a vacation, the telephone rang. It was my good friend Alexander Svobodin, a theater critic.

"Do you know that in six months Oleg Efremov will turn sixty?" he asked. "Isn't it a great opportunity to make a film about him? I already spoke to him, and he had no objections. I will be happy to write a script for you."

I said yes immediately. Efremov was my idol. A brilliant actor and director, he and his friends from a theater school in 1956 had created the Sovremennik (Contemporary) Theater. It was the first liberal theater to emerge in the USSR after the era of Stalin's brutal dictatorship. Efremov ran this "beautiful child" of his until 1970, when he took on rescuing the Moscow Art Theater, which had been founded by Konstantin Stanislavsky and Vladimir Nemirovich-Danchenko in 1897 and was the pride of Russian culture. In the 1960s and 1970s the Art Theater was rapidly deteriorating. As its newly appointed artistic director, Efremov began to turn things around and had revitalized it in a few years.

I went to my studio executives and immediately got their approval to start the film. That by itself was a sign of coming changes. Never before would it have been possible to get such a quick okay for a new project that was not already in the studio plan. I was thrilled and expected to have a lot of fun working on a subject I liked so much.

But no sooner had I begun filming than a drama started to unfold, not onstage but within the troupe. Efremov had decided that it was time to modernize the theater and create a new foundation for its artistic work. The existing troupe of 160 people was unmanageable. Many actors in the repertory company performed only once or twice a month but received a full salary nevertheless.

Efremov didn't want to work with actors he considered to be of a lower caliber. They, in their turn, didn't want to work under his direction and instead supported Tatiana Doronina, a renowned actress who was opposed to Efremov's ideas. The troupe was in disarray, and the theater was on the brink of collapse. Efremov felt that the only way to resolve the crisis was to rebuild the whole organization.

Passions were flaring, and my film crew and I were in the middle of the battle. It is a real stroke of luck for a documentary filmmaker to capture conflict as it develops. In the mid-1980s, it was very unusual to do so. The time and effort to start a film production took much longer than nowadays—so long that we would have missed the entire event. But I was in the right place at the right time, with all my equipment and the whole film crew, when the conflict started to unfold.

Efremov was rehearsing a new play by Mikhail Roshchin with his favorite actors, all very popular stars. Under different circumstances this by itself would make a remarkable film. But the actors were agitated, to say the least, and the director could hardly concentrate on the work. The rehearsals were a disaster.

Every day the conflict deepened, and the two opposing groups were swiftly turning into enemies. It was as if a volcano had erupted, and lava was pouring out.

I had no problems in filming Efremov's side. He trusted me 100 percent, openly expressing his discontent and concerns and answering any question I asked. I spent hours in his office, filming his efforts to restructure the theater and to find a rational solution to an irrational problem.

Once he said to one of his friends: "Do you understand that I am balancing on the edge of a knife?" And here I was, creating a profile of Efremov as he was balancing on the edge of a knife.

The actors from the other side of the conflict tried to block my filming. They all refused to talk to me or to be interviewed. I met with Doronina several times, trying to develop a human contact with her—to no avail.

But I still wanted to show a full picture—not just one side of the conflict. One time I had to pay for my attempts with a few unpleasant moments. I was shooting the meeting of the whole company with the minister of culture, who tried to resolve the situation. I caught a very ugly exchange of words between both sides. I had found a good spot upstairs in the sound booth from were I could observe the whole room.

Suddenly I felt a blow on the head and lost consciousness for a second or so. I slowly sank to the floor, with my heavy camera continuing to shoot. Somebody caught me and helped me to sit up. My camera was shaky, as can be seen in the film. Doronina was in the shot, speaking angrily from the stage to

Efremov. I don't know who hit me, but it's clear that it wasn't anyone from Efremov's side. The scene fit the film perfectly and added sharpness to it.

One of the most important sequences in the film was taken during a night meeting of Efremov's supporters. I got a call at 10 p.m., informing me that something important was about to happen. I called my sound person, and we both rushed to the theater. Efremov made a powerful speech, which triggered a highly emotional discussion. Innokenty Smoktunovsky, Yevgeny Evstigneev, Mark Prudkin, Angelina Stepanova, Oleg Borisov, and other giants of the Moscow Art Theater participated—they were fired up and furious. Never in my life had I seen such an outpouring of emotions, and I certainly had never filmed anything like that. Now, as I look back at these scenes, I recognize how lucky I was to get all that on film. This sequence became a historical document of the painful break up of the Moscow Art Theater, a Russian legend.

Many of the speakers are no longer with us. It is all history now. The theater, observed and captured at a moment of collapse, was something never seen before on-screen. If I had made this film earlier, before the winds of perestroika started to blow, I would never have been allowed to show what I did. All the contradictions, conflicts, and negative sides would have ended up on the cutting-room floor.

This picture, titled *For the Theater to Be . . . (Oleg Efremov),* marked a transition from one era to another. We thought that we finally would get the freedom to think, speak, and act, to follow conscience and reason, and everything would fall into place.

We couldn't predict then how painful the road ahead would be.

Solovki Power

Of my thirty-two films, I think that *Solovki Power* remains the most significant, because of its subject and the influence it had on the public when it was first released in 1988. Indeed, the inspiration for this book arose when ten years later, in 1998, I learned that the original negative of the film had been destroyed, preventing the creation of any more copies. I couldn't accept that it could be lost to history, and I felt it was my duty to preserve the memory of the film and the people whose stories it portrays. They are all gone now.

I began making the film in 1987, at the genesis of perestroika. While Mikhail Gorbachev asserted that "the process was under way" and the country started to change, the change was feeble, affecting few of the country's essential systems.

It never occurred to me that mine would be the first film about the Gulag, an insidious network of prison camps created by the Bolshevik totalitarian regime after the revolution in 1917. The film's title became a metaphor for the criminal regime that created these institutions.*

The film evolved in a strange and unexpected manner, in a way that confirms that nothing in life is random; one barely visible bit of fluff catches onto another, and so on, until you have an entire shawl. In the 1970s–1980s, Dima Chukovsky and I made several films with the renowned academician Dmitri Likhachev. His area of expertise was ancient literature and Russian history. The author of *Reflections on Russia,* a book that dealt profoundly and wisely with Russian culture, Likhachev was the unofficial "last member of the old

---

*In Russian, the film is called *Vlast' Solovetskaya,* a reference to "Vlast' Sovetskaya" (Soviet regime). "Vlast'" can be translated as both "power" and "regime." The Bolsheviks established concentration camps for suspected counterrevolutionaries in 1918. During the 1920s, "class enemies" and criminals were confined in the Northern Special Purpose Camps on the Solovki Islands in the White Sea near Arkhangelsk on the mainland.

Russian aristocracy," which was destroyed during the revolution of 1917. Permitted to go a bit further than other people, Likhachev was a kind man who gradually trusted and befriended us. At one point, I remember him saying, "It would be good to make a film about Solovki. I spent four years there, and I'll never forget it." The name hung in the air when he said it. I knew very little about the prison camp at which he had been an inmate. We knew the camp existed, of course — Alexander Solzhenitsyn had written about it in his banned, yet illegally circulated *Gulag Archipelago* — but we knew little else. Interestingly, Solzhenitsyn's depiction of the Solovki camp is based in great part on reminiscences that Likhachev shared with him. Because the authorities knew the names of all the former inmates who had helped the writer — Solzhenitsyn had been expelled from the USSR in 1974 and even stripped of Soviet citizenship — Likhachev's freedoms were strictly curtailed. For at least a decade he was not allowed to leave the country and could not participate in international conferences.

By 1986, more pieces fell into place. Vitya Listov, a historian, archivist, and film scholar, mentioned that, while doing research for a film on Soviet theater in the 1920s, he had discovered in the archives in Krasnogorsk film footage from the late 1920s about the theater on Solovki Islands. It appeared to be a part of a propaganda film called *Solovki,* made between 1927 and 1928. Dima and I immediately requested a screening of this film, but permission was denied.

When we told Likhachev about the existence of this film, he grew excited because he remembered some visiting filmmakers shooting in the camp while he was there. As a member of the Academy of Sciences, Likhachev managed to overcome resistance and got exclusive permission to see the film. It knocked him off his feet. A few months later, after he turned eighty, he called us to say that he was ready to speak out and record his memories of the Solovki camp right away. "I don't want my memories to die with me," he said.

It was impossible to get a film camera and sound recording equipment to shoot anything on a topic like prison camps at this time. Everything was under the strict control of the studio authorities. So Dima borrowed a friend's amateur video camera, and we went to videotape Likhachev.

For four hours Likhachev spoke, and I nervously recorded him. I had read *The Gulag Archipelago* back in the 1970s when it was circulating underground (I remember reading it secretly at night — doing so was dangerous and could have led to a prison term). But I had trouble processing what Likhachev was saying. It's one thing to read about it and quite another to hear from someone who went through it. When I returned home, I hid the tape in the closet, showing it only to my mother, who got scared and asked that I promise neither to show nor to tell anyone about it.

Now anxious to make the film, I couldn't figure out a single studio that would dare to put it into production, even though life had become a little bit more free and political changes were in the air. Television was certainly not an option, and the Documentary Film Studio was no better, as the executives there would have died of fright before even finishing reading the proposal.

Some time later the topic of making a film using Likhachev's recollections on Solovki came up in a conversation with director Sergei Solovyov. An old friend from the film school, Solovyov had recently been appointed head of a film unit at Mosfilm, the country's main film studio. Though it was a feature film studio, Mosfilm had occasionally produced documentaries, the most memorable being Mikhail Romm's *Ordinary Fascism* (1966). Excited by the material I presented, Seryozha Solovyov, a bold, freethinking, adventurous man, immediately wanted to make it into a movie. His words stunned me and appeared to be the height of audacity.

"Seryozha," I said. "It's dangerous! Who'd ever give us permission?"

"Everything has to be done wisely" he replied. "Let's do everything wisely."

And so we began. Solovyov, Vitya Listov, Alik Lipkov (the studio's chief editor), Dima Chukovsky, and I sat down and started thinking. Solovyov proposed a ninety-minute, feature-length film. We would describe the subject in vague half-truths as we wrote a fake proposal that would clear the Soviet censors.

Vitya Listov wrote the screenplay. Approximately fifty-nine pages of the script were dedicated to the history of the Solovki Islands and their archeology, religion, architecture, and art. Basically the script included everything about Solovki as a historical monument, leaving only one page that mentioned in passing the prison camp that had been located in the monastery and on the territory of the islands in the 1920s.

Seryozha got it approved by the artistic board of his film unit. It was also sent to Goskino and passed through the high film executives smoothly, without any problems. The script looked quite innocent from an ideological point of view, did not contain any anti-Soviet motifs, and promised a fresh and interesting film. Goskino, the ministry that controlled Mosfilm studios, appropriated 300,000 rubles for the picture—in those days a very large budget—and we began production.

At that time, it was hard to predict which way things would turn in the country, as a life-and-death struggle went on between the pro- and anti-Gorbachev factions in the Party and the government. I believed that in order to make an honest and powerful film about Stalin's Terror, I had to work fearlessly without looking over my shoulder. I had to feel free and to be free. So I decided to resign from Ekran, where I had been on staff for twenty-five years. And I left.

When we began working, our plan was simple. We would show Likhachev the 1928 propaganda movie, film his reaction, record his reminiscences, put that all together with the old footage and other archival material, and that would be our film. (By this time we succeeded in obtaining permission to use the footage from the 1928 documentary *Solovki*.)

As planned, we set up a VCR with a monitor and played the old film, with Likhachev watching and remembering. After filming for four days in a row, we started to realize that we didn't have enough dramatic material to make a compelling film. Though the information was interesting, Likhachev related it too calmly, without anger, bitterness, or inner drama. A devout Christian, he had forgiven everyone and everything a long time ago.

On top of that, we learned that my Leningrad friend Slava Vinogradov was also making a film about Likhachev, allegedly about the war period, during the Nazi blockade of Leningrad. For some reason, Vinogradov was also interested in the Solovki years and moreover had asked for the Solovki film in Krasnogorsk. This made me wary. So I called Slava immediately.

"Slava, what's going on?" I asked.

"Nothing. I'm doing a picture about the siege of Leningrad."

"And why are you interested in Solovki?"

"Well, we may touch on it a bit. It's a page from Likhachev's biography, after all."

"Slava, we're already doing a film with Likhachev. We started first—you know that."

"I know, but there's nothing terrible here. Even if we deal with Solovki, it will be brief. A five-minute sequence, no more."

I calmed down. We had always been friends and had gone to the Film School together. I trusted him, and so I stopped thinking about it. But then Dima Chukovsky learned for sure that Slava was seriously digging in the Solovki period, traveling to Solovki, and had gotten all the materials from the Krasnogorsk Archive, using the same film we had found. This was troubling information. And then came confirmation that at least half of Slava's film would be devoted to Solovki.

Of course, I was deeply hurt. Indeed, Slava and I are no longer on speaking terms, which is sad. He is talented and always behaved decently, but something must have happened to him then. Perhaps when you're making a film, all other considerations pale (before getting it done). I'm not judging him. I can look back calmly now; time has passed and healed the wound. I still recall with nostalgia my college years and all my student friends, the ones who are now gone and the ones still living. I don't want to think badly of any of them. In a way I'm grateful to Slava. If I hadn't started worrying then, our film would have been poorer. The truth is, everything that happens is for the best.

So we started to understand that we had to expand the scope of our film beyond Likhachev. The situation was complicated by the fact that the clock was ticking. It was a month since we had gotten the go-ahead. And we had only seven months for everything: preproduction, filming, and editing. We couldn't miss the deadline. That would have created problems for Mosfilm, which worked to a strict production schedule for the year. So our whole crew worked around the clock. Nothing but the picture existed.

Whatever the topic of a film, there is always something much more far-reaching than its events and characters. In our case we had to go beyond this one prison camp on Solovki Island. We had to show that this one camp was a microcosm of the whole totalitarian system. Likhachev had told us several times that the guards used to shout at the prisoners: "Remember, we don't live under the Soviet regime here. We follow a special Solovki regime." But in practice, the entire country lived under that Soviet-Solovki regime for almost seventy years. Using the example of Solovki prison camp and showing how it functioned, we wanted to reveal the essence of the criminal Soviet regime. To make this metaphor work, we needed more witnesses, more stories, more examples, and as many documents as possible. The thesis had to have a solid grounding, with solid proof and justification. That is why we began to look for other characters.

Two protagonists were right under our noses. Both lived in Moscow and were mentioned by Solzhenitsyn in his *Gulag Archipelago*. The first was Oleg Volkov. The second was Olga Adamova-Sliozberg. It took only a few days to locate them, and we hurried to meet them.

First Volkov. He appeared to be a gift for the film. Very handsome, with a big white beard, sharp light blue eyes, and a tragic face. Angry. I don't know if he was angry by nature, but he certainly hated the Soviet regime. He had spent twenty-seven years in camps, prisons, and exile. He hated the system passionately with every fiber of his being. His fierce fury, so pronounced in his memoirs, became an important dramaturgical spring in the film.

He was almost ninety when we met. He and Likhachev were polar opposites. Likhachev ended up in Solovki by accident, through youthful naïveté and a lack of understanding of what was going on around him. He was arrested for being a part of a student group interested in linguistics and the norms of grammar. Volkov was arrested because he understood very well what the regime was, and he did not want to obey. He refused to do what he considered to be unacceptable. He spoke six languages and worked as an interpreter in the Greek embassy. One day two young men approached him and asked him to work for the secret police. He answered that he would never be a snitch.

"You'll regret this," they said.

"There's nothing you can do to me," he replied.

He ended up in the Solovki camp soon after. First he was given three years, then another three were added, then some more. He showed me photographs of his younger self; he had been handsome and elegant. And he remained so in old age. He had expressive movements, long hands, and long, nervous fingers. His manner of speech was harsh, fragmented, and abrupt. He spoke slowly, with pauses, and had an upper-class rolling R. He had a cultivated way of formulating his thoughts, right to the point. It's very rare to come across people who can express themselves so clearly and emotionally and say exactly what they mean. He radiated nobility.

He also had a heightened sense of his own worth, and sometimes his behavior was slightly arrogant. His wife tried to soften his sharp edges and was helpful in establishing a good, trusting relationship between us. He was respectful from the start and helped in every way he could.

We showed him the Solovki film too. He was completely stunned, and a wave of reminiscences flooded him. I couldn't stop filming. Everything he said was powerful. He remembered dramatic events and incidents we knew nothing about. He brought up amazing characters, describing the prison camp atmosphere with lots of expressive details and little anecdotes. He was a great storyteller. The narrative started to become flesh and blood.

Likhachev and Volkov, two old men, completely different, talking about the same things in very different ways, giving different examples and details but essentially saying what we wanted to express. It was all about Soviet power and Solovki power.

Volkov told a story about the torture of members of a sect, the so-called Christers, whose religion would not let them work for the Antichrist. They refused to do camp labor. They would be stripped and left without protection against mosquitoes. In June the air is thick with mosquitoes in Solovki; they can eat a person alive. The guards would force the Christers to stand naked on the rocks and did not allow them to move. Volkov wept as he told the story. He was a courageous, strong, and controlled man—yet the tears poured out of his eyes. He gestured feebly at the camera to make us stop.

I didn't stop the camera, but when I edited that sequence, I blacked out his face; it was unthinkable to show that man crying. And the black strip actually worked more powerfully than the image.

Once we had Volkov in the film, I calmed down, even though I was still worried about how we would manage to build a story. The plot had to develop in time, with twists and collisions, peaks and valleys.

Our next contact was with Olga Adamova-Sliozberg. Olga brought gentleness, femininity, and warmth to the film. She exemplified not only the ruined lives of those who had been accused of being "enemies of the people," had been imprisoned but also those who were left behind—their family members. She gave a vivid portrayal of the abyss of suffering into which that generation had been plunged. Her fate was to be the wife of a man who was arrested and executed, and then to spend eighteen years herself in prisons and camps.

She was around eighty-five when we were filming, but she retained her natural charm. She gave me her pictures; she looked lovely when she was young. I still remember her deep green-gray eyes—they were velvety and beautiful. It was hard to believe that she had lived through everything she described.

I always ask the protagonists of my documentaries to speak of concrete things, of concrete events in their lives. There is nothing worse for a film than generalizations—no matter about what. Even if generalizations are interesting, even if they are basically needed for the development of the point, as a rule they don't work in a picture. What works is a story that the person tells about himself or herself, with all the details, the remembered particulars. Especially interesting is the process of recollection, searching for words, digging into the memory. When captured on camera, this turns the viewer into a collaborator, a witness.

Adamova-Sliozberg had an amazing visual memory. With stunning details she described the events of the winter of 1937 when her happy family had been completely destroyed by the Stalin purges. First she told about her husband and how he was arrested. She described her total confusion—she did not know and could not believe that the person whom she had lived with for so many years and knew everything about, the father of her children, was sent to prison as a spy and "an enemy of the people." She had two kids, and in order for them to survive, she had to work very hard. Being a stenographer, she took the work home and made the transcripts day and night, trying to make a little bit of money. In about a month after her husband's arrest, three secret police officers broke into her flat late in the evening when she was still working in her room. They announced that she was arrested too and had to get ready to leave immediately. She was so shocked that she couldn't think straight. She said, "I cannot go. I have to finish the transcription." One of the men arresting her said, "You'd better not lose time. Say good-bye to your children."

"I went to the bedroom," she recalled. "My boy was sleeping on his tummy, and I turned him over. My girl was sleeping on her back. I kissed my kids, and they took me away."

One of the striking images in the film is her story about how, after three years' imprisonment, she and others were transferred to Siberia. At some transit point on the way, the women came across a mirror.

"Everyone hurried over to see herself," she said. "There were lots of us, and I couldn't figure out which one I was. And suddenly I saw my mother, her exhausted, sorrowful face. That was me."

How perceptive, how bitter was her story . . .

Now we had Likhachev, Volkov and Adamova-Sliozberg. But was this enough?

Would we be able to build a narrative? Would we find other interesting characters with extraordinary lives? Without them, there would be no intense and coherent story. We continued our search for witnesses.

I always try to make my films as representative as possible and to include people of different social strata, professions, interests, generations, and gender. We looked for former inmates everywhere. We tried to expand the search all over Russia, finding people from all walks of life, to show the era through them as fully as possible, demonstrating our conclusion that the Solovki experience was the experience of the entire country.

Our search for other witnesses was feverish. Naturally, everyone we found led us to others. From Adamova-Sliozberg we learned about Zoya Marchenko. She herself hadn't been at Solovki, but her brother Grigory died there. I went to see her, and we liked each other from the start, feeling as if we were old acquaintances. She took out her brother's photos and letters, spread them out on the table in front of me, and began reading parts. There were no tears in her eyes, but, oh, how she read these letters!

She wore a pink knitted shawl with big holes in the fabric. She bundled herself in it, as if hiding from the world in her shawl. I'll never forget that shawl and her eyes—dry and alienated. She was telling her story, and she was talking to herself, not to me. She was thinking aloud.

As she spoke of her brother, she gave me an excellent hook for linking Solovki with the mainland. It was her story that gave the factual evidence: the Solovki camp was nothing but a model of the entire country and its political system.

Her story made it clear what was going on in that watershed year of 1929 when her brother was arrested. Her brother was an enthusiastic follower of Trotsky, who by that time had been exiled by Stalin.

Grigory Marchenko did not hide his views. He and his friends met in his home, in a big communal flat in the center of Moscow. Once they saw a man sitting on the first-floor landing, reading a book. Her brother's friends joked, "Look, they've put a stoolie there!"

The man was still there when they were leaving late at night. They did not yet realize what danger they were in, and they laughed, not understanding the monstrous reality that was emerging. It was the new and terrible era that few even suspected then. A secret police agent was placed in the house around the clock. These details reflected the times. People hadn't noticed that the country was being transformed step by step into a giant concentration camp. No one had yet imagined what was coming. These were small hints, but the end was a tragedy.

Zoya told me how the imminent arrest moved nearer. How her brother was taken, how they searched his room while she was there. How she visited him in prison. She gave a very vivid description of their last meeting, before secret police officers took him away to Solovki. She brought him a sheepskin coat and felt boots, which she got from friends. Her brother told her some details of the interrogations, which she wrote down when she got home. Those notes were found during a search, and she was arrested too. All in all, she spent twenty-one years in prison and exile.

We were lucky with our characters. Each was unique. Each was an individual with a special charm and personal vision, with a rare ability to remember and bring up striking details, which often became metaphors. Zoya Marchenko was definitely such a unique type. She spoke with such precision and expression that each phrase seemed etched in stone. I listened, notebook and pen in hand, writing down the things I thought I'd like her to repeat during the shoot. She repeated them in front of the camera with the same intensity and inner pain. Many of the other characters in this film had the same gift of being able to repeat for the camera what they'd said, while making it sound as if they were saying it for the first time. This was a revelation for me.

In the past I never asked my characters to do anything especially for the shoot. I was convinced that people speak naturally and in an interesting way only when they recount something for the first time and that, if you've missed the moment, you can never make it up. This appeared to be not true. Indeed, this was the only time in my entire film career that I worked with the characters as if I were the director of a narrative film, often rehearsing their answers

before starting the shoot and sometimes making several takes of the same episode until the result was exactly the one I wanted to achieve. It worked pretty
well but kept me nervous all the time. I didn't like this way of dealing with
real people. I knew how difficult it was for them to repeat the painful stories of
their past, but I had no choice. I was desperately short on film. The shooting
ration was only 10:1, which means that for every ten meters of film stock we
shot, we could use only one meter. I had to worry about every meter of film
stock. I am grateful to my protagonists for their complete understanding and
willingness to do anything to make this film happen.

Zoya became a close friend of mine. I make new friends with every film.
The people I film are not simply my characters, but they are people whose fate
I am no longer indifferent to. I meet frequently with them during the filming,
I put so much emotion into communicating with them and they respond in
kind, and ultimately we become so close that I love them and want to continue seeing them. But then the film ends and with it this part of my life. And
I start another project, immersing myself in a new set of challenges, making
new friends who become part of this new life, and all of a sudden I lack spiritual energy, strength, and time for my older friends.

I recently gave a talk at the Russian State University for the Humanities. A
sweet young woman came up to me and said, "Mrs. Goldovskaya, hello." I was
taken aback, not accustomed to being called "Mrs." in Russian. She told me
she was the granddaughter of Zoya Marchenko, whom I hadn't seen in over a
year. Zoya had passed away six months earlier.

Zoya Marchenko was our fourth witness. She led me to several other people
who were invaluable to the film. When I start making a documentary, I often
have no idea how things will develop. But God seems to direct me. I'm not
religious, but I can't rid myself of the feeling that there is a force guiding me,
that someone wants things to unfold this way. This miracle happened several
times during the making of *Solovki Power*.

It was Zoya Marchenko who gave me the telephone number of another
former Solovki prisoner. She had met him on a tourist excursion outside Moscow. His name was Samuil Epshtein. I called him right away.

"Hello," I began. "Zoya Marchenko gave me your number. Is it true that
you were in the Solovki prison?"

After a pause he said, "Yes . . . it's true." He spoke very slowly, as if he wanted
to weigh and consider each word he said. I had a hard time convincing him
that we should meet. At last he agreed.

He lived in a small apartment on the outskirts of town. It took me a long
time to get to his place, and I climbed up to the top floor. He opened the door,

wearing pajamas and slippers. I saw a tiny old woman, with the face of a mouse, sitting at the table. She looked at me with horror-filled eyes. I had come with flowers and a cake. We began chatting and sat down for tea. That always helps reduce tensions at a first meeting.

She never said a word, but she held her husband's hand, and whenever he remembered anything concrete about his terrible years in Solovki, she would press it and murmur, "Please don't talk. I'm scared. Don't say that." This had an awful effect on him. He kept looking at her and said very little. But from what he did say, I could tell that he knew much more. He was colorful-looking. He had a birthmark on the right side of his almost bald head, exactly like Gorbachev's. He was more than eighty years old, but his memory was absolutely clear. He seemed to remember everything.

I sometimes wondered why those who did time in the camps aged better than many of those who remained outside. Could it be that as inmates they knew their terrible destiny? They had nothing to lose. They didn't have to lie, to pretend, to second-guess, while people on the outside lived double lives in an atmosphere of imaginary freedom, always under psychological pressure, forced to compromise, scared to tell the truth, doing everything possible not to be sent to the camps.

Samuil Epshtein was an intelligent and very well-educated man. He kept wonderful details in his memory. He spoke excruciatingly slowly, but each word made a point. In the late 1920s and 1930s he was a Komsomol activist and, incidentally, a Trotskyite.

We spent about an hour and a half together, and I realized that he was extremely important for the film. He was sent to Solovki in 1935 and stayed there until 1939. We knew very little about this period of Solovki history. We knew only that in 1934 the camp had been transformed into a harsh, merciless prison in which the inmates were not allowed to leave their cells even for a short time. He told us that in 1939 the camp was shut down on Stalin's order, and the surviving prisoners were transferred to prisons in Siberia. Before meeting Epshtein, we knew nothing about this. Here was a precious opportunity to illuminate that page of history.

We touched on few details, but I sensed that he could tell me immeasurably more if not for his wife.

I said, "Let me film you. The film won't work without you."

"Oh, I don't know."

His wife grabbed his hand. "No, not that! Not that! Don't you realize what will happen if they come back?"

She meant the Stalinist times. I said nothing.

A few days before meeting Epshtein, I had watched Claude Lanzmann's *Shoah*. There was a scene in the film where the director was persuading a barber who had been in Auschwitz to talk about his experience. But the barber did not want to be in the film. "If you don't do it, and I don't do it," the director said, "then who will?"

When I was leaving, I asked Epshtein to see me to the lobby. We got in the elevator, he in his worn blue slippers. At the front door, I told him what Lanzmann had said to the Auschwitz inmate. "I realize that this is very difficult for you," I continued, "but you and I must do this. Otherwise it will be lost. You're eighty years old. You must understand that there may never be another chance like this. If not you, if not me, then who?"

"What for?" he asked.

"We must, we absolutely must do this! It's our history."

Epshtein looked at me closely. "All right, I'll think about it. Just don't call me. I'll call you myself."

Two or three days later, he called. "I agree. But I can't be filmed at home."

"We will find a place to do it," I promised.

We interviewed him in a Mosfilm office. There was modest, plain furniture in the room, not very beautiful but not ugly either. It looked quite homey. The filming justified my hopes. Epshtein spoke with such conviction and power that the story took on another dimension.

Toward the end of the 1920s, Epshtein had been a fiery Komsomol member who became a victim of his obsession, his convictions and misconceptions. He had true faith in the Communist idea; he could not understand or explain why he had been arrested. He spent fourteen years behind bars, three in Solovki, the rest in Kolyma, where he was sent with the last ship to leave Solovki. His first wife had been arrested too. He had known that, but he did not know that she had perished in the camps. He learned about that only when he returned. Then he married her sister, the woman I met.

How could I blame her for being so scared? It's hard to believe that all this horror lasted for so long. And even now, when it is in the past, many people still feel the fear. It is ingrained in their cells. The old people lived their entire lives with it. Thank God, our children do not feel the same way; they never experienced anything like that. But Russia is unpredictable. Who knows which way the wind will blow tomorrow?

I told myself that I was walking on thin ice. I had spent my entire conscious life under the Soviet regime. My generation, and particularly the older generation, knew what it was. My mother, who remembered the 1930s, 1940s, and 1950s, who knew the Cheka, the NKVD, and the KGB, was terrified for me.

When she heard about the film I was planning, she almost wept. "Do you realize what you're doing?" she asked. "It's suicide." But on the other hand, there was my son, Seryozha, who said, "If you don't make this picture, I'll lose respect for you. You have to do it. Remember grandfather." I was afraid when I decided to make *Solovki Power*, afraid while I was making it, and afraid after I made it. But I never regretted it for a second, never doubted that I was doing the right thing. Yes, I was afraid, but there was no turning back.

The information that Epshtein gave us was invaluable. We hadn't known that in 1931 the majority of the prison camp inmates were sent to work on the construction of the Belomor-Baltic Canal, where most died. (After the film came out, I had a call from a lawyer, Anatoly Chukhin, who was researching the Petrozavodsk archives. He wrote a book, *Canal Army*, based on the materials he had discovered. He told me that he had located the files on thirty thousand people who had vanished in the construction of the canal. They had been sent there from the Solovki camp.)

Samuil Epshtein made another major contribution to the film. He introduced me to the friend who shared his cell—another amazing person, Alexander Prokhorov.

An engineer and metro builder, he was sent to America in 1934 to study the latest technologies and come back with new knowledge, observations, and experience. He returned to Moscow in 1936 and ended up in prison in 1937. He had been sent to America by People's Commissar Sergio Ordzhonikidze. By the time Prokhorov returned to Russia, Ordzhonikidze was dead, either by suicide or murder—who knows what went on in those terrible years?

When I met Prokhorov, he looked fifty, but he was in his eighties. Handsome and full of life, humor, and youthful energy, he even flirted with me, which was funny, to say the least. He spoke with humor and passion. He told us his story and gave us his version of the years spent in prison. Now we had three people describing it: Adamova-Sliozberg, Epshtein, and Prokhorov. The accounts of people who were such powerful individuals expanded and deepened the theme, making it multifaceted and polyphonic.

The film was turning into a history of Solovki, one of the first prison camps (if not the first) of the enormous Gulag system, from its creation to its abolition. This chronology was becoming the basis of the narrative of the film. But for this kind of composition we were missing an essential element: the starting point. We knew when and how it ended; Prokhorov and Epshtein had talked about it. They left Solovki for Siberia in the fall of 1939 on the last ship, the *Semyon Budyonny*. We were lucky to find a photo of the ship. But we still didn't know how and when the camp began.

It was Zoya Marchenko who helped us to find this information. In our first conversation, I had asked whether she knew anyone who had been on Solovki when the camp started in the 1920s.

"No, I don't know anyone," she said, "although perhaps there is a man. He's a Chekist [he worked for the KGB]. He wrote his memoirs. When I came back from exile, I worked as a typist. I typed his memoirs. He started working for the Cheka in 1918, after he overheard a conversation about Fanny Kaplan's plan to assassinate Lenin and reported it to the secret police."

"How did it happen that he overheard that conversation?" I asked.

"I don't believe him, actually. I have the feeling that he made it up," she said. But she continued, "Once, he mentioned in passing that he had been in Solovki."

"In what capacity?"

"I don't know much about him. He's not the kind of man you want to have personal conversations with. Not very pleasant. I disliked him from the very start. He was a guard, and I was a prisoner! How else could I have felt about him? I haven't talked to him since."

And she gave me the telephone number of this former Chekist, Andrei Roshchin. Fortunately, his number had not changed. I called him, told him that I'd heard he had written his reminiscences of Fanny Kaplan, and they interested me. I knew I couldn't breathe a word to him about Solovki and our film. He said I could visit him.

I brought flowers, tea, and a cake and went to his house.

That was an unforgettable experience. I entered an apartment reeking of urine. It turned out he was very ill and on dialysis. (A few months later I brought him an apparatus from Hungary that helped detoxify the body.) We started talking. As a true Cheka officer, he was very suspicious: What are you doing? What are you filming? What is it about? I again told him that the whole Fanny Kaplan story interested me. He told me all the details. When he was fifteen, in 1917, he came to Moscow from a nearby village, fleeing the famine, and he got a job in a cobbler's shop. There was nowhere to live, so he slept in doorways. One sunny day he got off work early. He lay down on the grass in Alexander Park and fell asleep. He was awakened by loud voices. Three people were sitting on a bench nearby—an agitated brunette and two men. One man was simple-looking, perhaps a sailor; the other, young and intellectual, with glasses. They were discussing something, and he could tell that an assassination was being planned. They kept saying "Lenin" and the places he was planning to visit in the following week. Roshchin jumped up, ran to the local Cheka headquarters, and told the officers that he had heard a suspicious conversation.

One of the staff told him, "Write a report and leave. If you're needed, you'll be called." He wrote as well as he could, since he was barely literate, and left. A few days later they came for him, took him to the Cheka, and asked him what the people looked like. An attempt on Lenin's life had taken place that day.

He told me the story with lots of colorful details. It was interesting, but useless for me. I began asking him more about his life. He told me that he started working for the Cheka in 1918 and had participated in the assassination of Yakov Blyumkin, also a Cheka officer, who had organized the killing of Count Mirbach, the German ambassador in Moscow.

"And after that?" I asked.

He told me that in 1923 during a Cheka operation he had made a grave error. He and his colleagues were supposed to arrest someone at the scene of the crime. But something went wrong, and he ended up shooting and killing the wrong man. He was imprisoned and then exiled. But by 1934 he had returned to Moscow and was made a guard at the Bolshoi Theater.

"How interesting," I said and asked him about his work as a guard. He told me.

"And where were you in exile?" I asked.

"I was sent to Solovki."

"What? You were a prisoner in the Solovki camp?"

"Yes, but I was there as a Chekist. I was a guard there."

"So were you exiled there, or were you working there?"

"You see, Chekists were exiled there too. But we worked while we were there. We worked as guards, kept an eye on the inmates, and maintained order."

This was indeed interesting to me. I tried to find out more, but he didn't want to talk about it.

"Well, all right," I said. "I can see I've tired you. That's enough for one day. Thank you—it was all fascinating. I think that maybe you and I will be able to work together. Maybe I'll film some of your reminiscences."

As I was leaving, I asked, "Do you need anything? I have a car, so if I can bring anything . . ."

"You have a car!" He was very pleased. "You know, I have a very big favor to ask. Could you bring us potatoes and other vegetables? I don't go out of the house. My wife does the shopping, and it's too heavy for her. We have a son, our only child, and he is always busy."

"No problem. I'll be happy to help. What do you need?"

He gave me a rather long list, and I went shopping, buying quite a lot more than he had asked for.

I was back the next day with shopping bags and another cake and another bouquet. I sat down to listen to his story some more. He told me about Fanny Kaplan again, and then I turned him toward Solovki and got some fascinating information. It was exactly what we needed so badly—it gave our film its beginning.

Roshchin had arrived with the first ship of prisoners at Solovki on June 6, 1923. What an amazing revelation: 1923. Not 1924, as we had thought before. It all happened during Lenin's lifetime, which meant that the camps had been started by Lenin and not by Stalin, as we were led to believe. This was even more shocking, as the country in general seemed to be on its way to a more peaceful future after the destruction wrought by the revolution and the Civil War. In 1922 the New Economic Policy was instituted, and entrepreneurship was encouraged. The regime seemed to allow a freer and quieter life. And at the same time in 1922, behind this facade, a cruel, inhuman regime was taking hold. The idea of concentration camps was not only born but already forcefully implemented by Lenin and his cohorts. (Much later, in the mid-1990s, we learned that camps like Solovki had existed even earlier, around 1918–1919, in Potma, on the Portominskie Islands in the White Sea. These were horrible camps, where people were shot by the hundreds, perhaps by the thousands.)

Now the structure of the film became clear. Roshchin was the starting point of the narrative, and Epshtein and Prokhorov the end. The first transport to the islands and the final transport from the islands—we had to fit the story into this space. As soon as I found this time line, I knew that the film's backbone was firmly in place: the history of Solovki prison camp from the first day to the last.

Roshchin turned out to be photogenic and a good storyteller. His face wasn't the most pleasant I've ever seen, but that worked for the film. A guard had to look like that.

It's one thing to film a person you like, expecting that the viewer will like him too. It's another thing when you don't like that person and know that you can't hide it. You feel guilty. Of course, I never said anything bad about Roshchin. It's just that his image and everything he recounted were not likely to win people's hearts.

"The inmates in the Savvatiev monastery had absolute freedom. They lived in a house surrounded by barbed wire, and they were allowed to walk around the house," he recollected, not even realizing how ridiculous and terrifying his statement was. He sincerely believed that people who stayed behind barbed wire could feel free.

Roshchin gave us his photograph taken there, confirmation of his account. When his ship arrived, he said, the monastery was in ruins, burned down. The prisoners began rebuilding. Roshchin claimed that the monks had set fire to the monastery. Later, with the help of the museum staff on Solovki, we found pictures of the monastery after the fire. We permitted ourselves only one commentary to Roshchin's claim: "It is not really clear who set the fire: the monks or people from neighboring villages, who burned the monastery after robbing it." Even back then, in 1922, the terrible thievery and the terrible methods of covering up events so prevalent in Soviet society were present.

Roshchin recalled a unique episode: the suppression of the first and probably the only uprising in the Solovki camp. In December 1923, members of the Socialist Revolutionary Party (SRs) who were incarcerated there protested the three-hour limit on being in the fresh air. They demonstrated with banners and posters, singing the old revolutionary songs with words like "Shame on you, tyrants!" Professional revolutionaries, they were used to the conditions in the tsarist prisons, where they were allowed to go on hunger strikes, hold protests, and so on. But the new regime, which they actually helped bring to power, was less tolerant. Six shots rang out; six people were dead. The Red Army guards shot from their towers. The guards, who were mostly uneducated peasants, felt a strong class hatred toward the Socialist Revolutionaries, who were all intellectuals. SRs walked around the guard towers, shouting "You are animals! You have been deceived by the Bolsheviks! We will get out of here and take revenge! You'll always remember us!" The guards in turn used their weapons at the first opportunity. Two women were among the dead. We later found an article about this incident in a 1923 issue of *Izvestiya* and used it in the film.

All the characters we had filmed so far belonged to the intelligentsia, but among the Solovki prisoners there were many others—workers, peasants, clergymen. Anyone could be imprisoned during the Stalin regime. So we needed someone from among these groups as well. But how to find such a person? Again the staff at the Solovki museum helped. They were amazing young people who adored their work and had no interest in money. From them we learned that once they had a visitor, a very simple man who said he had been a prisoner there. He was from somewhere in the southern part of Russia, from the Krasnodar region. We got his address and wrote to him. Efim Lagutin's response came quickly.

Yes, Lagutin wrote, he had been in the camp from 1926 until 1929. Then he was transported to Siberia, was released, and ended up around Norilsk. He had spent a total of seventeen years in prisons and camps.

Lagutin was my favorite character of the film. Well, "favorite" isn't really accurate, for I came to love them all, and I cherish them all, but he was the most touching, the most pathetic, and for sure the most innocent. A holy man. All the others had had time to do something in their lives before their imprisonment. They had matured as people and at least could understand what had happened to them and why. But Lagutin ended up in the camps as a fourteen-year-old. He was an orphan, lived in Belorussia, and dreamed of travel. He had read about ships that traversed the seas to Argentina and Brazil, and he wanted to try his luck. He went to Odessa, where he dreamed of finding a foreign ship at the port, stowing away, and sailing across the ocean. But the secret police weren't sleeping. They caught the lad, arrested him for treason, and sent him to be "reeducated" in Solovki.

Lagutin added an incredibly moving layer to the film. I think he was often viciously beaten in Solovki, and I wouldn't be surprised if he had been castrated. His voice was a falsetto. I didn't ask what happened to him, I didn't want to open old wounds. He was a gentle, sensitive man, with delicate blue eyes, so helpless and lacking in self-esteem and very cautious. He was the exact opposite of Volkov. The latter was full of himself and his ego, whereas the former was shy and tried to go unnoticed.

Lagutin wrote that he would be pleased to take part in the film. We headed out to his village. Our whole crew—consisting of twelve people, including assistants, gaffers, production manager, and so on—and all the 35 mm film, lighting, and sound equipment arrived by bus. All these people and machinery intimidated Lagutin, and I felt that first we had to get to know each other and discuss the film we wanted to make.

I asked him if I could stay with him and his wife in their house overnight, and I decided to send the crew to a hotel in the neighboring village. He was quite surprised and looked at me as if I was crazy.

"You really want to stay with us?" he asked.

"Yes."

He hesitated. "Well, please. Of course, you are most welcome to stay."

It was a small house, just two small rooms. He lived with his wife, a woman of colossal size with swollen legs, clearly very ill. They seemed to live happily and showed each other care and support. It was only much later that I understood why my request had shocked him.

After filming him, we became friends and met several times. We corresponded. I invited him to Moscow to look at the rushes and then to travel with us to Solovki, to the place where he had been imprisoned.

During his visit to Moscow he stayed in my place.

I tried to be hospitable, to make him cozy and to feed him good food as much as time allowed. Before he went home, he embraced me and said, "Marina, I'm so grateful to you! You're the first and only person in my life who wasn't afraid to have me in her house."

I didn't understand what he meant. "Why?"

"Well . . . Ever since I got out, even my relatives won't let me in their houses, and they don't come to mine. We've practically lost touch. Well, a few letters now and then. But they're embarrassed and afraid of me."

"Why?"

"Don't you understand? I spent eighteen years in prison even though I was completely innocent, yet my relatives never believed me. They trusted and feared the authorities and treated me as a criminal . . ."

"God," I thought, "imagine living your whole life branded a criminal whom people avoid like the plague! What horrors the so-called enemies of the people and their children and families had to suffer!"

But let's go back to that first day I spent in Lagutin's house. Initially it was difficult to get the conversation going. Lagutin was shy, and his wife didn't say a lot. But after a while when he brought out his homemade red wine and we started eating potatoes, things lightened up. Lagutin started relating the unbearably sad story of his life, recalling important details and circumstances. I kept pushing for more and more, and he responded.

I always asked each of my characters for photographs of their youth. Most of them had none because they had been confiscated when they were arrested. Some had a few, and each one was precious for us. I asked Lagutin too. "Do you have any photos from that time?"

"How could I! I was just a kid when I was sent to Solovki. I was fourteen and stayed until I was seventeen. But in Solovki they were making a film, and I was in a shot. I'm almost certain that I was in it.

"I was sitting on a bench, reading *Pravda*. I remember it was an article about one of General Nobile's expeditions to the North Pole. I heard a noise and turned my head and saw that I was being filmed."

It was like being struck by lightning. What if he actually was in the 1928 film *Solovki*? It was a fifty-minute film, and I couldn't remember every shot.

I couldn't wait to return to Moscow: I wanted to watch *Solovki* again. Lagutin described it very well. I found the scene immediately. A boy wearing a cap is sitting on a bench with his back to the camera; then he turns and looks at the camera, right at me. It was him, Efim Lagutin. What a lucky find!

Later, we filmed him in Solovki, at the very same place. The bench was gone, but he told us where it had been and where he had sat. It was an amazing bridge from that time into ours.

One morning when I was working in the editing room, the telephone rang. It was my school friend Naum Kleiman from the Film Museum. "You won't believe this," he said. "I was just visited by the wife of the cameraman Savenko. He filmed the 1928 film *Solovki,* which you are working with. She brought me the camera he used then. I bought it for our museum. And can you imagine? Savenko is still alive and lives fifteen minutes away from your editing room!"

I froze in my chair. It seemed so unlikely that Savenko could be found that we didn't even try. And now his wife showed up on her own. I got her number and called. "I don't know if you'll be able to film him," she replied. "His memory is not great, but you can try. Maybe he'll remember a few things."

We were there the next day. Savely Savenko was a bit over ninety and didn't have much to say. But the two coherent sentences he uttered were pretty funny, and we used them in the film: "I shot *Solovki.* It was the best film I ever made."

In the film, we showed him at the age of twenty-nine with his camera and some scenes he had shot with it. He truly did beautiful cinematography. Savenko tried to explain why he thought that this film was his best one. His speech was slurred and confused, but we understood. All his life he had been making educational and technical films to earn his living in a small provincial studio. It must have been a pretty boring job. But in Solovki, he filmed people—the most varied, outstanding, and often unique people. What a collection! Academicians, professors, philologists, historians, military commanders, priests, philosophers, engineers. They were all prisoners in the Solovki camp. Some of them were the brightest people of Russia.

Finding himself in such company was a stroke of luck—of course, he knew that he was free to leave. And he was. He heard interesting conversations and enjoyed dealing with people of a level he would never meet again.

Solovki was a typical Soviet propaganda film, made to show how the government was reeducating criminals. Savenko made beautiful shots of the landscapes of the islands and the monastery, and he created sequences of cultural work—the publication of a newspaper, the amateur theater, even a small zoo—and of course, of the rehabilitation through labor. The movie showed how labor heals people and turns them into decent citizens.

Over the entrance gate to the camp was a big sign with Stalin's favorite slogan: "Labor is the work of honor, glory, courage, and heroism." Later Hitler copied him. Over the gates of Buchenwald, he put "Arbeit macht frei" (Work brings freedom).

An interesting detail: When the film was completed in 1928, it was shown and discussed in workers' collectives. We found in the archives a transcript of one such discussion. Some of the speakers were really angry and demanded, "What is going on in this country? Free and loyal Soviet citizens suffer, we have no place to live and nothing to eat, we have to stand in line in the unemployment office, while these criminals in prisons and camps are well fed and given housing and work."

This reaction pushed the authorities to shelve the film. It was shown only outside the USSR. Actually, it was made primarily for foreign countries. It was intended to counter the accusations made in *The Island Hell: A Soviet Prison in the Far North,* a book published in 1926 in London. Its author, Sozerko Malsagov, and a few other inmates had managed to escape from the Solovki camp a year before. Apparently the guard system was not yet well organized at that time. They had to swim though the icy-cold water of the White Sea. Desperate people take wild risks. They escaped to Finland and from there on to England, where Malsagov published his book about the horrors of Solovki.

When the book came out, the foreign press was appalled and fiercely attacked the Soviet regime. The film *Solovki* was the reply intended to show that all the accusations were nothing but lies. In it, everything about Solovki looked great, even dignified. Everyone was kempt and well-dressed, the beds had clean sheets, and the food looked quite good. There were even white tablecloths. Watching this footage, both Volkov and Lagutin kept repeating, "What nonsense! It was nothing like that!"

Of course, all those lovely scenes were scripted and staged. This was real falsification, lies, fake—as our protagonists called it. The miserable prisoners, slaves of the Solovki camp, were forced to act in a propaganda film. Later, in 1943, a similar film was made in Terezinstadt, a horrible Nazi concentration camp. The style of totalitarian regimes is always the same.

The sequence with and about Savenko added another important dimension to the picture. It was as if God gave us these discoveries, one after the other. And they kept coming.

One day Dima Chukovsky came in with news: "You know, I just learned that Uspensky, the Solovki guard who took part in the execution of three hundred people in late 1929, is alive and lives in Moscow."

Dmitri Likhachev told us that he had been an eyewitness to this execution. Once when his parents came to visit him (that was still allowed in those years), they had rented a room from one of the guards, and Likhachev stayed with them. One night a fellow inmate rushed in and warned Likhachev that the guards had come looking for him.

He later learned that one of the prisoners, Innokenty Kozhevnikov, formerly a Red Army officer and hero of the Civil War, had escaped with Shepchinsky, his former aide. They were found in the woods two weeks later and almost beaten to death by the guards, who suspected that they had been part of a conspiracy. The guards learned nothing and shot them. Then the prison camp authorities decided to carry out a mass execution in order to scare the rest of the prisoners. That was the usual reason for such actions, which occurred constantly.

After receiving the warning from his friend, Likhachev told his parents that he had to go to work and ran off to hide instead. He spent the rest of the night in a haystack. In the morning, when he returned, it was all over, and no one was looking for him anymore. Meanwhile three hundred people had been murdered.

He remembered the execution and the executioners all his life. One of the guards who actively participated in the killings was Uspensky.

So when we learned that Uspensky was still around and living in Moscow, Dima called him and spoke with his wife. She said, "Please don't bother him. He is sick and old. He won't recall anything. I don't want anyone meeting him—I won't let anyone in."

I called a few days later, trying to speak to her, woman to woman. "Please understand how important this is," I said. "Eyewitness information, firsthand. We won't dig up the past. We simply need his clarification on a few issues that we can't figure out."

Naturally, I didn't tell her what we really needed him for. We would never get in if I did. Nevertheless, his wife remained adamant: "Stop calling me. I'm so sick of him! I'm sick and tired of him! He's a disgusting man. I've had enough. And I don't need you around. Let us live out our lives and die quietly —both him and me."

I realized that there was no reasoning with her. Well, then, we'd do something else. I wasn't worried about ethics here, in view of the character and the situation.

Dima Chukovsky found the address and began watching Uspensky's house. The building was on Prospect Mira, not far from the center of the city. It belonged to the KGB. Most of the inhabitants were KGB employees and had received their flats from that organization. Dima asked the neighbors for Uspensky's apartment and soon discovered his daily routine. Every day at 12:45 p.m., with military punctuality, he headed for the bakery. A fresh delivery of bread usually came at 12:30, and the store closed for lunch at 1 p.m.

We drove up to his building, parked in the courtyard, and waited for Uspensky to come out. He appeared as expected at 12:45, went to the bakery, and returned fifteen minutes later with a shopping bag full of fresh bread. Now I knew what he looked like.

The next day, I went there with my assistant Sasha and two still cameras.

I parked in the yard not far from Uspensky's doorway. We waited. Sasha was hiding in the bushes. He had put a long focus lens on his camera; I had a wide-angle lens. Exactly at 12:45, Uspensky emerged.

And again an invisible force was helping us. Uspensky seemed to have dressed just for this occasion. He was headed for the bakery in a black suit with many rows of medals and orders pinned to his jacket, carrying a cane and a shopping bag. He, a criminal, looked like a respectable and honored war veteran.

I followed him all the way to the bakery and took pictures. Then I waited in a telephone booth and made some closer shots. He didn't notice anything. I continued following him and got a few shots of his back.

Sasha was waiting on the other side, and he made several wonderful close-ups. Later I used those pictures in the film as visual commentary to Likhachev's story about Uspensky and the execution. Likhachev had asked us not to use the man's name: "He may have children, grandchildren. So many traitors, snitches, and executioners still live among us! He's not the only one. Please don't use his name."

We complied with his request. I even placed a black strip over Uspensky's eyes, to make him less recognizable. But he still was somehow recognized. When the film was shown in many Moscow theaters and received wide recognition, the son of Uspensky called me, infuriated. "What right did you have to do that?" he shouted. "There's no proof that it was my father! It could have been some other Uspensky. What have you done? The neighbors are driving me crazy, saying that my father is a killer. You should be sued!"

By amazing coincidence, the very morning that Uspensky's son called me, I had been at KGB headquarters to see the head of the archives. It took me a long time and a lot of effort to get an appointment. But I really wanted to get some additional background on a few people in my film, and one of them was Uspensky. I wanted to know more about him. I wanted to get confirmation of who he really was. What if he was the wrong Uspensky?

This was my first visit to Lubyanka. I went to the office of Colonel Korneyev. An intellectual-looking man stood up to shake my hand. (I later learned from our conversation that he was born in 1937 on the day his father was executed.) I explained the reason for my visit. "All right," he said, "let's check that."

He made a call and explained what he needed: Uspensky, Dmitri, born 1903, was in Solovki. Ten minutes later—I was astonished by the speed—the file was brought in. It was the first KGB archive file I had ever seen. It was labeled with Uspensky's name and date of birth and stamped "Keep Forever." That stunned me.

He opened the file. I saw the face of the man we had photographed. He looked thirty or forty years younger in the file picture, but it was the same man. No mistake. I read in his file that he came to Solovki from Arkhangelsk in 1929, punished, like Roshchin, for committing murder. He served his time and stayed on as a prison guard.

Everything about him in our film was the truth. He did participate in the execution. The incident was later investigated when a special commission came from Moscow, and Uspensky and the other executioners were sentenced to various terms. But the sentences were quickly commuted, and all of the executioners returned to the mainland. He was sent to serve in the army in the East and retired in the rank of a general with a lot of military awards.

So when Uspensky's son called, I could say, "I sympathize. I know you had nothing to do with this—you executed no one. But, unfortunately, your father did. I held his file in my hands today. If you're interested, you can see it for yourself."

He couldn't argue with that. He told me that he was a diplomat, and all this was horrible for him, his career, and his family. He didn't deserve this, and he couldn't believe that his father could have done anything like that. "I am sorry, but there's nothing else I can tell you," I replied. That's how our conversation ended.

We filmed a total of thirteen people. Because we had different personalities, different fates, and different stories, and we could edit and juxtapose them, we had volume and many facets of events. From simple stories, we could build a research document. It was different from a scholarly piece, because ours had a cinematic structure and visual stylistics.

We went to the islands twice, in summer and in winter. Russia cannot be filmed only in summer; Russia is winter. When we were there in winter, it was terribly cold, around minus thirty degrees centigrade, and everything was covered with ice and snow—incredibly beautiful. Those white trees and frozen landscapes created an atmosphere of horror, discomfort, and hopelessness. The images by themselves were a strong metaphor.

In summer the images were formed by the beauty of the greenery, the trees and blue lakes, turning silvery in the changing light, and the monastery, with its thick stone walls and solid, sturdy architecture. Horror and beauty.

Our guide, our "everything," in Solovki was Yuri Brodsky, artist and photographer. A touching, marvelous man, he was invaluable for the film. He was obsessed with Solovki; he devoted every spare moment to the islands and took wonderful photographs. He helped us appreciate the beauty, majesty, and spirit of this fascinating place.

We lived in the cells of the monastery both in winter and in summer. The first time, it was winter. Thick stone walls, tiny windows. It was terribly cold. I felt the horror of incarceration on my own skin. I don't know if they had central heating when it was a prison camp. It did exist when we were there, but it wasn't of much help. It was freezing even with the heat on. I slept under two blankets, in my fur coat and three sweaters. I could see my own breath.

The next time, we came to Solovki in summer. The museum employee who met us told us along the way that a journal from 1929 had recently been found in one of the cells that had been part of the camp. An inmate who worked as a bookkeeper had made notes of every delivery of provisions, how much was stored, how much was used, what was on the menus, what went into the soup, and how many people were sent to what jobs. Very boring housekeeping information. But it was important for us to understand that there was still a lot to be discovered on Solovki premises.

We learned from our museum friends that they had not yet studied the church situated on the Sekirnaya Hill. It was the most frightening part of the island. It was a prison within Solovki's prison camp, a horrible place where people were tortured and killed.

I've said this before, but I'll repeat it. I don't know whether there is a God, but I am certain that there is a power that leads me when I'm making a film. I've encountered it many times and hope that feeling will never leave while I continue working. Actually, I am convinced that this is a special quality of documentary filmmaking. Maybe that is the reason for my addiction to and obsession with this genre. It is something (I call it "my inner voice") that tells me, "Do that"—as if it knows that something must and will happen.

It was raining, a dark and gloomy day, not one for filming. The museum workers had gone ahead to the site. We drove up there. I had heavy equipment —two 35 mm cameras, tripod, magazines with film. I knew that the ruined church-turned-prison would not have electricity. We didn't have an electric generator with us—it would have been too expensive and complicated to bring one to that place. I had just two portable battery lights. I hoped it would be enough.

We got to the site. It was still dank and dark. We began unloading. I took the portable Konvas camera and went inside the decrepit, defiled church. It was so dark in there that it was impossible to film. I started up to the top with the camera. The museum workers were already looking for hiding places, checking cracks and crevices. It would have been silly to ask them to wait for better light. I kept looking out the window to see if there was any clearing. And suddenly I saw breaks in the clouds. God, help me, I thought. I was almost at the top, with the sound man and his assistant, when I heard the voices: "Marina, hurry, hurry!"

I reached the cupola, with its low vaulted ceilings and a rickety floor full of holes. I saw that the workers were digging up piles of papers and newspapers, showering dust. I turned on the camera, and at that very moment, as in a fairytale, the sun came out, a streaming ray burst in, and the dust swirled in it. Honest, that's how it happened.

"What is it? What have you found?" I asked.

"Look, look! Here are letters, letters!"

They began tearing the sealed envelopes and reading. And that became the opening sequence, the prologue of the film.

Dust particles tumbling in the sunlight, young men and women reading the newly discovered letters; voices of the writers like messengers from the past . . . God gave us that episode, and I used it throughout the film. I asked Tonya Melnik, a museum researcher, to read an excerpt from Taras Shevchenko's "Neophytes," which she had found on a torn-out page, stuffed into a letter. Here are excerpts from the poem, written in 1857 by the Ukrainian poet, who was exiled to Siberia by the Russian tsar for his revolutionary activity:

> They hung St. Peter upside down
> And took the neophytes to Syracuse in chains.
> And they took your son Achid, your beloved child.
> Your one and only, your dear love,
> And he rots in captivity, in chains.
> You mourn and do not know where he lies and suffers.
> You go and look for him in Siberia . . .
> And are you the only one?
> Mother of God, save us and protect us from misfortune!
>
> O cruel Nero! The sudden, righteous judgment of God
> Will strike you down.
> The martyrs will come, the children of holy freedom,
> And stand around your deathbed fetters
> And forgive you: for they are Christians.
> But you are a tormentor! A hundred times worse than a beast!

There is a point of view among scholars that Russian history goes in circles, and not much changes from century to century. I am not a historian; I am only a filmmaker. But to hear this particular poem in this particular setting was more than I could take. It affected me so deeply that I could barely continue shooting.

The voices from the past, of the dead, gave the film its intonation. I could have never planned such a sequence ahead of time. It came unexpectedly toward the end of our shoot, as if it were a gift from destiny or a message from those innocent people who perished in these cells.

And that's what documentary is all about.

Accidents, random moments began to add up, gradually forming the living substance of the film. For instance, Lagutin sang a camp song. I filmed it. His voice alone, broken and abnormally high-pitched, revealed so much of his painful experiences. The song spoke of his whole life. Later, on Solovki, I filmed piercing landscapes. I don't know what tree it was—it looked like a birch—but the birch has black spots on white bark, while this tree has rusty spots, the color of dried blood. We found an abandoned cemetery, wooden crosses tilted and skewed in the thick underbrush. I filmed it. Lagutin's song worked powerfully with these images.

Naturally, the question of how to end the picture came up. I knew that it should be a memorial for all camp inmates—the ones who remained forever in Solovki soil and the few who survived, as well as for all the others who were imprisoned over the years of Soviet-Solovki power.

It had to be filled with pain, bitterness, and the desire to understand what had happened to us all. It had to be filled with reverence for the greatness of the human spirit; all the inmates we had filmed had managed to preserve their spiritual integrity. We were looking for some symbolic shot that could, in a metaphoric sense, become a monument to those who served and suffered on Solovki land. And this shot would be our final shot as well.

We thought long and hard about an appropriate sign. First we wanted to erect a cross with memorial words on it. But what kind of cross? And what words? It seemed too easy, too trivial, maybe too artificial. We needed something more organic, coming from this place, this nature, this history.

We postponed the decision of this pivotal question until the last days of shooting. And again, long live documentary! We found a huge boulder sticking out of the water of the White Sea, surrounded by the untouched nature of the North. Giant boulders, and icy waters pounding against them. What could be more powerful than to make it simple and eternal—to chisel dates on the boulder "1923–1939," the years when the camp was here? At high tide, the numbers would be underwater. At low tide, they would appear above the water, those wordless and terrible numbers. And they would stay there forever.

We filmed Efim Lagutin and Volodya from the museum chiseling the dates. This was probably the most expressive memorial we could create.

When we were working on the film, we had almost no written information on Solovki's history in Soviet times. It was only after I went to America, Germany, and Australia with our film that I received many books and articles about the camp from Russian émigrés who had left after the revolution of 1917 and from their children. I hadn't even suspected that so much information existed. Little was accessible to us in the USSR, and we had very little time for research because of our crazy deadline. We were the first after Solzhenitsyn to dig into this area.

We did independent research, step by step, restoring the truth about the Solovki camps and about Solovki power. We found and mastered this truth for ourselves, living through it in pain and horror.

While shooting, we decided not to ask KGB for help. We didn't want to draw attention to our work. That may have been an overreaction on our part, but I was truly expecting that the film would be shut down at any moment. We sent requests to other archives, like the Academy of National Economy, where Belyakov, a cellmate of one of our protagonists, worked. We asked for his photograph; the answer came back that they had nothing on Belyakov, he had been arrested in 1937, according to the archives, and we should apply to the KGB for information. We didn't, just in case.

We had the same problem with camp commander Fedor Eikhmans. Luckily, in the museum in Solovki we found his photograph and that of his predecessor, Alexander Nogtev. They both were later arrested and executed. We also found a photo of Gleb Boikii, a big shot in the secret police, who also died in the camps. But we could not find photos of most of the people mentioned by our protagonists. At the very end of our work, we did turn to the KGB, but it was of no help. So we decided that the absence of photos could work in an even more powerful way. We figured a black screen could be more effective than a photograph. We wrote on a black signboard: "Nikolai Belyakov, arrested in 1937. Rehabilitated posthumously. No photograph remains." No person, no photograph, nothing . . .

For the entire seven months, we tried to keep our work secret. We selected a crew of reliable people. I don't think that we were completely successful: it would be impossible to hide the production of a film costing 300,000 rubles from the two thousand people working at Mosfilm Studios.

But the times had changed. Even those who might have rushed to turn us in sensed that there was no great interest in their vigilance and that, in fact, the authorities might not have approved of their telling tales.

We worked feverishly, in an exalted, agitated state. Solovyov, who as head of the film unit carried all the weight of responsibility, said more than once, "Let's make a film that will be shelved." He didn't want it to be shelved by the Soviet authorities, of course. He simply wanted a powerful, honest, and passionate film.

I was hesitant only in the beginning when I was deciding whether or not to do the film. After that, I thought only about how to do it, how to structure it, how to imbue it with emotion. Of course, then there came other worries: Would the film succeed? Would it strike people in the solar plexus or not? I wanted our film to be severe and frightening, but not embittered. I wanted it to be a call for understanding, not for revenge. I didn't formulate it for myself that way. During the work process I don't usually think things through—I simply made the picture the way I felt it.

This was a test on every level for me. I was working for the first time at Mosfilm, the studio with the highest artistic and technical level in the country. After a long hiatus, I was using 35 mm technology again; I had grown unaccustomed to the bulky, heavy equipment that required a large crew. This was the first time I was making a film not for television but for movie theaters; it called for a very high-quality image. As usual, I did the cinematography myself—I couldn't trust anyone else with the work. Of course, Mosfilm had many skilled cameramen who were much more experienced than I was. But it was easier for me to do the camerawork myself than to explain to someone else what I wanted. Ideas and decisions usually come in the course of shooting.

Making a film with so much research, searching for characters, and shooting and editing in just seven months was a heroic effort. The entire crew worked selflessly, without complaints, totally enthused from morning till night.

In most of my previous films I tried to avoid narration. I didn't want to impose my point of view on the audience. I wanted them to get it from the material itself. But this film was a different one. Its subject required serious analysis, which was impossible without text that had to be extremely precise, accurate, and reserved. The main burden fell on Vitya Listov, our writer. He literally did not leave the editing room until the work was finished.

This is how we worked: Vitya would write a piece of narration, we would try it with the image, and I would say, "Marvelous" or "Not really." Sometimes something didn't work for him, and I would reedit the piece to make it acceptable to both of us. We understood each other—and the result we wanted to achieve—so well that our work progressed without any strain. All our ambitions were funneled into one goal: to do the best we could. And that was the feeling of our entire crew.

Now came the time to record the text, but I still didn't know who the narrator would be. I couldn't find the voice that made me say, "That's him!" I knew it had to be a man's voice, very dry, steady, without intonation, but with a muted tragic tone. I thought, I sought, I watched films and listened to voices. Sasha Khasin, our sound man, brought me tapes from here and there. But they were all wrong. And we were running out of time.

Just then I was invited for a weekend conference in Edinburgh to show *Arkhangelsk Muzhik*. Sasha Proshkin was also going with his film *Cold Summer of 1953*. We were good friends. He called me about the trip, and as he talked, I realized that this was the voice I needed.

"Sasha," I asked, "could you read the text for my film?"

"Of course I can. I used to be an actor. Is it for *Solovki Power*?

"Yes."

"I would be greatly honored."

He read it spectacularly. Besides the unique timbre of his voice, there was the intonation—dry, without tears, but on the verge of emotion; the pauses were precisely placed. He made a few changes in the text to make it his own. The result was much more powerful than I had imagined.

After almost twenty years as a director, I had discovered how much narration could add to the film.

As for music, I really wanted my dear friend Marina Krutoyarskaya to compose the score for the film. I had no doubts that she would do a wonderful job. We had been working together since 1976, and we understood each other intuitively. Mosfilm proposed Nikolai Karetnikov, a well-known composer who also happened to be one of Marina's friends. So I asked both to join our team.

We met and discussed every detail, and the composers got down to work. Nikolai wrote the music of light, goodness, and God, conveying the harmony of God's temple of peace. Marina contributed darkness, evil, and hell, conducting the demons and the abyss through her music. I am infinitely grateful to both for their brilliant job.

It goes without saying that I was expecting a lot of problems with the approval of the film, and I was prepared for a fight.

Strange as it may seem, the studio approved it, and without a single comment. When we screened the film for Alexander Kamshalov, then minister of cinema (Goskino), he found a few things he didn't like and asked for some changes. One of our protagonists, the writer Alexander Gorelov, a kind and naïve man who was chairman of the Leningrad Writers' Association, told us that when he was pushed into a cell in Solovki prison, another person was already in there. It was Nikolai Belyakov, Lenin's comrade-in-arms.

"Why aren't you taking off your coat? Get undressed!" Belyakov said.

"What for? I won't be here for long. They will probably let me out right away."

"Let you out!" Belyakov burst out into laughter. "You're in the hands of the fascists now."

"Why do you call them fascists?"

And Belyakov told him how he was beaten on the head with the book he himself had written about Lenin.

Kamshalov wanted me to take out the words "You're in the hands of the fascists now."

I protested: "These were Belyakov's very words—he said it. And anyway, the whole episode falls apart if I take that out."

Kamshalov relented.

But he was adamant about removing the mention of *The Gulag Archipelago*. The book had been banned, and Solzhenitsyn was persona non grata.

I couldn't accept that either. It would have been dishonest to pretend to be first in exploring this topic.

I called an old school buddy, Andrei Grachev. At that time he was in charge of the international sector of the Central Committee of the Communist Party. Later he became Gorbachev's press secretary.

"Andrei, I've made a film, and they want me to cut any reference to Solzhenitsyn," I said.

"You know, I think you can keep it in. *The Gulag Archipelago* is an anti-Stalin book, not an anti-Soviet one."

"Can I quote you?"

"Of course."

This rescued the sequence.

Kamshalov also demanded that we remove the parade shots on Red Square in which Stalin stands on top of the Mausoleum, watching the troops marching just like the Nazis.

"This has to be cut," he insisted.

"I can't do it. It would ruin the sequence and lose the needed parallel with fascism."

"Then the film will be shelved."

"Well, then I can't help it."

Honestly speaking, I remained calm because I felt that it wouldn't stay on the shelf for long.

And I was right. At first, everybody at Mosfilm seemed to have forgotten about the film, but then suddenly there was all this scurrying, phones ringing, and I was told that the negative had to be edited immediately.

A few months later, the film had a national premiere in Moscow and was then screened throughout Russia.

Amazing! Why? Apparently, the time for it had come.

The film opened the 1988 season at Dom Kino in Moscow. The theater was packed. There wasn't even a seat for me, so I stood throughout the screening. Then our protagonists came onstage. It was their day. They received a long standing ovation. The audience applauded them for surviving, withstanding, not breaking, remaining themselves.

During the discussion that followed the screening, Oleg Volkov was the first to speak. With his typical directness and great hatred of the proletarian leader, he said, "Why are we shutting our eyes to this? Why do we keep saying 'Stalin,' 'Stalin era,' 'Stalin's crimes'? It's time to call things by their proper names. It all began with Lenin. It was he who invented all this. Stalin was only his loyal student."

The audience burst into applause. Everyone clapped and looked at each other in horror. It was another small step toward admitting the bitter truth. Similar reactions occurred at the many other screenings that followed.

Institutes, clubs, schools, universities, and public organizations in Moscow and throughout the Soviet Union all wanted to see the film and talk to the film-makers. For almost six months we traveled the country with the film, screening it and speaking. Every show was followed by heated discussions. Sometimes we seemed to be on the verge of a fistfight—a mini civil war.

Later I came across Akhmatova's line written in 1938: "A time will come when the two Russias will meet face to face: those who were in prison and those who imprisoned them." I did not know those words then, but that was the mood. People from the audience shouted, "My father was shot!" "My mother was executed!" "My whole family perished!" "I grew up in an orphan-age!" "The communists are fascists!" Yet there were many who still admired and defended Stalin vigorously.

Two parts of a single nation were struggling to the death. What had hap-pened to us, to our country? Where were we heading? Every screening turned into a public demonstration going far beyond the film—an unforgettable ex-perience! That's when I understood the power of film and how much a docu-mentary can do.

Meetings with the public brought astounding discoveries. Once, after a screening at Moscow State University, a young man rose from his seat and asked: "Do you know anything about the man who escaped from Solovki and later wrote the book *Island Hell* that is mentioned in your film?"

"No. I know nothing about him."

"It was written by Malsagov. I want to thank you for at least mentioning his name. He was my grandfather."

I almost fell to the floor. Then I started corresponding with Malsagov's daughters and granddaughter and learned a bit about him. He was arrested in 1921 for being an officer in the tsarist army. When he was arrested, he had a young daughter, and his wife was pregnant with his second child, born in 1922. He never saw her. He escaped from Solovki to England via Finland. Then he moved to Poland to be closer to Russia, in the hope of reuniting with his family. But it didn't happen. He died in 1974. His story was like many others that were connected to Solovki; they could have become films in their own right. But it never came to pass. I still feel sorry that so much material was lost to history.

But more to the point: the film itself was close to being lost to history.

The negative had been ruined. Someone had made a mistake, ordering three hundred copies from the original instead of using an intermediate negative. As a result, the 35 mm negative of *Solovki Power* is gone forever. Fortunately, I found a new print of the film and transferred it to Digital Betacam format. So although all of the protagonists have passed away, *Solovki Power* exists and will live on.

The film was shown abroad at many international festivals—in America, Europe, Asia, and Australia—and received many awards. It gave me the opportunity to travel the world, and I still treasure the impressions of the screenings and the people I met.

Solovki Power taught me a lot. It taught me to understand and appreciate every human being as a precious source of memory and history. Under the influence of this experience, my interests shifted toward documentary film as a record of the spirit and emotion of the passing times.

Life Is More Talented Than We Are

In the fall of 1988, shortly after I had finished *Solovki Power*, I got a call from Oleg Uralov, the director of a newly created studio called Videofilm. "I am glad you are done with *Solovki*," he said. "Now you have to start on the film for us. I included *Anastasia Tsvetayeva* in our studio's plan, and it has to be finished by December 30. We cannot miss the deadline."

This telephone call was unexpected and made me feel sick. I was absolutely not ready to start a new film. Seven months of intense work on *Solovki* had exhausted me, mentally and physically. And then there had been all the travel with the film around the country, screenings, discussions. I was on the verge of a nervous breakdown. But I couldn't tell Oleg I didn't have the strength to do the picture. Anyway, one should strike while the iron is hot. If he dropped the film from this year's plan, it might not get into the next one.

When runners reach the finish line, their legs keep pumping to prevent a heart attack. I was in the same past-the-finish-line state when I completed editing. I was ready for the nuthouse. I couldn't think of anything but the film. I couldn't read the papers or watch TV or talk to anyone. That happens with every film: neither experience nor age has made me wiser.

Relaxing after a film is over is even harder for me to handle. I plunge into depression, and I get all these illnesses, like lower back pain and insomnia, even though I'm basically very healthy.

That condition is apparently normal for a director. But people don't talk about it much. Why admit to weakness? And everyone tends to think that he or she is the only crazy person around. But one day when I thought I was truly losing it, I ran into my old friend, director Seryozha Solovyov. When he saw the crazed look on my face, he asked, "Are you all right? Are you sick?"

I didn't hold back. I forgot about professional correctness, and for the first time in my life I let loose with all my problems.

"Big deal! I go through that with every picture," he said. "How else? Movies aren't born without the suffering. You gave birth to your son—you know what it takes."

I had run into him just in time. His words soothed my frazzled soul. So I was normal, and what I was going through was normal.

Bet let's get back to the story. Of course I wanted to make the film about Anastasia Tsvetayeva. She was a special personality in our Russian cultural history. A daughter of Ivan Tsvetayev, a famous art historian who founded the Moscow Museum of Fine Arts, and a sister of Marina Tsvetayeva, one of the greatest Russian poets of the twentieth century, Anastasia was also a writer. She never got the attention of the media, though. She and her sister Marina were personae non grata for television. They both had a dubious émigré past; their lives took a tragic turn when they returned to the Soviet Union. Marina committed suicide in 1941, and Anastasia spent seventeen years in the Gulag camps.

Marina's poetry or Anastasia's memoirs could be published in small printings, but talking about them to a television audience of millions was out of the question. Neither their lives nor their works fit the facade of false optimism presented by Soviet television.

The film concept of *Anastasia Tsvetayeva* arose on its own, without any effort on my part. Usually a director has to fight for every topic, convince and wheedle, and figure out how to hide the dangerous parts. With this project, everything happened easily and nicely, in a very pleasant way.

It all began in 1983 with a call from a former student, a journalist named Tanya Alexandrova.

"Anastasia Tsvetayeva is here," Tanya told me. "She rarely visits Moscow. I got to know her in Estonia, at the Pukhtitsa Convent. She has agreed to be filmed. Wouldn't you like to do it?"

"I will do it with pleasure."

"Can you get a camera? Let's not miss the opportunity."

At that time there was no way to get official permission for this filming. Nobody at my studio would have allowed it. So I decided to organize an "underground" filming. Fortunately, by then, video cameras were no longer rare commodities. I had mastered the technology, so I asked some friends from the video department at the television studio to lend me a camera for the day.

I saw Tsvetayeva for the first time when I arrived for the shoot. Of course, I had read her memoirs, which gave a clear account of the tense relations between her and her sister, the genius poet Marina. It was a love-hate relationship. I expected to see a majestic woman, used to attention and even fame. But Anastasia Tsvetayeva completely surprised me. She was small, hunched, with a low monotone voice and an inability to look a person in the eye. She had just turned ninety.

My first reaction was "How can I film someone so unattractive?" But as soon as I turned on the camera and did a close-up, I had an entirely different reaction: "God, is she photogenic! She looks so significant. It's fascinating to observe her."

And she spoke marvelously, with image-filled literary turns of phrase, comparisons, and metaphors. I hadn't expected the colossal enjoyment her stories and her image gave me.

I filmed her in her little one-room apartment, full of books and pictures. There was a Christmas tree, and she talked about her sister, their childhood, stories from the past. She went over to the window, knocked her knuckles and fingernails gently on the pane, and hummed "pidgie, pidgie" at the pigeons on the sill. It was very touching. I went back to the studio with a warm feeling from our encounter. At that moment I didn't think about why I had filmed it; I just did.

About a year later, in 1984, Tanya called again. "Could you get a camera once more?" she asked. "Anastasia is back in Moscow. They're making a decision about Marina Tsvetayeva's museum, and she wants to see the building."

"Marvelous," I said. "I'll try to get a camera."

I did. We went to Marina Tsvetayeva's former apartment, now intended to become a museum. It was late autumn. The apartment was full of leaks, and the ceilings were dripping. Anastasia talked about how she and her sister had lived in this apartment in the early 1920s, about Marina, and about her own life. Then we took her to the Museum of Fine Arts, which her father had built in 1911. I filmed her inside and outside the museum and also walking in the streets—another hour of material.

In the fall of 1986, Tanya called yet again. "Anastasia Tsvetayeva has come to town," she announced. "Would you like to go to Peredelkino to film her there?" Peredelkino is a writer's colony outside Moscow.

I borrowed a camera for a couple of hours and filmed another short piece. Now we had three hours of footage.

In the spring of 1987, Tanya called once more. "She's in Peredelkino again, and tomorrow she will be meeting her friends Evgenia Kunina, a poet, and Tatiana Leschenko-Sukhomlina, a writer.

At the time I was editing *Solovki*. And that's when I called Oleg Uralov, the director of Videofilm Studio. "Oleg, lend me a camera for a day," I said. "I'm going to film Anastasia Tsvetayeva."

"Will there be a movie?"

"Give me the camera, and there will be a movie."

He gave me a camera with a full crew, and we went to Peredelkino. The three women were happy to be together and paid no attention to us. We were shooting them walking in the garden, chatting, laughing, recollecting their past, and reciting poetry. It was a delight to film these three amazing women, whose combined age was almost three hundred.

I got another good hour of footage.

And then, a few months later, came the phone message from Uralov with which I started this chapter. My first feeling was despair. I was planning to take a rest, which was badly needed. But then I calmed down. Thank God, I would be able to make a film I wanted to make and, without any effort, get it approved by the studio executives.

When I began editing the Tsvetayeva footage, I kept thinking that this film was going to be a sequel to *Solovki Power;* I even gave it the working title *Solovki Power II.* For it wasn't just about Anastasia Tsvetayeva. Her story was typical of the fate of the Russian intelligentsia under Soviet rule.

While editing, I realized that although the material was original and good, it was too monotonous. An elderly woman couldn't hold the audience this long. Fortunately, Tanya found several unknown photographs of Tsvetayeva's family, which helped. But still it was a professional challenge to make something artistic out of material that lacked diversity.

How to shape the film? The sequences were shot at different times, randomly, naturally, with no script, with four years between first and last. The sequences were also not related to each other. I decided to break up the film into chapters. I had no other way to handle such scattered material. The chapters fell into place, and the picture took on an elegant shape.

I used quotations from Anastasia's recollections as chapter headings. And for the title I used a line from Anastasia's poem: *I Am 90, My Steps Are Light.* And Marina Krutoyarskaya wrote a lovely score.

Finally, it turned out to be a pure, elegant film, one of my favorites. I'm as proud of it as of *Solovki Power.* It taught me something new, a film structure I had never used before.

When the film was finished, Marina Krutoyarskaya mentioned that Elena Obraztsova, a famous Soviet opera singer, was in Moscow for a few days between tours. She usually spent more time abroad than in Moscow. She had agreed to be filmed. We could have two whole shooting days. And again: "Let's not miss the opportunity."

In the morning, we arrived at her home with all the equipment. We were introduced. Then came her accompanist, Vazha Chachava, whom I had met before. We had tea to get used to each other and to feel more comfortable. I asked them what they were planning to do these two days. They said they were going to rehearse a new program. Great! When they began rehearsing, we started filming. In between, they told stories about their lives and their work together. They were both good storytellers. Then Obraztsova sang several gypsy songs. That pleased me because it would give us some variety of style in the music.

I filmed from morning till night for two days. I had no idea what the film would be about. I was dealing with a great singer and a marvelous pianist. With such striking protagonists, something had to come out.

But the question of what the film was about bothered me all the time. Why Obraztsova? Why Chachava? What did we want to say with this film? The usual questions that plague me when I'm making a film. But this was a special case: I had only two days to find the point and to capture the unique relations between these two people, and also to get enough material for a feature-length film. We wouldn't have another opportunity to get any additional footage. Both were leaving the country for an extended tour.

Only two days! By the middle of the second day, I was beginning to feel desperate. The enchanting singing and brilliant playing could remain forever in the cassettes as raw material unless something happened. And then it did.

At one point, quite unexpectedly, I caught Chachava looking at Obraztsova with such admiration in his eyes! The camera was on him, and I had captured the moment. It wasn't being in love with the woman—I don't think that women interested him. It was a manifestation of their joint love of music.

Filming Obraztsova in the remaining hours we had, I kept trying to catch a similar look in her eyes. But she is a tougher and more closed person, and she did not radiate her feelings the way Chachava did. Nevertheless, she opened up, talking with great sincerity and emotion about what Chachava and music mean to her.

Chachava's glance helped me find the theme of the film. When I decided to make this picture, I was hoping that, while shooting, some miracle would happen and Nabokov's formula that "life is more talented than we are" would come true. Chachava's glance was that miracle. I gave the film the title *More Than Love*. It was about music.

The film was fifty-eight minutes long. Two people in one room with a piano. And nothing more. They talk about music. She sings; he accompanies. And snow falls outside the window . . .

Perestroika: **Another Life**

*P*erestroika, which started after Gorbachev took over in the mid-1980s, divided my life in two: what came before and what came after. Before, everything was very clear. Clear that changes were on the way. Clear that one had to do one's work well, and clear how to do it. I made films for an audience I understood, in a situation I understood, where I knew who were my viewers and who weren't. I knew for whom my films were meant.

With the advent of the changes, everything became mixed up. We couldn't tell yet that we were living through a revolution, but the ice had cracked. Television grew more open, with new shows like *Twelfth Floor,* which teased us all, calling on us to talk about the big issues. And my own experience showed that new daring things could be done. I remember that in 1987 at an artistic council meeting, one of our directors, Igor Belyayev said, "We are undergoing a revolution." And I thought, "God! He likes overblown phrases. This is not a revolution. Just changes. Serious changes, but nothing more." I didn't realize that it was a revolution until much later, probably only in 1991, during the days of the attempted coup, what we called the putsch.

When you live in times of change, it's hard to appreciate what's going on around you. The sociologist Boris Grushin, whom I filmed in 1992 for *The Shattered Mirror,* said, "I was in San Francisco during an earthquake. It was hard to understand what was happening. We're living through the same thing now." Grushin called it a socioquake. I think that's an excellent term, very precise. We were living at the epicenter of colossal systemic shifts, and the consequences were not obvious. We did not see them until much later. Those enormous shifts continue to this day. And we still have trouble understanding just what we are witnessing. It may take twenty years, if not more, for us to mature and to be able to evaluate or acknowledge the events we lived through.

In any case, my sense of a different life came after 1991. Perestroika touched only the area of glasnost, or openness. We were allowed to say what we were

not permitted to say before. Live coverage of the Congress of People's Deputies ran all day. The speeches created a shock. Parliamentarians said things people used to be afraid even to think.

The cataclysms that emerged from of perestroika brought a sense of insta-
bility. People wondered what was going on. Everyone had expected light and
joy. It never occurred to anyone at the start of perestroika that the whole country would fall apart. No one could have imagined that the Soviet Union might
cease to exist in the course of one day.

Political life was in turmoil, but there were no changes in daily life. The
stores were still empty. I remember coming back from a film festival in France
and bringing my mother cheese, sausage, and cookies. She was ill and, after
her hospital stay, was confined to her house for a long period. Her first trip
was, of course, to our beloved Dom Kino. This was in late 1988. The audience
met with journalists, writers, and directors for a discussion about perestroika.
Mother was stunned and horrified. She kept grabbing my arm and saying, "My
God! What are they saying? What does that mean? Am I dreaming?" Things
had changed so much it felt as if we were on another planet.

Of course, the fact that they had opened the sluices and let truth, for which
we all longed, come pouring out made us euphoric. We thought, "Now everyone will stop lying, there will be an end to the demagoguery, and things will
fall into place. We'll start living like normal people."

But suddenly we found ourselves in the midst of the many frightening and
unusual events that foreordained the disintegration of the Soviet Union: the
war in Karabakh, the bloody events in Tbilisi, Baku, and Vilnius. For the first
time in my life, all these horrors were reported by the newspapers that always
had kept silent about any political upheaval. The old Soviet joke "There is no
news in *Pravda* [which mean "Truth"], and no truth in *Izvestiya* [which means
"News"] was replaced by the perestroika joke: "Did you read that article in
Pravda?" "Shh, don't talk about it on the phone. It could be bugged." *Pravda*
and *Izvestiya* were the most influential Soviet newspapers.

Now as I try to recall that period, I find that much is confused, that details
and chronology are lost. What I do remember is that excitement was always in
the air. We went from delight and joy to despair and horror, from disappoint-
ment to hope.

Things were changing in my professional life as well. While television journalism flowered, documentary film withered. There had always been trouble
finding room for documentary films in the broadcast schedule. And now the
people from our studio, Ekran, had to find something new for at least peaceful coexistence with TV journalism.

This was not the best time for Ekran. Crises are normal in any creative collective after ten or fifteen years of existence. The documentary unit of Ekran, created in 1968, was almost twenty years old. The constant struggle to get our productions on the air—when television was not particularly interested in quality documentary film and preferred cheaper and more timely programs—and our feverish attempts to find a way out of this dead-end situation made our relationship with the bosses even worse. Hidden conflicts, personal ambitions, and petty hurts long nursed and that no one remembers anymore all surfaced. This was poison to the collective. Our longtime director Khessin was fired and replaced by a stranger at the end of 1986. Bickering and squabbling in our unit increased. This too was a sign of the times, the negative side of changes, which we had not thought about in the heady early days of perestroika. The totalitarian oppression eased, and the ensuing chaos overtook common sense. Self-destructive tendencies came to the fore.

I don't enjoy conflict. I simply can't live or work in a hostile atmosphere. We had several very unpleasant staff meetings. Then followed the proposal from the new director for me to become the artistic director of Ekran. I couldn't imagine trying to lead our crazed collective.

All these events coincided with the moment when I started working on *Solovki Power*. As mentioned earlier, I decided to leave the studio in the fall of 1987. I was hoping to continue working in Ekran as a freelance filmmaker.

In the late 1980s, when the international interest in Russia started to grow, I began traveling abroad a lot. In 1987 my *Arkhangelsk Muzhik* won the Grand Prix at the International Electronic Cinema Festival in Cannes. Invitations from film festivals, conferences, and symposia poured in. Thank goodness my parents had insisted that I learn several languages.

In 1988, as a sign of respect for the changes in our country, I was invited to head the jury of the documentary film festival in Cannes. There I met my idol, documentarian Richard Leacock, whom I had adored since I saw his film about the race driver Eddie Sachs. A member of the famous Drew Associates, a legend of American "direct cinema," and the cinematographer of Robert Flaherty's *Louisiana Story*, Leacock turned out to be an easy, cheerful, and sociable man, not what I had expected from a legend. We became instant friends. With time, I had the fortune to meet other legendary figures of documentary film, like Lionel Rogosin, D. A. Pennebaker, Robert Drew, Albert Maysles, George Stoney, Alexander Hammid, Jonas Mekas, and Allan King. I've been working with them for the last few years on an oral history of documentary film project, and I hope that the memoirs I've filmed will be released one day.

I also got to meet Chris Marker, the unique French master documentarian. He is not only an admired friend but also the godfather of *The Shattered Mirror,* one of my favorite films. If Marker had not sent me in 1992 to a producer he knew in Paris, I wouldn't have made that film or the others that followed.

The screenings and discussions of my films abroad during the period of late 1980s amazed me. I began to realize how little people knew about Russia and how much they needed to learn about our life and mentality. Often after screenings, people would stand up and thank me for the film, but then ask questions about "posthumous rehabilitation" and why so many people had been unjustly sentenced. What could I say? I would have to give them at least a two-hour lecture on the history of the USSR after 1917.

Naturally, that is just a small example of the general lack of knowledge about our history. And we Russians also know little about the life, character, and culture of other nations.

I came to America in 1990 to edit *A Taste of Freedom,* a film I made for TNT (Turner Network Television). The assistant editor was a huge, good-looking fellow named Steve. A recent high school graduate from the Midwest, he had moved to Los Angeles to go to college. He seemed to have a fairly good education. But the first week of our work, Steve dealt only with my editor and avoided communicating with me. However, from time to time I caught his hostile glances. It wasn't pleasant working in that atmosphere, and I knew I had to break the ice.

On Friday after work I put a bottle of lemon vodka, a can of red caviar, and a few other goodies on the table. We all had a drink and a snack. Steve relaxed and said, "You know, you're okay, quite a regular person." I decided not to take umbrage at why he might have thought me not a regular person. It turned out that since he was a child, he had been told that everyone in the USSR was an enemy of America and most probably a spy.

"Well, Steve," I replied, "you know, we were taught the same thing about Americans in school, but I didn't believe it."

After this intellectual and philosophical discourse, we had a good working relationship.

My time abroad and the opportunity to meet unofficially with foreigners revealed what I had never suspected: how little we know about one another, living on the same small planet.

Then, in 1991, I was invited to teach a semester at the University of California, San Diego, and I found myself in an unfamiliar world. It was a fascinating experience. I was completely distraught by my first class; I faced a group of young beach types in their twenties, with their feet up on their desks. Moreover, they just got up and left the room, without permission, and then returned as if nothing had happened and stretched their feet back up in the air. I took their behavior personally as a sign of disrespect for the teacher. I was used to the strict academic atmosphere of my beloved Moscow State University. Thank God, I had already restrained myself from expressing my indignation.

I went to the dean's office to find out what I should do. He heard me out and laughed. He explained that this was normal behavior accepted there and in many schools, something I found out for myself later.

After a few classes, I felt right at home. We were on a first-name basis with the students, and they invited me to their parties. The films they made were completely unlike the ones I was used to from my Moscow students, but they were fresh and original. I tried to get on their wavelength and to understand their viewpoint, and I think I succeeded. I had no other choice anyway. They gave me high evaluations (as I learned about half a year later), and I gave them grades, which were also good, and which they deserved. After the spring quarter was over, we parted, pleased with one another. I don't know if I taught them anything, but they taught me a lot. I had a much better understanding of what it meant to grow up in a free country without fear. Later I came to understand that things were much more complicated and ambiguous than I had thought. But that was later.

Back then, in San Diego, something happened that changed my life completely. My good friend Erwin Leiser, a documentary filmmaker from Switzerland, introduced me to George Herzfeld, his childhood friend. They had lived in a boarding school in Sweden during the war.

George was a real self-made man. In 1939 he and his family had emigrated from Austria to Sweden, where they had settled and started a new existence. After completing his basic schooling and a long military service in the Swedish Army, George had graduated from Sweden's Royal Institute of Technology, specializing in electronics, which in those years offered the best stepping-stone into the emerging field of data processing. In 1957 George had moved to California to continue advanced studies in computer technology and subsequently to embark on a successful business career with a number of leading companies in the USA, Europe, and Asia.

When I met him on April 21, 1991, he had his own company and was divorced. He was the most charming man I ever met. Six days later, George proposed. And a year later, in 1992, we were married. Suddenly I became a part of a big, loving family with two charming grown-up stepdaughters, an amazing mother-in-law, and numerous aunts, uncles, nieces, and nephews, living in different countries all over the world. This was a completely new and very emotional experience.

My transition to life in America didn't happen instantaneously. For at least four years I continued to live between two continents, lecturing at Moscow State University and working as a visiting professor in America: at Vassar College; California State University, Northridge; and the UCLA School of Theater, Film, and Television. I was making one film after another for different European channels in Russia and Los Angeles. I participated in numerous festivals and film conferences. My husband was joking, "You spend more time in the air, flying from one place to another, than on the ground!" I had always worked a lot, but never was the work so intense and challenging. Then, in 1996, I became a tenured professor at the UCLA School of Theater, Film, and Television, one of the best film schools in America. Teaching documentary production and the history of documentary film became my main job, which I love and cherish, but I never stopped being a filmmaker. I always believed that teaching and filmmaking nourish each other and are very much interconnected.

And this is the life I continue.

A Taste of Freedom

Perestroika brought us documentary filmmakers a long-awaited freedom from censorship. On the one hand, that was good; on the other, not so good. We were used to a metaphoric method of talking to the audience, hiding the most important thoughts between the lines, speaking in hints and references. It was a language that got past the censors but was understood by the audience, who could tell what we meant. And then the need for that indirect language was gone. We could speak to the audience openly. Strangely enough, it was not always for the best. Some filmmakers moved too much toward journalism and lost artistic energy.

For filmmakers of my generation, who had lived under totalitarianism, perestroika did not ease working conditions. I can't think of a single person whose greatest achievements were in the 1970s and 1980s and who adapted easily to the new situation. Why? Because our generation was not used to having to find funds or to fight over financing; everyone who had been working had received state funding. It's funny but true that both *Arkhangelsk Muzhik* and *Solovki Power* were filmed on government money. The Soviet state financed "anti-Soviet" films! But that was in the order of things. The state financed all the arts, film, theater, and, naturally, the main levers of ideology—television and radio.

Just take Tarkovsky's famous film *The Mirror* (1974), which he reshot twice. What producer in the West would allow him that freedom? But it was possible in state-financed cinema. Because of his independent thinking and rebellious spirit, the film bosses always treated Tarkovsky with suspicion. At the same time they supported him financially even if his films made political trouble; they knew that he was recognized as a genius by the West and by the Soviet intelligentsia. However, all this did not prevent them from shelving his film after the production was over.

That situation ended with perestroika. Money and politics were on everyone's mind. This was hard on the talented people who didn't know how to make their way in the new world. I know how difficult life became for many of my very talented friends.

If I had stayed in Russia, I doubt I could have gotten a good assignment on television. That's the way I am—I just don't know how to approach people with my hand out. I remember in late 1989, when I didn't have a firm commitment with anyone, I was considering several ideas, which I offered to the heads of various stations. They all turned me down. I didn't like making movies to suit the political situation before perestroika, and I didn't want to do it after. I wanted to make human films, about people, their lives, their personal crises, and these weren't in demand. Maybe I could have gotten one or two films done, but probably no more than that.

The perestroika years were full of events, and I often thought that the events had to be recorded. I remember that once, coming home from work around six (it was at the very dawn of perestroika, in mid-May of 1985), I parked and saw that Alexei Batalov's car was in the courtyard, and he was sitting in it without moving. The famous movie star was my neighbor. I wondered why he wasn't getting out of the car, whether he was sick. I went over, and he didn't even notice me. He was listening to the radio.

"What's going on?" I asked.

"Wait! Quiet! Listen!"

It was Gorbachev, the newly elected general secretary of the Communist Party. His speech engrossed me too. Gorbachev was saying what nobody had said before. He said that the economy needed to be reformed and that the Soviet people deserved to know the truth about the situation in the country. He said that the Soviet people have to condemn immodesty and empty talk, which had become the language of the party bureaucrats. For the first time in my life I heard from the top Party official the things we had all been discussing only in our homes behind locked doors.

"Do you realize what's going on?" Batalov demanded.

A thought flashed through my mind: "What a shame I didn't film this scene!" Batalov's emotional response to the political winds amazed me. Usually politics had nothing to do with us, but here it began to have a direct impact. I deeply regretted not having a camera with me. Later that feeling came to me almost daily. We were eyewitnesses to huge, crucial changes, and I worried that it would all disappear without a record. We forget what we were like, life goes on, and there's no time to look back. But we need to look back. We must. During the turbulent years of World War I, followed by the Russian Revolution of 1917 and then the Civil War, the writer Zinaida Gippius noted in her St. Petersburg diaries, "I will tell about the little things. The big things will be told by History."

I always think about that. The little things that we feel at every historic moment, every breaking point, are what interests me. After that moment with Batalov, I decided that I had to have a camera, even an amateur one. I would film for myself, so as not to forget.

As mentioned earlier, I was making a film in 1990 called *A Taste of Freedom* about Sasha Politkovsky, a former student of mine. It was my first work for American television. I was doing it for Ted Turner, and the producer was Roland Joffe, who directed *The Killing Fields*. I kept thinking about how to make it interesting for Americans so that they would understand what was happening to us. Of course, I wanted the film to be interesting for Russians too. Basically, I have to make a film with myself as the first audience—it's my viewpoint, my take on the events. But still, I always think of its effect on my friends, colleagues, and audience at large. Will it matter to them? I'm always balancing what I want to say with what people around are feeling.

I wanted to make a film about people, about life, about what was happening in our country. It would be a film without narration; things should be clear from what is seen and heard on the screen. For that, I have to pick my protagonists properly, concentrate on them, and await events; then I film the people when events unfold, and then the reaction of the protagonists, like the developer in photography, will reveal the feelings, hopes, and issues the whole country is living through. The film's point should not be explained by the narrator but must grow out of the events in the film and be comprehended by the audience. Viewers must draw conclusions on their own.

The Politkovsky family was a find in that sense. Sasha was at the height of his television fame, a charming, lively, and interesting man. His wife, Anna, also my former student, was photogenic and emotional, yet clear in formulating her thoughts and opinions. And they had two marvelous children.

It was my son's idea to film Politkovsky. "He's the best protagonist you could get," Seryozha said. "He's a journalist—his reports and his life are excellent reflections of the times."

I think that I was able to use their little world—a cozy two-room apartment on Herzen Street in the center of Moscow—to tell what was happening outside in the big world, what we all felt in 1990. The events in Azerbaijan (we had no idea how soon it would no longer be part of the USSR), the aftermath of Chernobyl, the Armenian pogroms in Baku, the first Russian refugees from the Soviet republics—Sasha was involved in them all, covering them as a journalist. I was with him, camera in hand. A multifaceted film was coming together in which a personal life mirrored the situation in the country.

Sasha's trips had a certain element of danger. In those days in Russia, journalism started to become a high-risk profession. Not everyone had an answering machine then, but the Politkovskys did. After each broadcast of *Vzglyad (Point of View)*, Sasha's weekly television program, Anna would find warnings and threats against Sasha on the machine.

These were turbulent times. The Communist Party was resisting the changes desperately, and Gorbachev was trying to placate both the Communists and the opposition. No one knew how things would play out. A demonstration was scheduled by the democratic forces for February 25 to demand the deletion from the Constitution of the article on the Communist Party's leading role. I started preparing to film that demonstration several days in advance. I filmed the events leading up to it. The authorities were afraid of a demonstration. The newspapers and television warned about possible disorder, provocations, and pogroms. Somebody filled mailboxes with leaflets calling for the beating and arrest of Jews, foreigners, and democrats. The extreme nationalistic organization Pamyat (Memory), also a product of perestroika, threatened to bring out its thugs to counter the demonstration. It was an agitated time. Mother begged me not to go. Who knew what would happen there? Who needs you to film? Think of your son—think of me! But she had to accept my decision. I went to film the demonstration.

Before that, I had filmed a few incidents that captured the atmosphere of those days. The Politkovskys had just gotten a Doberman puppy, an adorable creature that became a full-fledged cast member of the film. For instance, after it had its ears trimmed (which worked with our theme very well: like the poor Doberman, we were all whimpering over painful changes), Sasha and Anna talked about the coming demonstration. The atmosphere at home was charged with foreboding of important transformations that perhaps would bring unexpected consequences.

The next day, the demonstration took place. At least 500,000 people participated. They were saying no to the dictatorship of the Party in all spheres of life. It was an impressive, exciting sight. A few days earlier I had picked out a good vantage point on Zubovskaya Square, in an apartment of an acquaintance whose balcony looked over the Garden Ring Road. Everyone was expecting conflict and confrontation, and it was expected to happen exactly at the crossroads where I had placed my camera.

I came early in the morning and started filming long before any demonstrators showed up. The newly formed OMON (special police troops) came out with shields, clubs, and masks—just like in Hollywood blockbusters. There were soldiers, police officers, and covered trucks bringing in people. Soldiers, armed to the teeth, took up posts throughout the center of Moscow. The atmosphere was charged, and bloodshed seemed more than likely. But, thank God, there was none. The Pamyat did not show up. Its members either were too scared or had gotten orders to stay away.

From the balcony, I watched the demonstration approach. The Garden Ring Road was filled with people—countless police lined the street. A song by Bulat Okudzhava, a popular bard, blared through the loudspeaker: "Let's hold hands, friends, so as not to perish one by one." Holding hands, the demonstrators picked up the song. The sun was shining. I filmed, sobbing tears of joy, knowing that this was a historic moment and I had the fortune to witness and participate in it! This surge in democratic fervor was more than I had expected. It was a time of hope, of faith in a radiant future. We thought then that it was enough merely to tell the truth (one of the most powerful plays at that time was called *Speak Out!*) and hold hands, and everything horrible and inhuman that had been in our distorted Communist state would disappear. We discovered soon enough how naïve and trusting we had been when perestroika started. We were not experienced or sophisticated enough for politics.

But I don't regret a thing. It was a wonderful time, and I doubt it will ever be repeated—at least in my lifetime. I was truly happy at that moment: I had a camera in my hands, and I was filming history.

When I got home, I said to Mother, "These events must not be forgotten. Time will pass, and memories will fade. There's so much going on! So much I want to retain!"

I think that was when I first considered starting a diary.

I had bought one of the first Grundig camcorders a year earlier, in 1989. It used the new s-VHS format and gave a much better picture than the regular VHS camcorders. Life was swirling around me, filled with emotions and anxieties. After years of stagnation when nothing happened, there were important events every day, constantly urging me to capture them.

Once, I brought my camera to the university to show it to the students. It was a rarity back then.

That day, Vladimir Zhirinovsky was speaking. It was 1989, and Zhirinovsky was just starting out but he was already an infamous politician. After my class, I went with the students to listen to him and filmed his inflammatory speech. I watched it at home and saw that the quality of the tape was great and that the content was nightmarish. That was a good page for my diary. After that, many more pages followed.

The idea of making a documentary film consisting of diary pages did not leave me. But I didn't accomplish it until 1992. When I was on a business trip in Paris, I dropped in on Chris Marker and mentioned that I wanted to do a video diary. He liked the idea. "Write a proposal quickly," he said, and he called Pierre-André Boutang from ARTE.

"Marina Goldovskaya from Moscow is here with me," he told Boutang. "You know her film *Arkhangelsk Muzhik*—it received the 1987 Grand Prix of the International Electronic Cinema Festival in Cannes and was broadcast by ARTE. She has an interesting idea for a film about Russia."

"Tell her to come see me tomorrow morning," Boutang said.

I went to his office at ten in the morning, with the brief handwritten proposal I had created at the hotel the night before. I wrote that I wanted to make a video diary about a "time of trouble," to capture what we were feeling while living in a time of revolution. It was written hastily, but it expressed the thoughts that I had been mulling over for several years. Apparently it interested Pierre-André.

"Fine," he said. "How much money do you need?"

I made some quick calculations in my head. The sum was quite modest. That suited Boutang. That same day, he supplied me with the videotape I needed and the money, and I left. Using my semiprofessional Super VHS camera with a built-in mike, I began filming the picture that became one of my favorites, *The Shattered Mirror: A Diary of the Time of Trouble*. The title, however, came much later.

I filmed events that took place from February until May. So the story covered almost half a year of my life. The movie is not about me, of course. It is about the life of our country and how people lived in those difficult, watershed times.

My proposal had said that I would film only those people I knew well— friends, students, and colleagues. I asked all of them the questions that tormented me. I was very anxious then. The country seemed to be plunged into chaos. It was not clear where we were going, where we were being led, or whether we were being led at all. I think the film conveys the sense of nervousness and confusion that I and everyone around me felt.

Much later, while I was thinking about the concept of the next film, I visited the studio of the animal sculptor Valerian Martz. Among the figures of all kinds of animals, I saw a horrible metal fish, all turned inside out, with bared fangs.

"God, what's that?" I asked.

"I call it *Perestroika*. I began making it in 1990. I made it, feeling overwhelming fear and insecurity."

"God, that's what I was feeling," I thought. I had the same fish inside me, only I always thought of it as a hedgehog. So that hedgehog-fish is inside *The Shattered Mirror.* I used my personal story as a skewer, the plot skeleton needed in any film, be it documentary or not. A story is needed to cement all the component parts.

When I was planning the film, I had no idea how widespread the genre of video diary had become in documentary film outside Russia. In Russia my film was probably the first such attempt, and many of my colleagues were hostile to it. After one screening, the discussion got heated. There were voices saying, "Why has the director dragged her own life onto the screen? That's immodest. It's beyond the framework of art."

Such opinions discouraged me at first. Maybe I had done something wrong? The late Alyosha Gabrilovich was among the most opinionated: he really didn't like it. Interestingly, about three years later he asked me to come to his class at VGIK and show my films, including the diaries. I had three by then. And he and his students liked all three. Time really changes perceptions. As for me, I now watch my diary films with as much, if not more, emotion than I felt when I made them: I feel the freshness and aroma of my experiences then.

I recently asked my friend Olga Kuchkina, a journalist and writer, "Do you remember how scared you were in 1992?" (There's an interview with her in *The Shattered Mirror,* where she talks about the fear that fills her daily life.)

She was surprised. "I was scared? Why?"

It had been only ten years ago, yet her memory had faded. That's probably why my video diary is worth watching today. It preserves the emotional memory of a time gone by.

I had come to the idea of video diaries independently, not even knowing that the genre existed. Later, when I was teaching in America, I decided to study American documentary films more thoroughly. I had not seen a lot of them because they were rarely shown in the USSR. Some films I did see, among them Lionel Rogosin's *On the Bowery; The Savage Eye,* by Joseph Strick, Sidney Meyers, and Ben Maddow; *Koyaanisqatsi,* by Godfrey Reggio; and some others. But these infrequent screenings at Dom Kino couldn't give me a full picture. So when I was invited to teach at Vassar College in 1993, I spent every free minute watching American documentaries, and I learned a lot of interesting things.

Film diaries were not new. People began doing them in the late 1940s. Jonas Mekas, an émigré from Lithuania and a brilliant documentary filmmaker, began making pictures using a 16 mm amateur Bolex, adding a sound track while editing. He was not only a talented cinematographer but also a good writer, so his movies were an amalgam of original text and film intentionally shot in the style of home movies—jiggling camerawork, accelerated and slowed shots, with the camera stopping and other signs of amateur film. He filmed himself; his brother, Adolfus Mekas, also a cinematographer; his fellow Lithuanians who emigrated after the war and lived in New York; and his friends—underground artists, beat poets, and writers, including Andy Warhol, Stan Brakhage, Yoko Ono and John Lennon, Allen Ginsberg, William Burroughs, and Jack Kerouac. These are diary films.

I think this genre, coming in the postwar years, demonstrated a serious growing up of documentary film. It needed to go beyond the simple informational and educational functions it had performed since the late 1920s. Typical films in this style were made by the Grierson group and many other filmmakers all over the world. However, there were the few rare examples in documentary film (take Vertov's *Man with a Movie Camera* or Luis Bunuel's *Land without Bread*) when the directors even in the late 1920s and early 1930s found forms for self-expression that verged on a personal interpretation of reality belonging in the genre of literary diary. The kinship with literary and theatrical forms of looking at life, the expansion of genre variety that was visible in the 1960s and 1970s, showed that documentary film had started to branch out from journalism to art.

I think that the major influence on contemporary documentary film came in 1987 from Ross McElwee's *Sherman's March,* which has a strongly diaristic form and is both witty and charming. McElwee was Leacock's student at MIT, and Leacock's voice can be heard in the introductory episode of *Sherman's March,* which is no accident. The diary film is the next step in the development of direct cinema. McElwee's film re-creates the geographic journey of General Sherman during the American Civil War, but everything is seen through the eyes of the author, who is director, cinematographer, and soundman at the same time. In the course of 157 minutes the audience, not bored for a second, meets the director, his family, and numerous wonderful characters (mostly women) and gets a glimpse of life in the contemporary American South.

Another fascinating diary film appeared in 1989, *Silverlake Life: The View from Here*. Two homosexual lovers learn that they have AIDS and decide to film a chronicle of their final months. Both filmmakers, they felt the need to preserve the tragic experience of their path toward death, in the hope that it might help others understand something important and never before exposed.

When I first saw the film (which was made in S-VHS, like my *Shattered Mirror*), it moved me to the depths of my soul with its confessional mode, clinical details of the disease, and the relationship of the two men, who loved each other deeply. I always show this film in my History of Documentary Film course, and I am surprised every year that not only do the young men and women who see it for the first time weep, but so do I, who have seen it many times. It is a real masterpiece.

When I first screened *The Shattered Mirror*, some people hated it, others found it interesting and unusual, not only for how it captured this period of time but also for how it used cinematic language. It won several festival prizes, including the Golden Gate Award in San Francisco and a Golden Hugo in Chicago. It was also broadcast in Russia, Europe, and Canada. I understood that the diary was worth continuing.

After *The Shattered Mirror*, I made another video diary, *Lucky to Be Born in Russia*. It was 1993, and I wanted to show how things were settling down. My son kept telling me that life was better, more interesting, easier, that everything was heading in the right direction. I began making a film about that. I filmed my college friend Misha Sadkovich, who had become a businessman, and my co-author for *Arkhangelsk Muzhik*, Anatoly Strelyany, who was building a house in the country. I also filmed my former student, the journalist Seryozha Parkhomenko. He said he was living in paradise, because he could write about anything at all and could write the truth too.

But at the same time, life was throwing us all unexpected punches. On August 19, 1993, the anniversary of the putsch, all the former Communists and nationalists and fascists, the red and browns, as we called them, held a huge demonstration at the White House, where the Russian Parliament was housed. Rallying a crowd of thousands, the leaders of the antigovernment opposition called on people to take up arms, overthrow the democratic government, and impeach Boris Yeltsin. This was turning into a serious confrontation between the parliament and President Yeltsin. Several months later, when life came back to normal, I joked, "Yeltsin sensed that my film needed drama, so he decided to send tanks to the White House."

I filmed all the events of those anxious and dangerous revolutionary days that led to the firing upon the White House. Unexpectedly I had made a film about the fragility of democracy in Russia and about how the world had gone mad and only people with a solid grounding could stay sane. I asked all my protagonists the same, silly question: "What is the meaning of life?" It gave them a chance to tell sincere stories about their feelings, doubts, and anxieties.

The House on Arbat Street (1993)

Shooting from the helicopter

The attributes of a communal apartment

Eleonora Iossifovna Plyatt

An old music box

Denis Maslakov, poet

The house as the ship

Lucky to Be Born in Russia: Tanya Zakharova

The Shattered Mirror

Lucky to Be Born in Russia: a Communist at the antigovernment demonstration

A Taste of Freedom: Sasha Politkovsky

Lucky to Be Born in Russia: Moscow, the putsch (October 3, 1993)

The Shattered Mirror: in line for gasoline

The Shattered Mirror: shooting in the streets of Moscow

The Shattered Mirror: Marina Krutoyarskaya

The Children of Ivan Kuzmitch: Svetlana Nickolaevna Bukharina

The ruins of Meshchersky's castle

The Prince Is Back: Prince
Yevgeny Meshchersky

The ruins of Meshchersky's castle

Moscow State University: Professor Sergei Muratov, Richard Leacock, and I

At an international film conference
in Dortmund, Germany (1989)

At my Moscow home with my husband, George;
my son, Seryozha; and my dear friends Valya,
Sasha, Marina, and Masha (summer 1995)

My mother and my son (May 1991)

Once More about Scripts

Back in the 1920s and 1930s, Dziga Vertov, my countryman and genius documentary filmmaker, predicted that "scripts" as a "product of literary composition" will disappear. His dream could not become reality then: the system's censorship would not permit it. The film executives demanded a detailed script, everything spelled out from A to Z, edited, and censored. There was no room for improvisation—directors had to follow the approved script exactly. Naturally, in order to keep to the script, staging and reenactments were the basic method of filming.

Actually, this held true outside the Soviet Union too. Documentary films were made this way all over the world. Few people thought films should be made differently. This mind-set was tied directly to the technology, the heavy and cumbersome 35 mm equipment, the problems in recording sound, the insensitive film that demanded artificial lighting, and so on. Harry Watt, a director in the Grierson group, describes in his book, *Don't Look at the Camera,* how British documentary filmmakers worked in the 1930s and 1940s. Basically they filmed feature screenplays, playing them in real locations with real people who tried, after numerous rehearsals, to act naturally before the camera in the roles written for them.

There were some rare exceptions. Flaherty, for example, hardly even used screenplays. The script for *Industrial Britain,* which he made with Grierson in 1932, was a single sentence: "The film will consist of pictures of industrial Britain." Leacock, who worked with Flaherty on his last film, *Louisiana Story* (1948), recounted how Flaherty kept writing and rewriting the script, especially on rainy days when they couldn't film. The great master did it only because of his personal obligation to Standard Oil, which was financing the film. In reality not a single scene from all the many versions of the screenplay was used. Life was always more interesting than what Flaherty had planned. Nevertheless he sometimes used staged scenes, especially when dialogue was involved. But he hated the rehearsed scenes, and whenever he looked at them, he would ask in irritation, "Did I film that shit?"

The new technology of the 1960s, which introduced smaller cameras and synchronous recording, gave birth to both direct cinema and cinema verité styles. As a consequence, discussions about "filming without scripting" again started to surface.

Films made in these styles are impossible to plan—how can a director guess what will happen and when? What does a scriptwriter write in the script? The director plans one thing, and a different thing happens. But even then, at that new stage in documentary film stylistics, the authorities in the Soviet Union continued to require a detailed script. Scripts were written, seriously discussed, rewritten, and discussed again. All of the people involved knew that the paper was useless, but they wrote what allegedly would be on-screen and then filmed what real life offered.

I've always had a bad relationship with scripts. I trust life much more than any concept. But like everyone else, I had to deal with the reality in which I worked, and I made up phony scripts when I was the film's author.

And now my attitude toward "the script issue" has not changed. More than ever I am convinced that a precise and detailed script in documentary is pure fiction. What kind of a script can a person have for a video diary, for example? It is life itself.

However, we must not forget that nonfiction film is multifaceted. Of course it goes without saying that some genres of documentary film such as historical, biographical, research, and scientific films, which today represent the major part of the contemporary television documentary repertoire, do require scripting. But in films where the main point is the element of spontaneity, a script is something different. It's needed, but only as an outline, identifying the possible alternatives without giving a strict order of events.

There are some other reasons as well to have, if not a script, then at least a detailed proposal or a treatment. First of all, it's hard to get funding for a project without a detailed description. No one buys a pig in a poke. Second, the director also needs it, as it helps in formulating his or her vision and defining the goal the film is trying to achieve.

Naturally, in the work process, both in preproduction and production, a director will discover that although much of what was planned does not exist and much has changed, nevertheless much of what was hoped for is in the film. The vision had a theme, and it had characters, as well as a milieu and situations to observe or create. And the original proposal helped sort things out and keep the idea on course.

To interest a producer, the proposal must be striking and explain what will attract viewers. After all, documentary, as Flaherty said, is "a voyage of discovery." If there is no discovery—of material, a topic, an interesting hero, or the filmmaker's personality—there won't be a film. The director must state in advance what kind of discovery he or she is expecting to undertake.

Earthquake

In January 1994, after editing *Lucky to Be Born in Russia,* I returned to Los Angeles for the new semester, exhausted, wiped out completely. The film had taken everything out of me. Actually, this time what had worn me out was not the film itself so much as the events of October 1993, when I found myself in the epicenter of the political unrest. Back in California, I thought, "Now I'll be able to relax a little bit." I had lectures scheduled at the UCLA film school and I was just starting teaching, so naturally I was anxious, but I still hoped to get some rest.

I got back to LA on the January 15, and the night of the January 17 a terrible earthquake shattered our peace. It took many lives. My family was spared, but it reminded me that this wasn't the time to relax. It happened at 4:31 a.m. I had trouble sleeping because of jet lag, so I was in the kitchen reading. I had just gone back into the bedroom when the quake started and all the books in the hallway fell down. My husband had just built some bookshelves for me, but everything crashed and the books fell down. If I had gone back to bed five minutes later, the books would have squashed me. Everything fell out of the refrigerator; all our dishes landed on the kitchen floor, and even the heavy television set came tumbling down. I don't know how I did it, but in the darkness I managed to lift it up to clear my way. I picked it up and put it back. Later I tried to move it again but couldn't make it budge. It was too heavy. But under the shock of the earthquake, I didn't even sense its weight. That was the first earthquake I ever experienced.

It was very strong—6.7 on the Richter scale. The actual trembling wasn't so frightening. It lasted only about twenty seconds and then calmed down. It hadn't been pleasant, of course, but the worst part was that we didn't know what was happening. It was pitch-black, and the phones didn't work nor did the electricity. Our car was in the garage, but we couldn't get it out because the garage had power doors. We were worried too; we didn't know what had happened to George's daughter and her family. There was no way to get in touch with them.

Knowing that I could change nothing, I went into the closet and got out my camera. The batteries were low; I managed to shoot only a few short clips of the collapse around us. The next day, we went to my husband's office, which was close to the epicenter of the quake. The doors sagged and could not be opened. We had to climb through a window. Everything was on the floor: piles of computer parts, cords, spare parts, files . . . I filmed it all.

"We'll pick up the nuts and bolts later," I said. "Why don't we go see what's going on?" And we drove around. We reached a building where twenty-seven people died. Rescue workers were trying to get into the ground floor, hoping to find survivors. They brought out furniture, clothing, toys. People stood around, watching. It was a horrible sight. I filmed it all, not realizing then that I had started my new picture, *This Shaking World*.

The next week I had to go to Paris, to turn in *Lucky to Be Born in Russia*. The eleven-hour flight gave me time to think. Why not offer the French a proposal for a new film? The theme arose from my last months living in Moscow and Los Angeles, a kind of illustration for the famous joke: "Ivan, why do you keep flying back and forth? Just decide where you're going to live and settle down!" "You know, it's not great in either place. But I love the stopovers in Paris."

This Shaking World was supposed to be a film about being alive in this world. I wrote the proposal on the plane, handed it to my French producer, and went back to Los Angeles to teach. Once in a while I'd call Paris to see how things were going. "No decision yet" was always the answer. Then, in about five months, the answer came: "We've accepted your proposal. Make the picture." That terrified me. What I had planned to film was gone. Most freeways in Los Angeles had already been restored, the buildings rebuilt or razed. Construction is very fast in America, and few traces of the earthquake remained. By the time I got the okay for the filming, the city was back to normal. But turning down work is not in my character, and then the challenge excited me: could I find a way out of this seemingly hopeless situation? That's part of the profession too—finding solutions where there don't seem to be any.

Even if outwardly the signs of the earthquake were gone, traces still remained in people's minds. Some people, particularly the young, had to get medical care in psychiatric hospitals. People were traumatized not so much by the earthquake as by the continual aftershocks and the uncertainty.

I began searching for the hook for the film. How could I construct the story so that it developed and kept the viewers' interest? It was the usual set of questions that always arise when you start a film. I decided to cut from scenes of the earthquake and its consequences to the story of the city today, following a well-known genre in documentary known as the "city symphony" (from Walther Ruttman's famous 1927 film, *Berlin: Symphony of a Great City*). The film also included the O. J. Simpson case, which I had filmed in detail, since his wife, Nicole, had lived on our street. I had filmed everything from the puddles of blood the morning her body was found to people's reactions to the event. And then came subsequent events: the slow car "chase" on the freeway that all America watched, glued to the TV; the first court trial that found Simpson not guilty; the media frenzy; and the crazy tourists who came in crowds to the house of O. J. Simpson, former football star accused of killing his wife. But this episode was just a sidebar to the story about the people of Los Angeles—how they got back on their feet after the earthquake, how they lived through the stress, and how they felt after that experience.

We learn from all experiences, good or bad. I'm glad that I completed that difficult project. I had to create the picture out of thin air, from that delicate stuff known as human emotions. And I learned yet again that it is the most precious element in documentary. Making the film helped me lose my fear of the enormousness of Los Angeles. The city became understandable and dear to me; it became my home.

Ever since that film, I've been filming people's reactions to events. I had developed a taste for that with *The Shattered Mirror*. I film, often not knowing where the footage will be used, if at all. This is the most interesting thing I know: filming people at the crossroads of events, their emotional reaction, their behavior—shedding light on a situation through human reaction. This is a manifestation of my subconscious sense that history is made continually and that each of us is part of it.

The House on Arbat Street

In 1993, a year before the earthquake, I made *The House on Arbat Street,* a film about a communal apartment building situated on one of the oldest streets in Moscow. Actually, I started working on this film much earlier, but it took two years to sell the idea. At first I offered it to a TV channel in Moscow but was unsuccessful. Then I suggested the topic to Roland Joffe, my main producer on *A Taste of Freedom.* He liked the idea and said that he wanted to produce it. He passed my proposal on to Canal+. It lay there for a long time without a response. I didn't want to wait, so I started filming anyway. I had met two elderly and very sick women who used to live in the apartment house at Arbat 35. I was afraid that they might lose their fragile memory completely. They were essential to my film if it ever became reality.

I was just finishing editing *The Shattered Mirror* when I got a call from France: "Your proposal is under consideration. If you could come to talk about it, it would be good."

I flew to Paris. I was supposed to meet René Bonnel, who was in charge of film production at Canal+. I knew that this meeting would be decisive. If I couldn't convince Bonnel that Canal+ would simply cease to exist if it didn't take my film, then Canal+ wouldn't produce it. I was quite anxious and kept thinking about the best way to present my project. I strolled around the city to calm down. It was a beautiful sunny day. I crossed the Seine and saw a white ship. And suddenly it struck me: what a great metaphor this ship is for my film!

Filled with impressions of the walk and the white ship, I entered Bonnel's office. Using gestures and facial mimicry, I told him about the film. There were other people in the room besides Bonnel, who was a plump and pleasant-looking man of fifty or so and very important. I later got to know the others, including Catherine Lamour and Anna Glogowski, with whom I have worked on several films since then.

"This will be a film about Russia," I said. "This big communal apartment building on Arbat Street in Moscow will be a metaphor for Russia, a ship that survived and sailed through the century in spite of all odds." René Bonnel's eyes sparkled. I could tell he liked what I was saying. I liked it myself, for now I knew exactly what my film would be about.

I started work with that feeling. I knew that the house had to be a sailing ship. This was a difficult visual metaphor to be created. Arbat, one of the oldest streets in Moscow, is very narrow. To make "my" house with beautiful sculptures on the facade look like a ship required a 5.7 mm wide-angle lens, which was unavailable in Moscow at that time. Finally we got one. Now the house really would look like a ship if filmed from a low vantage spot. But in all the six weeks of shooting there were no clouds in the Moscow sky.

I've recognized one of the axioms of my life: "If you want something very much, it will happen." The very last day, when I had to turn in the camera, I woke up and saw that the sun was shining, but there were clouds in the sky. The clouds I had been waiting such a long time for! I grabbed the camera and a small tripod and rushed to Arbat, where I sat and waited for the sun to be at the right angle. I set the speed at the highest rate: I put the rapid-motor setting at seventy-five frames per second instead of the usual twenty-five; that slowed the movement of the clouds by three times. The clouds floated over the house, but it looked as if the house was moving.

The metaphor worked. The film was about how the house that was Russia sailed through the century. The image that came to me as I crossed over the Seine was the key to the entire film.

Whenever I make a picture, I try to fly over the location. I did that with *Solovki,* with *The Eighth Director,* with *Arkhangelsk Muzhik*—all of them. In Soviet times it was easy. Once we got permission for aerial filming, we went to the army base or the agricultural aviation base and got a helicopter for free. With perestroika, things changed. We had to pay for everything, and this venture was an expensive one. But I still decided to get a helicopter at any cost. I needed the sense of air and space.

I wanted to fly over this house. Before, helicopters were not allowed to fly over the city. But I was lucky. In October 1993, suddenly I saw one in the sky. It was an American helicopter, as I later learned, and it belonged to the Moscow police. We got the necessary permission, made financial arrangements, and started the shoot. I set the camera on high speed to make the aerial view slow and smooth.

There is always a problem with helicopter shots—the glass is in the way. If I shoot through it, the sharpness and quality are reduced. Pilots usually helped out; they either lowered a side window or slid the door open (on some models the doors slide rather than open out), so that I could film from a seat, tightly strapped in. There were never any problems except once I lost a shoe when flying over Voronezh. Now the question of glass in the helicopter arose for this film.

"Can you get rid of the glass?" I asked.

"That will cost extra."

Naturally, we paid. The pilots sat in front, and my assistant and I were in the back. We were strapped in. I had the camera in my hands. I was ready and waiting for them to open the window. Instead, brandishing screwdrivers, they started unscrewing the left door.

"Why are you doing that?"

"Don't you want to shoot without glass?"

"Yes."

"Well, the window pane doesn't lower. We'll have to remove the whole door."

"But I could fall out!"

"You're strapped in. You shouldn't fall out—it's tight."

"What about the camera?"

"Hold it tight."

"Could you tie the camera too?"

"We don't have anything for that. Hold the camera."

I thought, "God, I'm in for it now!" I had told them that I wanted to film the entire house. The pilots were experienced and bold, used to flying, which I was not. I have a fear of heights and get dizzy. I sat down and pushed my legs hard against the front seat; I felt pretty safe. But with the helicopter flying straight, there is no sense of the horizon. And I needed to get a flyover shot of the whole house, all 360 degrees. I said, "We need to tilt a little, so that I can see the city." He leaned a bit to the left. I thought it was the end for me, that I would fall out. I pushed as hard as I could against the front seat and gritted my teeth. I can't tell you how horrible it was. But I got my shots . . . all of them.

We landed. I didn't have the strength or energy to move. All the air was gone from my lungs. My arms and legs were like cotton, and the feeling stayed for two days. I just couldn't pull myself together, I couldn't sleep—I was miserable. I'll never forget it. But that flyover made the film. It was nice and smooth. I intercut the reminiscences of the protagonists with that flight; flying over the house, I returned to the characters, as if gathering them all under one roof. I filmed the people in the places they now lived, but the helicopter scene brought them all together.

The selection of protagonists is of paramount importance for any film. Probably 90 percent of the final result depends on this selection. I had a wide range of choices for *The House on Arbat Street*. Over the years, thousands of people had lived there. In the regional archive we found old books with all the information about the inhabitants of Arbat 35, including the addresses of the new apartments where they had moved when the house was vacated in 1976. Lyosha Kublitsky, my student at Moscow State University, was a great help in the research and the filming as my assistant. I couldn't have made the film in four months without him. Today he manages a film production company.

We started with a small group of people who knew one another and lived in two neighboring apartments. Then we expanded our search considerably and soon ended up with fourteen main characters.

The first one I met became my favorite—Eleonora Plyatt. A neighbor let us into her apartment; she was bedridden. Her son came to visit every third day, prepared food, and took care of her. She had the strength only to reach the toilet on her crutches.

When I first saw the woman, I knew she had to be filmed immediately. Her age and her illness meant that two or three months' delay might be too late. Even if she were still alive, she might not be able to recall what she still remembered now. I had never encountered a more expressive face. There was so much emotion in what she told us! And she spoke not only with words but with her eyes, hands, lips, and body. She was a person of rare expressiveness, spiritual purity, beauty, and naïveté.

I am always looking for interesting people whose stories reflect and represent their lives. Eleonora Plyatt spent her life marked as "the daughter of an enemy of the people," and her greatest emotion was fear. She had been afraid her entire life. First she feared for her parents: her father was executed, her mother spent fifteen years in prison. Then she was afraid for herself: she lived in a communal flat where everyone knew her parents were in prison. Her son later told us that one of the neighbors would get drunk and try to break down the door, brandishing an ax and yelling, "I don't want to live with a daughter of an enemy of the people! Destroy them all!"

She attempted suicide but failed. She got married because she was afraid to be alone. As she told it, she met someone and accepted his proposal only to feel safer. But she was afraid of him and did not love him. He was unreliable and insensitive. Her life was a daily struggle. The only bright spot was her son. She adored him. She said, "My only love is my son."

There was a man she had been in love with and who must have loved her too, but she never told him. She was married and had to keep her feelings pent up. And this woman, with her faith, naïveté, contradictions, and the horrors of her life, was a powerful expression of her times. She had to hide her noble ancestry, not speak of her arrested parents, and live with a husband she did not love. She was penniless and couldn't even buy her son a toy. She once bought him a bunny filled with sawdust for a few kopecks, but her husband berated her for being a spendthrift.

My second heroine, Lydia Belova, also did not marry out of love.

Her husband was a hero of the Civil War and worked in Gosplan (the State Planning Commission), where he earned a very good salary. It later turned out that he had served in the secret police as well. It was in the early 1920s, when life was very hard, there were no jobs, and Lydia's relatives were starving. And he would bring them black caviar, fish, and fruit. Lydia's family said, "What more could you want? Marry him!"

She hid from him whenever he visited. But she did marry him and then had to hide from him for real, staying with neighbors in their communal flat. He became abusive and filthy when he drank. She had the strength and common sense to leave him eventually. This was another mirror of the times.

The third protagonist was Elizaveta Belova, the daughter of an army commander who was chief of the Leningrad Military District in the 1930s. He was a dedicated Bolshevik, a true believer in the Communist idea, as was his wife, Elizaveta's mother. She was an intelligence agent in the Red Army and earned numerous medals and awards for her dangerous assignments. Then her husband left her, and she had a nervous breakdown. She never left the house; she spent her time sitting on a couch and shooting her pistol at the wall. She shot herself in 1935. In 1937 her ex-husband was arrested and executed.

Elizaveta, a large woman with a deep, masculine voice who smoked constantly, told us about the last time she saw her father. "I'll never forget," she said. "Father was sad, drunk, and he looked like a badgered animal. 'If anything happens to me, whatever they say about me, don't believe it. Daughter, the revolution is dying. The revolution is dying!' And I've remembered these words all my life."

This story also reflects the postrevolutionary history of my wretched country.

A compilation of such stories creates the image of the times—especially when the people who lived through it and show photographs and letters from family archives are capable of remembering and of putting things in context. I always asked them to talk about a concrete event (say, a mother's suicide). This technique gives rise to numerous, almost visible details for accuracy in describing their own destinies, which together form a portrait of the period.

Through people's stories, I wanted to create a picture of a big communal apartment building, the House on Arbat Street, and in a broader sense, the image of the whole country, the Soviet Union.

That's why I needed representatives of the various social strata who over the years found themselves in that communal residence. We found a former count: he was ninety-nine when we filmed him, but he looked sixty. His family used to own an apartment of eleven rooms (he still had charming color drawings he had made of the dining room, the living room, and the nursery), but the regime forced them into a single room. His face spoke of his noble birth. His account was the starting point of the film: he had been a child when the house was still under construction in 1912 and then he became one of its first residents. The second character was Nadezhda Sherishevskaya. She was more than eighty years old when I filmed her, and she had been born in the building. Her father was a doctor, and her mother was a pianist.

Then came a different life and different people. In the early 1920s and even a little before, in 1918–1920, Moscow had been flooded by the people who escaped from the battlefields and from the towns and villages destroyed by the revolution and the Civil War. They had no belongings and no place to live. So the city authorities forced the owners of private apartments to let these people, mostly peasants, share their living space. The so-called communal apartments became a norm, a standard way of living. Most of the Soviet citizens lived under such conditions until the mid-1950s.

I introduced several such dwellers in the film as well. We found Anna Daniloiva, the daughter of caretakers who had arrived in 1920 from a village and lived in a small room of a huge apartment. She recollected that at least one family occupied each of the other fifteen rooms.

And we found other amusing and interesting characters of different backgrounds. Step by step our narrative grew, re-creating the life of time gone by.

As usual, I used personal archives and old newsreels. On top of that, quite unexpectedly I also found two fiction films on communal life and used some of their footage. One was the first Soviet propaganda film, *Consolidation* (1918), with scenes showing the idyllic life of a professor and a worker's family who had been moved into his apartment by the new regime. The other one was *The House on Trubnaya Street* (1928) made by the great Soviet director Boris Barnet. It was a brilliant comedy, showing in a grotesque style the normal insanity of communal life: people shaking out their clothing on their neighbors' heads, chopping wood on the staircase and accidentally hitting passersby with a hammer, fights in the hallways, and so on. This was a good addition to some of my characters' stories; it brought an ambivalent flavor—humorous and bitter at the same time—to the whole concept of communal existence.

But the biggest discovery and real stroke of luck was the encounter with Anna, the niece of Elizaveta Belova. They lived in the same house, and I of course wanted to meet her and talk to her. Elizaveta gave me her telephone number but warned me that Anna was very sick, that she had multiple sclerosis and probably wouldn't want to be filmed.

When I heard her voice on the phone, I could hardly understand what she was trying to say. But there was something about her that made me think, "I absolutely need to see her." I asked, and she agreed.

I found a beautiful woman, relatively young (in her late forties). She lived in a marvelous apartment in one of the most prestigious Moscow buildings. She was the daughter of Elizaveta's brother and the granddaughter of army commander Vassily Belov, who had been executed in 1937.

She told me stories about her life. One stunned me, and I knew I had to film her.

"During the war," she said, "we had a lot of rats in the building. My father decided to get rid of them. One of his comrades said, 'Nothing to it! Let's catch one and burn it. The rest will run off.' But rats turned out to be very vengeful creatures. Can you imagine? When they burned that one rat, the other rats came that night and started biting us, the children. My brother, who was six, screamed, and our parents chased off the rats. But I was only ten weeks old, and I got a lot of rat bites. Who knows, maybe that was the source of the infection that caused my disease? I'm not getting any better after all these years."

While listening to her, I immediately pictured the chain of cause and effect. The rats were treated badly, the rats did harm to humans, the little girl suffered, and now she is an adult. The chain of evil leads from the past into the present and the future: "You mean that the future comes out of the past?" I asked her.

"Of course it does. Everything in life is interrelated," she answered.

That was the essence of the film I wanted to make. Nothing in life happens accidentally—everything has causes and consequences. And everything from which we suffer today, the situation in which we are now, has roots in the past. Anna Belova's life and personality made it possible to express this idea metaphorically on one level and directly on another.

Anna Belova spoke slowly, with great difficulty. It was not easy to listen to her, for it is not easy for any of us to understand and overcome the tragedy we all went through as a people. But that was exactly what my film needed.

In the search for protagonists, I always think about types and variety. One should be handsome, another not very, a third funny, a fourth sad, a fifth witty, a sixth tragic . . . I can film people who are not eloquent, even those who stutter. The variety adds multidimensionality and interest. I need the full palette of color that I find in life. Characters who do not resemble one another portray the range of human experience.

What force guides me when I make a film? Is it God, or is it the energy of the desire to achieve something? I often think about it, because there really is something or someone. When I want something very much, life itself starts to help me.

Working on *The House on Arbat Street,* I kept worrying about the age factor: "My youngest hero is fifty-two, and the oldest is ninety-nine. There can't be younger people, because the house was vacated in 1976 and it's 1993 now. So, is the story of this house over? Is life over? Is there any future? All right, no one lives in the building anymore; it's all offices. But still there has to be a young face in the picture."

I also wanted to give the film a poetic intonation. I was dreaming of finding a poet who would help me with that. But how and where could I find a poet on such short notice? I tried, tried hard, asked all my friends for suggestions, but nothing worked out.

I couldn't find the person to give the film a poetic flavor. But I did find a marvelous artist. A friend called one morning: "I heard you are looking for an artist who portrayed the life of Arbat Street? I know one. His name is Lev Baturin."

I visited him the very same day and immediately fell in love with his work. Later, I bought a few of his paintings, and now they hang on the walls of my home.

Before I met Baturin, I had already done a lot of shooting out of windows for this film from many apartments where my protagonists had lived—capturing the views from the house onto Arbat Street, the alleys, the street. I am always interested in the world around my characters, what they see every day. I love filming windows, taking a look from afar at the mysterious life that goes on beyond them. Baturin's paintings amazed me: they were all views from a window. There is always something in the foreground—a sewing machine on the sill, a tea set, or a cat, and beyond them the city, the Arbat and its courtyards. These pictures seemed to have been painted especially for me.

Baturin no longer lived on Arbat Street when I met him, but nearby. Like most Soviet people, he had lived in a communal flat. He spoke of this period of his life with such nostalgia, with such accuracy of atmosphere, with such lively descriptions of the residents! I could picture his former neighbors: the granny who wasn't related to anyone and lived in the kitchen, and the prostitute who brought all the cab drivers up to her room.

At the Krasnogorsk Archive, I found documentary footage showing life in the 1930s: apartment interiors, communal kitchens, bathrooms, furniture—a huge bed with big lace-covered pillows, a table with a sewing machine, kitchen utensils. This worked beautifully with Baturin's vivid recollections of his apartment, making it more full-blooded.

"Of course," he said, "life in a communal flat was horrible—no space to turn in the kitchen, a real Sodom, a mess—but I still have nostalgia for it. I was young; I had just come back from the army. I was full of energy and a desire to live, and nothing around me seemed unpleasant."

I edited his story and his paintings with the story of Iskra Goleinishcheva-Kutuzova, another colorful character I was lucky to find, who told about the horrors of communal life, the fights and squabbles, and the court cases that resulted. The scenes from *A House on Trubnaya Street* matched this atmosphere very well. The end result was a sense of something familiar and nostalgic. It was an uneven experience, but that's life: nothing is totally black or white. Even in the grimmest years people fell in love; had hopes, aspirations, and inspiration; and encountered important people and things. Even a prison cell has light from the window, through the bars.

The artist theme added some aesthetic flavor to the picture, but it still lacked poetry. And there was nothing I could do about the fact that all my protagonists were elderly people. This idea was uppermost in my mind, even as I found myself unexpectedly going off to the opening of a new college of contemporary art. It was out in the suburbs of Moscow.

"Mother, you've lost your mind!" said my son. "Your picture is in a shambles, you keep whining and complaining that you're in trouble, and yet you're wasting half a day to go who knows the hell how far to say a few unnecessary words, just because you don't want to let down a friend."

I went anyway. Something was pushing me to go. As I drove up to the school, I saw Sasha Aronov, a journalist and a poet. He was walking with a woman and a boy toward the same college where I was headed.

"Hey, Sasha!" I called out.

"I'd like you to meet someone," Sasha said. "This is Denis Maslakov, a poet. Not a wunderkind but a real poet."

I said something friendly from the car, parked, and, as I walked up to the building, thought, "God, he's just what I need! A marvelous little boy. That face. That smile."

The boy was wonderful. Very pretty, around ten or eleven, with an angelic face, beautiful eyes, gorgeous smile.

"If he only lived on the Arbat," I thought. But it was ridiculous even to imagine how he could possibly live on Arbat Street.

I entered the building and saw them: mother and son.

"Tell me, please," I asked. "Do you live on Arbat?"

"How did you know?" Alena, Denis's mother, replied. "Yes, Arbat 33."

I clutched my chest. My house was Arbat 35. Naturally, I stayed to hear the boy read his poetry. It was very good, the intonation was perfect—it was what the picture needed. Denis and I were on the same wavelength. I told Alena I wanted to show Denis the building. "Maybe he'll want to write a poem about it," I added.

The very next day, I showed Denis the house. It was an enormous building with a big courtyard, wide sweeping stairs, and beautiful stained-glass windows in one of the entrances. I took him out on a balcony and showed him the view, showed him the carved stone knights. We walked all over the building, and I kept telling him about the film. Not about its content but my feeling of it. About the people who had lived here once and had left their trace.

"So many of them passed through this house! I sometimes think their ghosts are still here."

He listened closely. The next day, his mother called. "Denis has written a poem. About the house."

"Read it to me!"

She started reading. I listened and wept. The tears just flowed—I couldn't stop them. There was nothing tear-jerking about it, but the poem struck exactly the mood I needed, and I knew the film was done: it had its poetry. The lines weren't rhymed, but the poetry was soulful, coming from the heart of a person starting out in life and for whom the building was more than just a building; it was a poetic image. Here are some lines from this poem:

> The Knights will let me cross the entrance
> They will even be glad I came.
> I am not their enemy, even if I come from Arbat Street,
> From the precipice of today.
> I run up the stairs through the century,
> I tame the house's secret,
> And souls smile as they hover
> In the misty darkness of the stained windows.
> No, knights will not leave Arbat street,
> They will not abandon us for traders of *matryoshkas*.
> We will always have the House with Knights,
> Its warmth and its faith . . .

Now I had a poet and a painter. I had beautiful pictures of Moscow in all seasons, the flights over the city and over the house, and majestic sculptures of the knights on the facade. I had everything I had envisioned.

Just as my protagonists no longer live on Arbat, I no longer live in my old home on Polyanka Street. I moved nearby, actually. Whenever I have time, I find an excuse to walk past the house where I grew up. It is filled with very different people now, and almost no one is left from the days of my childhood. But it's still my house, my "House with Knights," even though it never had knights on its facade. Now I can actually see a knight from my new apartment; the building across the street has a sculpture of a huge black knight. I look out my window, and what I see reminds me of *The House on Arbat Street*.

In his article "The Birth of Kino-Eye" (1924), Dziga Vertov wrote, ". . . once in Spring of 1918 — I was returning from the train station. The sighs and pounding of the departing steam engine still in my ears, . . . someone's swearing . . . a kiss . . . an exclamation. . . . Laughter, whistle, voices, the station bell ringing, the puffing of the steam engine. Whispers, exclamations, words of farewell. . . . And my thought: I have to have a camera that will not only describe but record, photograph those sounds. They can't be organized or edited otherwise. They flee, the way time flees . . ."

What a wonderful line! The story of the residents of a building on Arbat is also evidence of fleeing time. It vanishes like Atlantis. This film and my next, *The Children of Ivan Kuzmich,* were my attempt to keep a small particle of that mysterious vanished country from drowning.

Life with a Camera

The idea of *The Children of Ivan Kuzmich* was suggested to me by my old friend Maya Turovskaya, an outstanding scriptwriter and film scholar. She is also the scriptwriter of this film and one of its protagonists. Ivan Kuzmich was the principal of School 110 in Moscow, from which she graduated on June 21, 1941, a day before war was declared. Maya's classmates included many remarkable people: Svetlana Bukharina, the daughter of Nikolai Bukharin, a comrade-in-arms of Lenin's who was executed as an enemy of the people in 1937; Marcus Wolf, "the man without a face," the notorious chief of East Germany's Stasi (secret police) and the son of German Communist writer Friedrich Wolf; and Victor Fisher, who was the son of an American journalist working in Moscow in the 1930s and who became an Alaskan state senator. Some of her other classmates were Alexander Shcherbakov, a test pilot and the son of a Moscow Party bigwig who was close to Stalin; the nuclear physicist Alexander Rodionov; and the sculptor Daniel Mitlyansky, who made a monument for the school's students killed in the war. His *Dove* sculpture is a part of Berlin's Checkpoint Charlie Museum.

The destinies of all these people were fascinating and could make an interesting film. But as usual I was desperately trying to find answers to my recurring questions: Why was I considering making this film now? What did I want to say with it?

It was 1996. Corruption was rife, moral values were disregarded, and the country was poised between a return to the Communist past and the lawless and scary present. I personally consider it a basic truth that the only way to survive in such critical situations is to believe in human ethics and high moral standards—and to remain who you are.

So Maya and I decided to make a film not so much about who had been in that class but about their teacher, the principal of the school, Ivan Kuzmich Novikov, who had died fifty years earlier, in 1947, but who remained in the memory and consciousness of his students. It would be a film about a man who lived in the vile 1930s, when not only parents but also children were arrested, when friends and relatives denounced innocent victims of the regime, when conscience was declared a "remnant of the past." Ivan Kuzmich Novikov followed his beliefs and did not give in to the regime. He knew he was risking his life, but he never betrayed his students. He stood up and said, "Do not touch the children. The children are not guilty."

I can imagine what those children suffered once they got outside the school gate. Like Svetlana Bukharina, who must have become devastated and frightened when she heard, "Your father is an enemy of the people!" There were a lot of children like her in those days. School 110 gave them political asylum. They lived a normal child's life inside its walls, as if what was going on in the country had nothing to do with them. Politics was never discussed in school. Thanks to Ivan Kuzmich Novikov, they grew up, survived, and turned into decent human beings—honest, good, and successful. In the grimmest of times we can and must preserve our human dignity and humanity. That is what our film would be about, we decided. People like Ivan Kuzmich Novikov leave a permanent mark, influencing the lives of people around them and therefore the world.

Naturally, I wanted to film Svetlana Bukharina. I couldn't imagine the film without her; her story was going to be the linchpin. But there was a hitch: she refused to be filmed. It was too painful for her. It was hard just to get her to agree to meet with me. We did, and I brought along a camera, just in case. After ninety minutes of conversation, I knew: she must be our main protagonist. She was intelligent, had a tender heart, and was touching and courageous.

She had had a cloudless, sunny childhood. Her mother was kind and beautiful, her father one of the most vivid figures of the Soviet era. She showed me a photograph of herself at three, on Stalin's lap. The families were neighbors in the summer at the dacha.

The idyll ended quickly. First the parents divorced; then her father was arrested and executed after a horrible campaign of persecution. She and her mother were exiled once, and then again. When they came back to Moscow in the mid-1950s, she devoted herself to her mother. She also went back to the university, where she got her PhD in history.

She told me all of this, reluctantly at first but then in great detail, in the kitchen while she made the borscht she was going to feed me. At some point I felt that I could bring out my camera. She did not object.

I started filming, and I think she enjoyed it. She probably felt the need to speak out, and this was her chance. I was absolutely fascinated by her incredible destiny and could not stop. She kept bringing up new precious details and insights, which I didn't want to miss. All in all, I got eight hours of footage. But that was not the only result of our communication. We became friends and remained friends until her death on April 10, 2003.

The interview with Bukharina made me rethink my original plan to use 16 mm film. Because it would be much harder to save the priceless material on film than on video, I chose video.

Besides Svetlana, there were many more former students of School 110 with fascinating life experiences whose stories I wanted to become part of the film. Considering the length of the film and the number of characters I was planning to include, it was clear that I could only afford sequences of five to seven minutes each. The rest of the footage would end up "on the cutting-room floor," practically impossible to preserve.

I couldn't accept that. It seemed like murder—murder of memory, murder of history. For instance, there was Alexander Rodionov's story about the years he worked on the atom bomb and the atmosphere at the secret laboratory in Arzamas-16, now called the city of Sarov, where he was sent after he graduated without being told where or for how long he was going. He was not even allowed to leave the place for two days to be at his father's funeral. That story alone could become a film by itself.

I had recorded a marvelous interview with Elena Dzubinskaya. Her sister, Natasha, also had been a student at School 110, in the same class as Svetlana Bukharina. Natasha went to the front as an army nurse and was killed during the bombing of the hospital. Elena told me not only about Natasha and her family but also about her own life.

Elena had graduated from a technical college, married the man she loved, and moved to the Far North with him. She told me about bringing up her family in a small town, in small communal barracks, with no facilities at all. Once a week they could use a public bath, which was a half hour's walk from their house. And still she was happy. She loved her kids, her husband, and her work. It was interesting listening to her, watching her. I have her story on tape but was unable to use it in the film.

There was a long interview with Yevgenia Tint, another pupil in the same class. She became a pediatrician. There was nothing extraordinary in her life. But the way she spoke was special: sincere and reflexive. She was a thoughtful person, able to evaluate her own experience, her failures and achievements, and put them into the context of the country's history.

There were so many stories! I transcribed them all and hope to publish them someday. They represent an entire generation that deserves to be memorialized. And they reflect the times astonishingly well. Listening to these stories helps in understanding the Russian mentality and why we have trouble giving up our Soviet past. It is complicated to explain, but even though the Soviet years were hard, there was much that was good and that must be remembered. All my films of the 1990s, *The Children of Ivan Kuzmich* included, are an attempt to explain this period of Russian history.

As I go through the interviews now, I discover that I could make another film, and yet another, and again one more. Nowadays, you can make video books on DVDs. I hope to try that soon. I am not a historian, even though I've always had an interest in history. But my camera has given me a way of capturing history as part of my profession. This history is unique. What is important in it is not the facts and events by themselves but their resonance in people: what people feel and think about them. No description, especially written after the fact, can compare to what is recorded while the event is happening.

Svetlana Aleksievitch, a wonderful Belorussian writer, and I made a two-part film in 1990 about World War I called *From the Abyss*. The first part was *People of the Blockade*, about the siege of Leningrad, and the second was *People and War*, about what people on both sides—German and Russian—thought and felt. We spent a lot of time looking for protagonists who had great stories to tell and could relate them well. We shot 150 hours of unique footage on Betacam. Both films combined had to be two and a half hours long.

I did the final edit and mix in Austria and was told to leave the originals with the producer. So all those precious 150 hours of interviews remain in an Austrian vault. Even now, twelve years later, it makes me sick when I think about it. I promised myself that I would never do that again. I will keep everything that I have filmed.

So in 1996 when I started *The Children of Ivan Kuzmich*, I gave a lot of consideration to how to preserve the material that wouldn't go into the film. I thought: "Why not try the new mini digital format?" I had just bought a small Sony VX1000 camera. I tested this technique; the results exceeded my most optimistic expectations. I transferred the Mini DV tapes to Betacam, and there was almost no difference in image quality. It was a risky path, as Mini DV at that time was considered an amateur format. Still, I wanted to try it and shot all interviews on video. For location shots of Moscow, Alaska, Germany, and various images of nature and night shots, I used 16 mm Kodak film. Ever since, I have been using digital technology. And now most independent documentary filmmakers work this way.

Technology and Creativity

Once I got my own video camera in 1989, a new era began for me. I didn't have to be dependent on producers and networks, waiting for months and sometimes even more for an approval of an idea for a new film. I could start shooting right away. I could afford working on long-term projects without spending too much of my own money. So when I say that I can divide my professional life into those two stages—before the video camera and after—I really mean it.

Usually, the technology that documentary filmmakers use is more modest and simple than that in narrative cinema. The assortment of cameras, lenses, and accessories is, of course, endless, and if the budget permits, we can have anything we want. But in most cases, documentarians simply cannot lug all those luxuries around nor is there enough time or need to use them. The instant to be captured is fleeting. If we miss it, we can't do a retake. We can't prepare the shot or rehearse it. We can only guess, predict, and capture it.

So the technology has to be special: light, mobile, and reliable. And it has to be "smart." When needed, it should perform some of the cameraperson's functions without distracting from the most important thing—life flowing in front of the lens. I personally believe that the role of technology in our profession is more important than in fiction film. There have been four technological revolutions in the history of documentary film. The first, in the late 1920s and early 1930s, was connected with the advent of sound. It gave documentarians the opportunity to add music and narration to the images, which were powerful new tools to comprehend and interpret reality.

Documentarians striving to achieve a strong dramatic structure besides music and voice-over also started using interviews and dialogue as their colleagues from the narrative cinema did. But what was quite natural and organic for fiction didn't work for documentary. The heavy, cumbersome 35 mm equipment forced documentarians to use staging and reenactments. Even newsreels were often shot with scripted and staged sequences. Documentaries very often turned into bad copies of narrative films, which plunged the whole genre into a deep crisis.

The second technical revolution came in the late 1950s with the introduction of 16 mm film, which first was accepted by amateurs and war correspondents and later became the basic standard for television. Documentary film moved from the movie theaters and clubs to the television screen. In the 1960s two landmark films were made on 16 mm equipment with synchronous sound: in America, *Primary,* by Drew, Leacock, Maysles, and Pennebaker (the Drew Associates); and in France, *Chronicle of a Summer,* by Jean Rouch and Edgar Morin. Roman Kroitor and Wolf Koenig made films in a similar style in Canada. These films received a strong positive response and heralded the start of a new era in the documentary genre.

It is symptomatic that the revolutionary breakthrough occurred simultaneously in different countries. The time was ripe, and the dreams of the pioneers of documentary from the 1920s had come to pass. The Americans called this new way of documentary filmmaking "direct cinema style"; the French, cinema verité, in honor of Dziga Vertov. His Russian term *kinopravda* literally means "film truth." In the Soviet Union the more customary term for this style was "observational method."

I was lucky. I began working in television right at the moment this revolution was taking place, and I found myself in the middle of it. Fortunately Ekran, where I worked, was part of the State Committee for Television and Radio and was the only organization in our entire country that had the most modern foreign 16 mm equipment.

If I had worked at the Documentary Film Studio—where filmmakers always used, and use even now, only 35 mm film—I would not have been exposed to the new 16 mm technology and probably would have opposed switching from 35 mm to 16 mm, as did most of the "old school" documentarians. Some of them still are opposed to it. And in fact at first the image quality of 16 mm black-and-white reversal film, which was the main standard used in Soviet television, was very low and could in no way be compared to 35 mm. However, 16 mm opened the opportunity to come up close to life and gradually to move away from scripting, reenacting, and staging

For me, as a woman, it was always hard to handle 35 mm synchronous sound equipment. When for the first time I picked up the 16 mm Éclair, I realized this camera was for me! I could use it handheld and could go into the thick of life to capture its wonderful flow.

I remember how I felt after the first screenings of the material for *The Weav-*

ers, my first experience in direct cinema style. I shot it in 1968. I sat in the screening room, so excited, but practically wailing. The film stock was black-and-white reversal, and the image was lousy. I was beginning to despair. But I was also captivated by the vision of candid life observed, where everything flowed, everything was unpredictable, where I could capture the unexpected detail, gaze, gesture, the atmosphere. This for me was the precious essence of documentary film.

With time, the quality of 16 mm black-and-white film improved, and then came color 16 mm film with a high-quality picture. It is still in use. Many documentaries are made with it, free of script, staging, "artistic" lighting, and everything else that kept documentaries from being truly real.

The third revolution in documentary was video. At first, filmmakers resisted and refused to work with video. They had their reasons. The video technology of the late 1970s and early 1980s was far from perfect, with inconvenient linear editing and large, heavy cameras plugged into a suitcase-sized video recorder. I remember making *Monday, a Day Off* in 1983. The video engineer had to haul around a fifty-pound box behind me, and we were tied to each other by a cable. And even so, this was a revolution. I didn't have to think about the film ratio anymore. Tape was much cheaper than film, and I could shoot as much as I wanted because the tape could be reused over and over again. (In the USSR this was a hot issue; we were using only foreign film and video stock, which was very costly.)

Of course, the image quality was reduced and differed from that of film. At that time, video couldn't be projected on a large screen; it could be shown only on television. That seriously limited the opportunities for video filmmakers to screen their work theatrically, which was really frustrating.

Back then it was hard to imagine that soon the time would come when video would be shown in movie theaters and that it would be possible to transfer it to film with practically no loss of quality. Now it's a mundane matter.

Video technology has been improving so quickly that we hardly noticed the fourth technical revolution—the digital revolution. It had the greatest impact on documentary film. Digital cameras made it possible to reduce the crew to one person—the filmmaker—if needed. It has made the creation of a film cheaper and simpler, and the filmmaker has almost no technical limitations.

A small digital camera, like the Sony or Panasonic, can always be with the filmmaker, in a small bag. Cassettes and memory sticks are relatively inexpensive—we can film as much as we need and want.

The problem of artificial light also practically does not exist anymore. Camera operators can use either no light at all or just a little lamp, casting a small ray of light, and everything comes alive. All that is needed is a little experience.

So this is the cycle that has kept everything moving ever upward: the creative achievements stimulated development in technology, new opportunities that became available through new technology led to new artistic breakthroughs, and so on. When Alexandre Astruc stated in the late 1950s that the time would come when filmmakers would write with a camera the way a writer uses a ballpoint pen (*caméra-stylo,* as he called it), people took it as a metaphor. Today it's no metaphor—it's reality.

But I don't want to say that the digital camera is the crowning glory of a filmmaker's arsenal. There are filmmakers who continue to use 16 mm, 35 mm, and even 70 mm film. Technology completely serves artistic need. Ron Fricke, for example, shot *Baraka* in 70 mm format not because he couldn't handle, say, a digital Sony; nothing but 70 mm would have given that sense of scope, size, and even hyperrealism.

I myself enjoyed working with 16 mm and 35 mm, and if the opportunity arises, I'll be glad to get behind the film camera again. But to do that, I have to be certain that it is the best technique for the film I'm making and that I will have enough resources to use this technique to complete the film. Since I make most of my films through the observational method, a digital camera is ideal for me. Also I often start a film at my own expense. I cannot wait for money to come and risk losing the moment and, consequently, the story. Thanks to digital technology, with a moderate budget nowadays we can make the films we want and feel free to experiment.

Documentary film has traveled an enormously long path and has reached heights that the early founders like Flaherty and Vertov could only dream about.

The Prince

In 1998, after I finished *The Children of Ivan Kuzmich,* I began looking for the theme of my next film. I noticed an article in *Komsomolskaya Pravda* called "The Landlord Returns," about Yevgeny Meshchersky. The scion of a noted princely line, Meshchersky had returned to Alabino, a small village outside Moscow, to the ruins of the ransacked and bankrupt estate that had once belonged to his ancestors. According to the article, he had emigrated from Ukraine with his family and his serfs, to settle there and restore the family house.

That seemed notable and strange. There was something of the absurdity of our life in it. The prince's attempt to restore his rights to the estate and raise it out of the ruins seemed symptomatic of the day, reflecting the confusion in the country, caught between the desire of some to return everything to the way it was under Communism, and the desire of others to leap directly into capitalism. Suddenly the nobility sprung up out of nowhere, some of them real, some pretenders. There were assemblies of the nobility and balls, books of heraldry, and talk of the restitution of property confiscated by the Bolsheviks. Freedom of speech had reached the point when newspapers could print any lie you wanted without thinking of the truth or even common sense. Whose sick mind could have come up with the prince's serfs? Where would they have come from? If there was even a particle of truth in it, the law had to investigate. The law was asleep, however, and it didn't care about some prince and his mythical slaves. There were plenty of other problems around than the return of some prince.

I realized that this was an unusual and curious story that could be a film. I immediately pictured what kind of a film I could make: there could be an interesting narrative, filled with conflict, developing over time, and with an open finale. The action could unfold in one place, in one house. I had always wanted to make such a film with the structure of a theater play.

I imagined renting a room near the "estate" or maybe even moving into the ruins with the prince and his family. I could spend all summer there, which would let me observe their life very closely, twenty-four hours a day, if need be.

I remembered the palace ruins: when I was little, Mother and I walked near them when we visited friends in Alabino, and each time the ruins tugged at my heart. They were sad, tragic, and majestic. All that was left of the palace were a few broken columns and the facade. In the newspaper there was a photo of Meshchersky in front of the ruins, and it brought the childhood memories back. I was moved by the spindly branches of birch trees growing out of the collapsed roof. Ruins are a very powerful image of collapse and decay. I felt the drama and the conflict of the plot that was happening right now. It was the second day of creation: the prince was trying to make something out of nothing. That meant there would be development, so necessary for a narrative. There would be changes. Start from zero and end at 100 percent or at zero again. All the elements needed for a film were there.

A small but essential thing remained—to actually meet the protagonists: Meshchersky, his wife, and their children. If I liked them, if they agreed to be filmed, I could embark on a fascinating journey. Running ahead of myself, I can tell you that everything came to be just as I had imagined from reading that brief newspaper article.

I bought a ticket and flew from Los Angeles to Moscow for five days—it was spring and I couldn't leave my students for long. I headed straight for Alabino, where I met the family, and I liked them very much. They seemed to like me and made no objections to the filming. I decided to do the film. Through the microcosm of one family living on a small plot of Russian soil, I could talk about the bigger world, about what was happening in Russia, and about our strange times.

The prince seemed like a typical Soviet romantic. He had graduated from the Leningrad Technical Institute, and he liked going on expeditions, singing around campfires, communal life, and lots of company. But at the same time, he said that he had felt like a prince from childhood. However, I didn't see anything aristocratic about him, even when he put on a tuxedo.

His father, whom I met later in the summer when he came to visit, looked much more like a prince. He had a spade-shaped beard, an aristocratic drawl, and you could see some elements of noble breeding in him. We became friends. He was a pleasant, nice man who had lived a hard life. Meshchersky Senior told me how his own father had been arrested, how his mother took him from their house when he was little, and how they hid their ancestry. They weren't arrested, but they spent their life in a tiny town near Leningrad. Then he graduated from a law school. "I couldn't stand the paperwork," he said. "I hated my profession all my life."

"Then why did you go to law school?"

"Because I had to know how to deal with that regime, how to function."

He was a born engineer; he loved machinery and technology. And this quick-witted man with agile hands had spent all those years shuffling papers. He married a simple peasant woman from Belorussia because he thought it would make him more acceptable for the regime. "Before getting married I had an affair with a woman from the nobility," he said. "But I quickly realized that together we would not survive. She was unprepared for life, and I had no protection." And so, by keeping a low profile, he survived and even had a career. In any case, he had lived a quiet life. He also told me that he did not approve of his son's idea to get the family estate back. He had lived a long life, and his experience told him that nothing good could come out of this venture.

But the younger Meshchersky, Yevgeny, believed in the possibility of the impossible and decided to fight to get the estate back. He refused to accept that it was a doomed idea with zero chance of success, and he was persistent, optimistic, and filled with faith in his mission—a true romantic.

Yevgeny had come to the estate from the Ukraine, where he was well established. He built atomic power stations, including the one in Chernobyl. But he didn't like life in Chernobyl, and long before the 1986 accident he moved to Nikolayev, a city near the Black Sea, where his great-grandfather, an architect, had constructed the main building of the seaport in the early years of the twentieth century. Meshchersky was proud of this fact. He had always been interested in his ancestors.

He had divorced his first wife and did not want to return to Leningrad, where he used to live, especially since he had no housing. He gave the apartment to his wife and daughter. He met his present wife in Nikolayev, where she worked as a factory bookkeeper. They married and had three children.

Meshchersky was relatively young; he was forty-seven, his wife forty. She was a sweet, loving woman of a peasant background. Her grandparents had been exiled to Siberia in the 1930s for being kulaks (rich peasants), so she was afraid all her life and hid her antecedents. She was afraid now too, as they moved into the ruined estate without any permission, but she loved her husband and was ready to follow him to the ends of the earth. I could see that she had strong doubts and did not believe in his dream. The children were wonderful, aged fifteen, twelve, and five. Misha, the eldest, was a thinker and intellectual: on the one hand, he did not agree with his father on many things, but on the other, he loved him. Katya was pretty and just on the brink of becoming a teenager, charming and sincere. She didn't say much, but what she did say was always honest and direct. Mitya, the little one, was a funny chubby boy who certainly didn't look like a prince. He was a typical peasant farm boy.

In the beginning of perestroika, Yevgeny had started a construction company, but business practices were not for him. He didn't want to deal with the racketeers who wanted their share, and he tried to remain independent. He didn't like the new nationalistic regulations in Ukraine—he was Russian and wanted his children to learn Russian. But there were no more Russian schools. And after one of the financial crises in Ukraine, he lost all his savings.

During one of his trips to Moscow for the nobility assembly, Meshchersky visited Alabino, the old family estate. He was surprised to see that the houses were empty: all the tenants had left because the buildings were condemned. He decided to move there, even if they weren't really habitable. But once the buildings became empty, tramps moved in. They drank, made a mess, set fires, broke through the floors—even pigs aren't that swinish. When Meshchersky came with his family, he threw them out, hinting that he worked for the secret police.

The first time I saw the buildings, I thought it would take more than a hundred years to clean them up. The house, in which the family settled, was just as bad.

According to the new constitution, Meshchersky had the property rights to the Alabino estate, but only in theory. There were no legal regulations covering his situation for the agencies that registered and issued documents. On top of that, he had no papers to confirm his rights. To get the documents would take months or even years, because eighty years had passed since the estate had been nationalized by the government. So he was living in the house illegally, without a residence permit. When it was time for his son to get a passport, the authorities didn't want to give it to him, because he did not have the residence permit required by law. No one in the family could be hired legally either. It was a dead end.

Meshchersky was a real handyman. With his wife and two older children, he began fixing up the house. His dream was not only to get his own life in hand, but to save the history of his family and create a museum. Actually he wanted to turn the whole place into a historic site. The old Smolensk Road, along which Napoleon retreated in the War of 1812, ran by the estate. Meshchersky wanted to turn one of the outbuildings into a tourist hotel. He wanted to organize tourist excursions and performances re-creating historic events. He wanted to use the local army garrison to play Russian and French soldiers for battle reenactments that would draw visitors from all over the world.

The prince had a lot of ideas. He wanted to set up a souvenir factory to make key chains with tiny copies of the palace as it used to be; no one is ever likely to see the palace full-sized again. He also wanted to set up a technical school for local children. He wanted to have a theater again on the estate for plays and concerts as it used to be before the revolution . . .

Every day news plans came to him, each more utopian than the next.

I thought it interesting to watch him, his family, their relationships within it, and their relationships with the outside world. What do people think of the prince? Are they well-disposed, indifferent, or hostile? Do they help or not? What do they think of his ideas? Do they believe in them or not? This story would be a mirror reflecting the situation in Russia today.

Observing the Meshcherskys through my camera, I could capture the texture of their lives, their milieu with all its details. But most important, I had the chance to film the flow of life. That is what I love to do most.

So I decided to make the film. I realized that things would be changing very quickly and that I should start shooting as soon as possible. If I would go about it in the usual way — first with a proposal to get the funding, and then waiting for the response — I would miss everything and never make the film. "Well, then," I thought, "I'll try to do it all myself and then worry about the money." I had my digital Sony vx1000, a good selection of microphones, and a few small lights — easy to handle. This would be a unique opportunity to test digital technology. Would it really be like a *caméra-stylo*?

A month later, I came back to Alabino, settled in a tiny room in the Meshchersky house, and started shooting. I must confess that never before did I feel so good and free as during making of this film. I was risking nothing but my own time. And I didn't mind doing that — I felt great because I was filming what I really wanted to, unburdened by any obligations. Whenever you work for someone, you feel a sense of responsibility: they gave you money to film, and you must kill yourself to get it done on time. In this case, for the first time in my entire career, I was completely free.

Life was at full flow in the Meshchersky family. Everything was concentrated in a small space — around the ruins of the palace, in the dilapidated house where I lived with my protagonists, and in the enormous yard and parkland planted three hundred years ago along the riverbanks by Meshchersky's ancestors. The muted landscape of middle Russia is the one I love the most, with its flowers, little rivers and ponds, hills covered with grass and bushes, sunlight in the trees, all swaying in the wind.

Time had rolled over the house cruelly, turning it into a metaphor. I wanted to look back, beyond the present situation. I wanted to look at the history of the family and the house, which, like all the noble estates, had been destroyed by the Soviet regime, and, through that, at the history of the country in the twentieth century.

The whole time I lived with the Meshcherskys, I almost always had the camera in my hand. I changed mikes to suit the work and conditions. Life flowed around me, I was a participant in it, and my protagonists talked to me directly. And I talked to them while shooting. We made dinner together, watched television, and discussed the events. I helped them clean the house; together we went shopping.

I filmed the house being restored stone by stone and beginning to look habitable. I filmed Meshchersky working like a dog. He had to work on the water supply while knee-deep in water himself. He gave his all, worked until he dropped, and felt nothing but joy in the labor.

There isn't a single rehearsed scene in this film. Everything is born before our eyes, with no script. Life pulses. The life force is everywhere: Children playing, dogs and cats running about. A son trying to help his parents. Strangers visiting, looking with interest at what the Meshcherskys are doing. All kinds of people—village winos, local builders, a Moscow lawyer and his wife who came to help. Conversations continued throughout—about politics, the future, family problems. I filmed the news on the television set, which was always on, bringing the family's life into the "big" picture.

The prince's story unfolded, with his naïve hope that things had changed and he could reacquire the property; with his wife's story of a woman who did not share her husband's belief and was always filled with doubt; and with the story of his father, who came to visit and who was filled with bitterness and presentiments of doom. The kids helped their parents but dreamed of going back to the Ukraine, where they had been born and raised and had friends whom they badly missed.

In almost all my films, I used interviews. They are very helpful in building the narrative. But I always tried to keep them to a minimum. An interview sometimes appears as too direct and simple a solution. It's like a magic wand. When something remains unclear, when some important plot element is missing and the narrative thread is lost, we use an interview to fill in the blanks.

The way I saw *The Prince Is Back,* the story and the characters should reveal themselves without "directorial prompting." I did not want to use any narration. Everything had to be clear from the unfolding flow of life lived by the characters in the presence of my camera. I followed life, trying to capture the way people interact with each other, what they discuss, and how they express themselves. In other words, I was interested in the sphere of human relations.

It is what I find most interesting in documentary cinema today. Modern technology allows us to build a plot along literary lines, developing it naturally without pushing or making direct interjections and getting involved through interviews, and to follow the inner logic of the plot's development, using only what happens in life.

For instance, I knew that Meshchersky's father was coming and that I couldn't miss a moment of their meeting. If I had, I would have had to resort to other methods (narration, interview, titles) of explaining who he was and why he had come. But I caught it all, and everything is clear to the viewer without additional information from me. I had everything ready: the camera and microphone were always with me, so I sat for a few hours on a bench in front of the house and waited. And it all happened without strain. No one paid any attention to me. Father and son had not seen each other in a year, the grandchildren came running, and presents were handed out. It was a warm scene, and you could see their personalities and their relationships.

Here is another example: A friend of Meshchersky's, a French count married to a Russian woman, gave him a grand piano. It was delivered, and in the pouring rain four men struggled to get it into the house. You had to see it to believe it. First Meshchersky and his Moscow friend were moving it with the help of a local wino. The drunkard wanted only one thing: a drink. And he kept making insulting jokes: "What, descendant of the Romanov dynasty, tired already?" You could see the attitude of the locals toward the prince: hostile, condescending, and at the same time envious. Meshchersky brought him a glass of vodka, he drank it down in one long drink, perked up immediately, but left, since there was no reason to work anymore. Meshchersky was flabbergasted. Two men couldn't move the piano—it was too heavy, unless they dragged the keyboard through the puddles. The rain increased. The prince rushed to find help and returned with two soldiers. They got the grand into the house and set it on the weak, almost broken floor. I filmed it all and then selected the brightest moments for the film. It was funny and sad, and it gave another dimension to the prince's character.

Another sequence: A neighbor musician tried the piano for the first time. No one knew until then what shape it was in. She began playing Beethoven's *Moonlight Sonata*. The children and their mother listened, frozen in delight, in this dilapidated house with the rain lashing the windows. I was filming her at the piano when I saw the prince running up the steps. He entered the room, I panned to him, and . . . you had to see it. You couldn't act it. It's rare to catch something like this. He listened to the sounds of the sonata, his face radiated joy, he clasped his hands, his eyeglasses glinted in the light, and he smiled from ear to ear. I gasped. It was great luck for a documentary filmmaker to capture that reaction of unmitigated delight.

Filming was sheer pleasure. In those two and half months, we had rain coming down in buckets, and wind, and sun. Swaying branches and trees falling down. And the diesel horn of passing commuter trains, which had Chekhovian overtones. And landscapes in various weathers.

I did have frequent doubts during the filming about whether I could make the film I wanted. Was my prince as I had imagined him? Then I stopped worrying. If he interested me, then probably the audience would not find him boring either. I would show things as they were.

The prince and I came back from St. Petersburg, where the remains of the tsar's family had been given a burial. It was the only time I was shooting outside his estate. I needed this sequence to bring up his royal ambitions. Naturally, the burial was fodder for discussion. "Russia needs a monarchy," Meshchersky said. "It's obvious. After all, the Russian muzhik doesn't care who is in charge. But a monarch is the only one who can say when the president is behaving properly or not."

"And which of the Romanovs can be our monarch?"

"I want Russia to have a tsar, but not from the Romanov dynasty. A real tsar from the princes with a good ancestry."

"Would you want the throne?" I asked jokingly.

"It's very difficult," he replied seriously. "But if Russia needs it, I would be prepared to take on the burden. Because if not me, then who? I feel that this is our homeland, and we must fight for it. The princes were always in the lead, and the people followed. If the princes refuse, who will lead our Russia then? The others will plunder and loot and run off." I got that on film.

This prince was a mass of different elements.

Once I asked him what was the happiest day in his life. It was when he and his first wife and their seven-month-old baby climbed to the top of the highest mountain in the Carpathians. The baby was in a backpack. They didn't think they would make it to the summit, but they did. The sun was setting gloriously, and a gorgeous forest was spread at their feet.

And coexisting with this romanticism was pragmatism. Although not in everything. His friends and I tried many times to persuade him to give up on the palace—"They won't let you have it as property. At best, they'll let you be the director of the museum. And in that case, maybe the minister of culture might help you out." But the prince would not listen. He wanted to be the owner of his ancestral home.

The financial crisis of August 1998 took place while I was living with the prince's family. I filmed him and his wife hauling in two sacks of flour and a tub of sunflower oil. He was so happy that he managed to put the one hundred dollars he had exchanged for rubles to good use. He bought enough supplies to last for two months. They discussed their dilemma in such sad and funny ways. Tears and laughter . . . These private concerns were also history. A document of the times. *The Prince* doesn't have reminiscences and stories of the past; it is in the moment. It is a testimony about a slice of our history. Time will pass, and the film will resurrect how we lived and what we thought and hoped in those days in that little spot near Moscow.

There are many sounds in the film that I collected carefully during the filming. This is the first time I did the film's sound design myself. It was a useful experience. I better understood its full importance when I handled it myself.

Tanya Samoilova, the editor I've been working with for almost twenty years, edited the film with me. It's very important to find a friend and highly creative person who understands you and whose artistic sensibility and taste are combined with the ability to work hard. We put the film together in three months and made a fine cut and postproduction. Then we transferred it from Mini DV to Digital Betacam and made color correction. The image quality was better than we expected.

Marina Krutoyarskaya composed wonderful music. We worked at a distance. Tanya and I were editing in the United States (I was teaching at UCLA at the same time), and Marina was home in Berlin. Sometimes she'd call and say, "Listen to what I've written." We'd listen over the phone to her playing. I will probably never find another composer with whom I am so much in tune.

The result is the film I had wanted to make: a film about the hopelessness of dreaming and yet still about hope. It's a very Russian trait—having romantic faith despite the odds. *The Dreamer of Alabino* was the original title I had in mind, although it ultimately became *The Prince Is Back*. It is imbued with the life and reality of the country in that period, with all the twists and turns, the absurdity and the hope. That small family microcosm was part of the greater mad, mad, mad world in which we all live.

The Prince Is Back, I think, is closer to literature than any of my other films. The form is novelistic, a literary work written down by the *caméra-stylo*. It is also close to theater. I set myself a purely artistic goal: to preserve the unity of time, place, and action. It all happens here—in this house, this yard. At the outset of the film, which shows a model of the estate, I delineate the limits of the territory and never leave it. History is immersed in a concrete environment, which is part of the world, an expression of the world in which these people live and act. The milieu takes on the fabric of fate, the story of each character.

The characters became particularly important to me. They were always important, but here I treat them as dramatis personae onstage. Each has his own theme, each personifies some idea, each is an instrument with its part to play. All together they form an ensemble playing the same melody, telling a specific story that carries a larger message.

Take the prince. I filmed him, trying to reveal everything important about him, to show the viewer who he was, where he came from, why he was the way he was. I let the audience know what came "before" and what will happen "after." The same holds for his father, wife, and children. I tried to write my characters the way a writer does, but only with a camera. Each of them is important for me. Their relationships must be shown within the plot but also must fit into the life flowing around them; they develop in the three-dimensional space that has atmosphere, mood, and air. This is what interests me most in documentary film. These are the kind of films I want to make.

I can count on my fingers the characters in the film: five family members and another five neighbors and friends who took part in the action and commented on them. Time, like place, was limited. I began in winter, showed spring, then summer, then winter again. But the main action took place in one summer. The winter scenes in the finale mark time and give a postscript to the film.

What was the film about? I can't give a precise answer. Perhaps about how an obsessed man fights to the end, that the human spirit is invincible even when defeat is inevitable. And it is about a very interesting personality.

Thinking how to end the film, I once asked Lyuda, Yevgeny's wife, "What do you think the finale of our film should be?"

She thought about it, then said, "You know, you should film the two of us. We're walking away from the camera into the distance, carrying empty pails. And it's not clear whether we'll return with full ones."

And the prince added, "Even if it doesn't work out, we lived these years beautifully."

That's probably what the film is about.

I love this picture. I think I've tied up all the loose ends. Visually, it works—it "smells" of life. When I filmed the rain, I tried to give the viewer a sense of how wet, and raw, and bloated everything was, so that the audience can feel the texture and smell the scent of the rain.

When watching the film on a big screen in a theater, viewers sense all these things much more deeply. There is the rain, the grass redolent after the rain, the sky filled with ragged clouds . . . the bushes, grass, daisies torn by the gusts of wind, the birches growing up out of the columns, so thin and frail, so green and touching. The viewer wants to reach out and touch the leaves, they are so tender. They are filled with hope and hopelessness—it's all in the picture. The grass is fragrant. The film is very sensual. (At Le Nombre d'Or International Widescreen Festival in Amsterdam, where *The Prince Is Back* was awarded the Silver Rembrandt for artistic achievement in digital film, the picture was shown on a huge screen with a high-grade projector, and the image quality was great.)

I can say this about myself: I had always sought this, always tried to capture it, always thought and dreamed about it. Even in the films where I was only the cinematographer, I tried to capture the wealth of emotions elicited by nature. I always loved it, but I think that it was only in *The Prince Is Back* that I could fully achieve it and create that texture and atmosphere. It all came together for me.

And I also believe that this film portrays the same human spirit that captivated me in Flaherty's *Man of Aran,* the spirit of unyielding stubbornness and will in a man prepared to resist all circumstances—no matter what, no matter who.

Postscript: Four years after the film was shot, the prince and his family were evicted from the house—legally, by the police. I filmed the eviction and made an updated version of the film.

On Ethics

The question of ethics became a major issue in documentary film with the advent of 16 mm technology. When we were making *The Weavers* in 1968, Nikita Khubov and I sensed at one point that we had crossed the line and had violated the privacy of our heroines' private lives, by entering where we had not been invited. I had this feeling back then: "Oh, boy! This is dangerous! Where will it end?"

Later, in 1972, I wrote an article, "Delicate Camera," about the ethics of documentary film for *Zhurnalist* magazine. We film people, but they don't know what we are doing with them. And we cannot really explain anything, because they will feel less natural, and in the end it will kill the truth and spontaneity of life that we are seeking. But if people don't know we're filming them, there is the danger that we will take advantage of situations that are not meant to be public and we will hurt them. After all, when the film is made and shown, they have to continue their normal lives, and they have relatives and friends and work colleagues. Basically, not everything is meant for the screen.

I always tell my protagonists, "I'm filming. Try to pay no attention to me." The operative word is "try." It's silly to say, "Don't pay attention," because they will. But when they are busy, they will forget about you if you yourself will not remind them that you are filming. If they trust you, you will capture their lives. But I always tell them: "Don't worry. When the picture is done, I won't show it to anyone until you see it first." And I always keep the promise, if, of course, my protagonists want it.

Now that cameras are so perfected and available, many directors don't think too much of the consequences of making a film, especially since so many more people are making films. Some people seem to think that anyone can make a documentary. Film with a little toy digital camera, quickly collate the material on the computer, add a few patches of text and some music, and anyone has got a movie and can call himself or herself a director. Many such people are around now — without training, without any idea of the history and essence of documentary film, with no understanding of the problems it raises for the subjects and for the person with a movie camera. Many, too many, people think that documentary film is so easy to make. If only it were so! Documentary film demands serious preparation and very cautious treatment of the people being filmed. It requires sensitivity, respect both for them and for oneself as the filmmaker, and a great sense of responsibility.

In truth, the questions of ethics are faced in equal measure by directors of feature films and directors of documentaries. If a feature film includes a rape scene, the question is an aesthetic one: how frank can one be in depicting this act? But if the same act is shown in a documentary film . . . Fortunately, I've never seen a rape in a documentary, and I hope I never do. A person would have to be an immoral monster to film that act passively instead of intervening to defend the victim and stop a crime. For the documentary filmmaker, unlike the director of feature films, exists in the same reality as the protagonists. A director of a feature film is in a sense a virtual figure, everywhere and nowhere, down among the invented characters and in the skies above them. The protagonists are played by actors, which means they can be killed (they spring back to life after the scene), beaten in fierce battles (stunt people do it without bruises or scratches), or cut up with chainsaws (computer technology allows a director to film whatever the screenwriters make up). In documentary film, the director cannot use any computer tricks, except in the titles and credits. The audience has to be sure that everything shown is the real truth; otherwise, the audience does not treat the document as a document and instead watches the film like fiction. There are living people in documentary film. They can be hurt, physically and morally. Sometimes a filmmaker even makes trouble for them by showing them in a good light—some people are envious, and they don't forgive those who suddenly find fame. I had that happen with my hero in *The Eighth Director*. Of course, Litvinenko had expected that and was prepared for it.

There have been many cases of filmmakers damaging people's lives. I remember the film *Family Circle,* made by my friends Marik Zelikin and Alyosha Gabrilovich in 1976. They decided to use the observation method on the first year of marriage of a couple—naturally, with their permission. But the marriage ended in divorce after the filming was over. A much more famous story involves *An American Family* (1973), where the director got the family's permission to show the television series, after they had all watched it. But then came the reviews, and some reviewers delved into the characters of the people they saw on-screen, which the family didn't like. Then the family attacked the filmmakers for ruining their image. It seems silly to blame the mirror.

There are also cases of a different kind, when the protagonists want fame, even notoriety, and they expose themselves all over the screen. The mass media always want the unusual, scandalous, and entertaining, pushing documentary filmmakers into becoming paparazzi and filming through keyholes. It is hard to resist that pressure if one doesn't have a strong moral backbone.

I am horrified by some of the talk shows on American television, and now on Russian TV as well, where allegedly real-life guests, sometimes played by bad actors, recount their and other people's intimate problems and domestic scandals, holding back no details or expressions. They are telling the audience there is nothing to be ashamed of, that shame is merely a superstition, and see, we're famous, we're on television, be like us. As a result, the ecology of our communal existence is gradually turning into a garbage dump, and we'll have to deal with the consequences in the future.

Ethics are ethics because they are not regulated by law; they are a question of conscience. Conscience is very personal, and each of us determines what is acceptable. Thus the question of ethics in documentary film is much more important than in feature film, where we deal with models of all kinds of human behavior. In documentaries, we have real situations, not models. This raises the responsibility of the filmmaker and the demands on his or her human qualities. They say that being a good person is not a profession. And, in documentary, being a good person doesn't mean being a good filmmaker. But if you're not a good person with strong moral beliefs, it's better not to become a documentary filmmaker, in my old-fashioned view.

These problems were always an issue, but they are particularly acute now, when technology permits literally everything—we can penetrate into people's lives with unprecedented intimacy, and hidden cameras let us film in bedrooms and bathrooms. That means limits are necessary. I'm not talking about external censorship, which is ineffective in our day. There has to be an internal brake, an internal guard who says, "Do not go beyond this point."

The camera is a powerful tool and, therefore, a dangerous one, both for those who are being filmed and those doing the filming. Vladimir Sappak, the first Soviet television critic, said at the dawn of that era, "Television is the X-ray of character."

A documentary film is also an X-ray of character. The protagonists are revealed by the camera, but the camera first reveals the director. Whether directors want it to or not, they create not only the images of their protagonists but also their own self-portraits.

Life with a Camera (Continued)

Ever since fate brought me to America, I consider it a matter of principal importance that I continue making films about Russia. When you live in two countries, it helps you to remember who you are. It's important not to lose contact with your roots when you spend most of your time abroad. Perhaps because I traveled to Russia frequently—usually at least three times a year—and made films and kept an eye on what was happening in Russia, the connecting thread did not break. In America, I always felt Russian, and I follow Russian issues no less than anyone living in Russia. It's important to know who you are at all times. I know who I am. Now I am a Russian American.

In America, the issue of self-identification—Who do you think you are? Who are you?—is very intense. America is a land of immigrants, and Americans are a mixed nation. The country has an enormous number of people of Asian, African, and Latin American descent—quite a cocktail. There are many U.S.-made documentary films about ties to one's roots. People try to preserve their roots, and many of my students make films about their search for their ancestry. I can relate to that.

One of my students, a Coptic Christian from Egypt, made such a film; then so did an Iranian American, and then two Chinese students. Interestingly, they were all female—I think documentary film is becoming more a woman's world. They do it all: filming, editing, postproduction. It doesn't bring in a lot of money, but documentary film brings its rewards intellectually. Naturally, I have young male students, very promising ones, too. But when I was starting out in the Soviet Union, I was practically the only female director-cinematographer, and now that is no longer a rare thing.

I am a documentarian; I film life. And what is life? Not only events, not only the reaction of my protagonists to events, but also the protagonists themselves, who vanish as does time itself.

Everything I've done in recent years, since *Solovki Power,* covers the history of the passing age. Including the oral history of documentary film that I am doing for my university, filming the legends of documentary film. Including the memoirs I filmed in Russia. And including *Russian Chronicles: A Diary of Change*, the film that I plan to make now, to tell about what happened in Russia in the last twenty years. I've been collecting that material, bit by bit—events; conversations; people's reactions, thoughts, and feelings; how the times changed, and the people with the times; what changed in their lives; how everything keeps changing.

I hope that the people I filmed in Komsomolsk-on-Amur in 2000 live for a long time, but they were in their nineties when I filmed them, and some could barely remember their lives. After they're gone, who will be able to tell about what they went through? Who will tell about the wretched old women in the village of Zakharovka, where I went when I was making *The Children of Ivan Kuzmich*, because he was born there. The most interesting things I filmed were not about him but about the time when I was doing the filming. Yeltsin had just been reelected. The old women told me that they weren't getting their pensions, that Yeltsin hadn't done a damn thing for them and never would. One woman took me to see the house where she had lived during World War II. She told me how the Germans had come to the village and mistreated them. I thought, "God! The Russians come and rob them, the Germans come and rob them, the Communists rob, the capitalists rob! This poor woman lived through it all, but who will ever remember her? Who will let her tell her story?"

I'm making a video diary of passing times. What happens today will be different tomorrow, completely different the day after, and a year later no one will even remember what happened. Memory is impermanent. When I try to remember what happened in 1990 and what in 1995, I get things mixed up, details blur, and one year is indistinguishable from another. It's very different when I can look at the video material I've taped. I can see everything. I'm so glad I managed to preserve at least some things.

I can't say that I intend to continue making films following purely literary forms (for the diary is also a literary genre), but journalism is simply no longer interesting to me now. I'm interested in pondering life through my protagonists and my films. In capturing the lives of my characters and telling their stories, I put things into the broader context of what is going on in the world. Let my protagonists think about life—I'll think along with them. Bulgakov once said, "Someone dipped me in an inkwell and wrote *Theatrical Novel* with me." And I feel as if someone has dipped me in the camera and is using me to describe life.

Documentary Trip

Before I take on a topic, I have to hear a little bell ring inside me. My intuition prompts me to take it; I actually feel a nudge. I think, "Yes, here's a theme I can do." No one can predict how it will turn out, but it will be interesting. It responds to something in me.

So I say, "Take off!" and start work. Then come the doubts, horror, nightmares, lack of confidence. I regret that I ever started; I swear I'll never do it again. But deep inside, there's another voice, a confident one that says, "Don't be afraid. Everything will be fine. Keep working." I can't explain what prompts me to decide what films to make. I ask my friends for advice, I share my worries, but inside I already know that I'm on it.

What I think about primarily is whether I will be able to tell the story I want to tell. Are the characters interesting enough? What events can I expect during filming, and which will I have to provoke? I also think about what I will be able to witness (if it's a diary film) through lengthy observation. Do I have a strong concept? What do I want to say with the film, and why am I making it now? Will I be able to express the idea troubling me at the moment with this material? Will I be able to reveal it here? What do I want to change in the world with this film? Will I be able to move the world toward progress? I'm joking here, of course: no film makes anything progress, but it's useful at least to have the illusion (even misapprehensions have their energy) that at least some good will be generated by the film.

At first, I have only a vague idea of what the film will be like. I don't see or understand it yet—I have only a glimmer of it. It's growing in me, a small living thing, existing only in my subconscious. Then it grows and crystallizes, and I can visualize a lot of it, joining bits together into sections that will grow on the editing table. The sections grow into bigger parts, and the parts into the whole.

Documentary film, as I see it, is first of all a movement from not knowing to knowing. I start at zero. I have an idea of my characters, only an outline of my theme, and I decide to make the film in the hope of learning about them. Flaherty compared documentary film to a voyage into the open world. This was his view, and even though he was not a popular-science director but a true documentarian, he always stressed the necessity of research for the sake of discovery. Along the way, I learn something new, make revelations, and find new fuel for my curiosity. That is probably the distinguishing trait of documentary film. It deals with living reality, which I have to understand myself before showing it to the audience. The most interesting aspect is when that discovery happens in the process of the film, and the audience is witness to it along with the filmmaker, and we both discover something new, important, and exciting together.

In making films, I learn something about life. When I start, I basically say to myself, "I'm making this film because I want to master this piece of reality and understand what's happening in it, to travel this road along with the audience." Both the audience and I have to be interested in the journey, discovering something new along the way, doing an archeological dig, whether we're digging into history or into today. There is wide scope for digging today.

For instance, when I was filming *The Prince Is Back,* I tried to go beyond the surface of events into the psychology and mind of my hero, into the economy and situation of our society, trying to find out what was going on in our country. Just being in contact with reality makes me want to understand it.

As I start a film, I have an idea of what it is about—I formulate that rather clearly for myself. Naturally, in the process of filming, I deviate a lot from my original plan. I plan to film one thing, and something completely different happens. Whether I want to or not, I have to refocus and change. But the main direction has to remain the same—although sometimes, I have to change everything, even the topic.

Unexpected situations always arise when filming. Consequently, I start looking for ways of getting out of such situations without straying too far away from my original concept. I struggle to reformulate my main task, to get back in my original stream or to find another one more suitable to the actual situation. Usually, at the very start, I make a notation of three or four lines about what I want to say with the film and what it will be about. It is very important for me to do that. I write in a notebook, and then, after a while, I return to my notation. Then I add, "I wanted to do this, but changed my mind. Now I want to do something slightly different—the theme has changed." In more time, the concept may change again, it may transform, and then I will make new notations, keeping track of my progress in the creation of the film.

At last, the entire picture is shot. Now, in order to build it, I have to digest the material. I have to remember all the nuances, all the details, all the shots. I have a good visual memory. I quickly forget what I read. But I remember film images. Once I've filmed something, I can remember: "Oh, yes, there's an interesting blinking in that spot, and this one has a gust of wind in the branches, and here a dog ran from right to left, and there, from left to right." That remains with me. I will remember details that occur in a shot even many years after filming it.

The first stage of editing is sorting the material and getting rid of everything that doesn't work, everything that is of poor technical quality. I dump all that ruthlessly. I also throw away quite a bit of material that clearly has nothing to do with the topic. It often happens that I get carried away with the scenery or the characters. I enjoy filming them, and it may even be beautiful, but I know it doesn't belong in the film.

By the time I start editing, I have all the cassettes transcribed. I write a detailed description of each of them; if I suddenly do need something I've discarded, I can find it easily. So I filmed seventy hours for *The Prince Is Back,* and after the first round of cutting, I ended up with ten. The film is supposed to last an hour; I start creating a story out of those ten. First I do a rough draft. I call it a sausage. It's formless, long, and without structure or rhythm. The longer I work with the material, the better I get into it, and the clearer it becomes how best to handle it. I lay out the story line. Now I have two hours left out of the ten. That's much easier, making one hour out of two. I start polishing, giving the film its shape, and cutting out everything extraneous.

It is very important for me to use the "golden mean" or "golden section" as a principal for my structural composition. The golden mean is the most harmonic and most organically perceived proportion; the ancients ascribed magical properties to it. The line is divided at a point so that the ratio of the two parts, the smaller to the larger, is the same as the ratio of the larger part to the whole line. I can think of it as making the central focus approximately two-thirds or three-fifths along the way, rather than right in the middle. Many masterpieces in painting, sculpture, and architecture follow this principle. The designers of the Parthenon used it. Sergei Eisenstein used it for *Battleship Potemkin,* universally recognized as one of the greatest films. He consciously built it along the proportions of the golden mean; The culminating point—the shot of the raised red flag, the only color shot in the black-and-white film—is right at the point of the golden section.

It is crucial to introduce the characters and announce the theme at the very beginning of the film. The audience has to be attracted, intrigued, and hooked. What kind of film will this be? What is it about? Who are these people? Everything has to be laid out as if on a chessboard before the game begins. The audience has to understand the rules of the game from the outset. I give this five minutes, no more, and then it's time to move the pieces.

I try to unfold the action gently and easily so that each scene moves the story along. It has to develop, never stopping for a second, each episode leading the viewer up a ladder and revealing something new. The audience's curiosity should be piqued: "Oh, I didn't know that! And what's that? And that?" The viewer should never feel the reins loosen. I can give a slight break after a strong scene of information and emotion. The pause can be atmospheric or musical, but not empty in any case. Dramaturgy does not tolerate emptiness in a film; everything has to be saturated. And since I can't test anything in a documentary film ahead of time, I have to keep seeking. I seek as I film. I seek in the editing room—I look at the screen and ask: Does it work or not? If it doesn't, what do I do to make it work?

Somewhere around the end of the second third of the film, at the very point of the golden section, it's time to reach the culmination, the climax of the film. Something has to happen that will surprise and astonish the viewers, make them say, "Wow!" This is almost obligatory. Without it, the film will lack catharsis. The audience needs to be stunned. Of course, documentary film isn't feature film—sometimes I never get the material that can really shock people—but this has to be the most emotional point of the film.

As an example, I show my students *Place of Birth,* by the Polish filmmaker Pawel Lozinski. It's the story of an American writer who travels to the Polish village where he was born, and where he, as a five-year-old, with his father, mother, and year-old brother hid from the Nazis and the Poles. The Poles gave up the baby brother to the Germans, who shot him. His father was killed by the Poles, but he and his mother survived miraculously and eventually got to America. So he returns in 1992 to see the place of his birth and to understand how his father died, something he and his mother did not know.

For fifty minutes, the audience moves with the author as he learns. Step by step his family comes alive in the tales of the Polish peasants. The audience sees today's life and realizes what it was like for the family fifty years ago. Characters appear on-screen, each very different from the others, some pleasant, some not, like the drunkards with red noses, who are vicious and envious. God, all these people went through so much—the Poles and the Jews who lived among them. Many Poles were anti-Semitic and often turned Jews in to the Nazis, who gladly exterminated them. Sometimes the Poles killed them, just to get their last cow, which is what happened to the protagonist's father.

The director leads his protagonist (and us) toward that information. The writer finds the killer and his father's grave. The peasants help him dig up the spot. First they find a bottle; the protagonist recognizes it—his father always brought him milk in that bottle, and as a boy, he always drank from it. The body should be near the bottle, the peasants say. Let's look for it. And they find his father's skull, smashed by an ax. That skull is the culminating shot. It hits the viewers in the solar plexus so they can't catch their breath. I always give my students a break after the screening of that film. "Let's take a walk," I say. "It's impossible to discuss the film right after seeing it."

That is the paradigm for a film. Of course, documentarians don't often find a story like that and get to shape it with an effect as powerful. But that is the artistry of the documentary filmmaker—to find a subject and build a story that will excite and move the audience. This one picture is better than everything else done about the Holocaust. I've never seen anything more powerful on the topic.

Once I've created the plotline, it's time to polish the picture. I go over every scene, dropping two seconds here, another second there, and second by second, scene by scene, sometimes taking out only one or two frames, I tighten and compress and give the film shape. That is how I achieve line and finish.

Then I start dressing up the film by adding sounds like ornaments, and thinking about the music—where it will be louder? where softer? I keep the music to a minimum, using it only where it is necessary. Then I carefully add the text. To my taste, there should be as little as possible. At this stage I am playing with the tiniest details. Everything must be in its place. Everything must be done cleanly. In that regard, today's computer technology, from my point of view, spoils filmmakers and keeps them from learning how to work cleanly. They still can, of course, but it comes too easily. And when it's too easy, they tend to do a sloppy job.

Recently a student brought me a small film. It was well done, but it needed much more work. I asked him, "How many versions did you do?"

"What do you mean?"

"How many versions did you do?"

"This one, one version."

"Just the one?"

"Yes, one."

"Do you know how many versions I do? At least twelve to fifteen. And Leacock does twenty-five."

"Twenty-five?"

"Yes."

He couldn't believe it. But if students are serious about their work, that's the only way. Writers work with text the same way: they write, rewrite, rewrite again, until they feel the piece is ready. I know it seems old-fashioned in today's computer age. In the olden days, letters were not written quickly; they were re-written and edited before mailing. Now people just rattle off an email and click "Send" without rereading. I get real satisfaction from work when everything is polished and no rough edges are left—that's when the work is completed.

In principle, it would be good to set aside a film when it's done for a month or two, get some sleep and some distance, and then take a fresh look at it. Then I wouldn't have those terrible moments that I often experience. After a while, when my enchantment with the film fades a bit, I watch it and think, "Oh, my God, how could I? That should have been taken out, this bit shortened . . ." and so on. But I have spent my life making films not for myself but for television, on order. I had deadlines, and I was always in a rush. I never had a month to let a film settle, not even three days.

It's interesting that when I finish a film, it turns out to be the very thing that I had imagined and sensed at the beginning. I don't know how accurate that perception is. The border dissolves between myself before and my present self and between what I used to think and how I now perceive what I thought then. But there are original documents, proposals, notations, which I can compare with the completed film, and the comparison tells me that I am not mistaken.

Work on a movie gives rise to so many unexpected events and turns, all kinds of circumstances demanding enormous spiritual energy; it is simulta-neously so exhausting and so attractive, that I don't know of anything else that brings such joy. I have become addicted.

It's a strange profession. I never know where it will lead me. I never know whether what I wrote in the script or proposal will work. I have to be pre-pared for the most unexpected changes and not get lost, not be afraid, and not give up. Making a film is like running through a dark tunnel; somewhere at the very end there is light. Sometimes I lose sight of that light, and everything is dark and I bump into the walls, getting bruised and bashed. But if I have the strength to keep going (and thank God, so far, I have), I'll suddenly see the light at the end of the tunnel and I'll run out into it. The best part of docu-mentary filmmaking is the unpredictability of the result. I never know how things will end when I'm filming. That gives the spontaneity and freshness to the screen. And my next film starts at zero again. Every director starts at zero, no matter how successful his or her past films.

Sergei Gerassimov, the great Soviet feature filmmaker, used to say that you spend the first ten years working for a reputation and then the reputation works for you. It's important to have a solid reputation: it's easier to get financing, to put together a team, and so on. And still, when you start a film, if you're a real director, you start at zero. There is always the unpredictability, the anxiety, the infinite number of uncertainties—especially in documentary film. In features films, I'm sure it's somewhat simpler. At least the director has a script. Add good actors, a good cameraperson, a good editor—and the feature director finally makes a good film. But in documentary film, you are one-on-one with life. And how can you guess what trick it's going to pull tomorrow?

It is always very important for me that the film is constructed visually. I begin with the high points. I wrote about the importance of the helicopter shots in *The House on Arbat Street*. The same held for *Solovki Power*. I couldn't imagine the film without aerial shots above the Solovki Islands. I also sensed that I had to have winter footage. I didn't know how things looked there in winter, but since it was the North, the White Sea, the movie wouldn't have worked without shots of the cold wintry forest and snowy vistas. And there definitely had to be aerial shots of the sea with the clouds reflected in it.

That was the situation for *Arkhangelsk Muzhik* and for *The Shattered Mirror* and almost all my films. For *Mirror,* I knew the film had to have a lot of the streets, noisy, chaotic, with vendors and Hare Krishnas wandering around Moscow. It was a madhouse that appeared during the madness of perestroika. I needed chaos, noise, bustle, cacophony, disharmony, the gabble of voices. I hadn't clearly envisioned the film yet, but I could hear it.

When I first begin thinking about a film, when the concept is taking form, it resounds in me. I can't say that I hear actual music—I'm not a musician—but I hear the film, and I can sense what it should be. I hear the "music" of the film before I see any specific shots. The film is already alive and playing inside me. It's not a rational cognitive process; it's intuitive sensation.

Every film begins with sensations for me. Then gradually the noise of the picture grows and develops, filling me up with concrete images and taking on clearer traits. The logic of the narrative develops as well. But at first the only thing I know is what I want to say and why.

Perhaps because it is important for me to hear myself and understand what I want to say that I continue making films mostly about Russia, where I was born and grew up, where such a large part of my life took place.

As my plane makes the final approach toward Moscow, I start worrying. I don't know what it's about, but when I set foot on that soil, I feel that everything there is mine, and everything fills me with anxiety and pain. It's just as when my grandson is sick—everything hurts inside me. I fear for him. When someone else's child is sick, I feel pain too, but in a different way. I suppose

I can't take up a film without that feeling, for it would lack tension. The final product would be passionless; there would be no thrumming strings in the film.

I sometimes wonder if I'm not imagining all this, whipping up my own emotional state. I can't work any other way; I need to be vibrating inside. I can't formulate exactly what it is, but I know that, without it, the screen is dead.

They say that documentary film is the shortest route to poverty. It's true that documentary filmmakers are not rich. They have difficulty finding money for their films; it is hard to work and hard to survive in any country. It's all hard. Everyone seeks a path. I found mine—not very lucrative but independent. I'm thankful that my father taught me to have several professions and to work in many fields. I'll never forget what he told me: "Work, bunny. Your experience will never be wasted."

I'm so glad that I teach. I love doing it, and I seem to be good at it; I make enough to live on. Sometimes even my films make money. But I have a profession that gives me real pleasure—and masses of problems too, and nervous crises during the work. But that's nothing compared with the great joy that comes from capturing an unforeseen emotion, to capture life suddenly turning an unexpected side to you.

Thank goodness that documentary film and I found each other. I am grateful to the confluence of circumstances, if that's what it was, or to God, if that's who determined what my life would be. My profession demands that I always be in good shape, making those synapses in my brain work, figuring out how best to get out of unexpected holes and how to sail safely out of unpredictable storms while keeping to the main concept of the film.

The camera is an indivisible part of me now. If I'm ever in a place where I think something interesting might happen and I don't have my camera, I lose interest. Without my camera, the event is only for me, and that's not interesting enough. Even if it's only my grandchildren who will find what I've filmed interesting, it was worth it. The camera emancipated me. With it I feel free and absolutely happy. When I don't have my camera, when I'm not making a film or have an agreement or contract for a film in the works, I get depressed.

I never get tired when I'm filming. I can work twenty hours without stopping. I've even worked longer than that. It's only when I put down the camera that I realize how tired I am. But the exhaustion vanishes if something happens in front of the camera again. Even now, at my age, I can work away without stop. I rarely use a tripod, it's all handheld work, and I don't get tired. That's probably because I love what I do. I was born for this, and documentary film was born for me. I have a sense of our mutual love.

It's for others to judge whether I've made a contribution to documentary film, although I believe I've made a few good pictures. But I know for a fact that I am the luckiest woman in the world, with the best profession in the world.

Filmography of Marina Goldovskaya

Art and Life: Finding the Thread—L.A. Diary with Peter Sellars (2004)
   Director, producer, cinematographer, writer

Telly Award 2005; screened at eight festivals around the world in 2005, including Multicultural Film Festival, Amherst, Massachusetts; Athens International Film and Video Festival, Athens, Ohio; Montreal Festival International du Film Sur l'Art, Montreal; FIPA—International Festival of Audiovisual Programs, Biarritz, France

Senior Year (thirteen-episode documentary, PBS, 2002)
   Consulting producer

The Prince Is Back (ARTE France/Germany, 1999)
   Director, cinematographer, producer, writer

Spirit of Moondance Award, Moondance International Film Festival, Boulder, Colorado, 2002; Feature Documentary, Honorable Mention, International Documentary Association, Los Angeles, 2000; Special Jury Prize, Athens International Film and Video Festival, Athens, Ohio, 2000; Silver Rembrandt, Le Nombre d'Or International Widescreen Festival, Amsterdam, 2000; Telly Award, Cincinnati, Ohio, 2000; screened at 24 film festivals worldwide in 2000

The Children of Ivan Kuzmich (Canal+ France, 1997)
   Director, cinematographer

MediaNet Award, Filmfest München, Munich, 1998; Special Jury Prize, Festival International de Programmes Audiovisuels, Biarritz, France, 1998

A Poet on the Lower East Side: A Docu-Diary with Allen Ginsberg (USA, 1998)
    Cinematographer

Sixth Titanic International Film Festival, Budapest, 1998; Budapest Autumn Festival, 1998; "Beatniks and Poets," Museum of Fine Arts, Boston, 2002

This Shaking World (ARTE France, 1995)
    Director, cinematographer, writer, producer

Lucky to Be Born in Russia (ARTE France, 1994)
    Director, cinematographer, writer, producer

Golden Gate Certificate of Merit, San Francisco International Film Festival, 1995

The House on Arbat Street (Canal+ France, 1993)
    Director, cinematographer, co-writer, producer

Best European Documentary Programme, Prix Europa, Porto, Portugal, 1994; Planet Award, International Documentary Film Festival of Marseilles, 1994; Grand Prix, International Festival in Monte Carlo, 1994; Best Film of the Year, Earthwatch Film Awards, Washington DC, 1994; screened at 28 national and international documentary festivals

The Shattered Mirror: A Diary of the Time of Trouble (ARTE France, 1992)
    Director, writer, cinematographer, producer

Golden Gate Award, San Francisco International Film Festival, 1993; Gold Hugo Award, Chicago International Film Festival, 1993

Aus dem Abgrund (From the Abyss) (Oko-Media, Austria, 1991)
    Director, cinematographer

Part 1: *People of the Blockade* (60 min); Part 2: *People and War* (90 min)

A Taste of Freedom (Turner Network Television, USA, 1991)
    Director, cinematographer

Denver International Film Festival, Denver, Colorado, 1991; Telluride Film Festival, Telluride, Colorado, 1992

More Than Love (TTL Studios, Moscow, 1991)
    Director, writer, cinematographer

I Am 90, My Steps Are Light (Anastasia Tsvetayeva) (Videofilm, Moscow, 1989)
  Director, cinematographer, writer

Solovki Power (Mosfilm Studios, USSR, 1988)
  Director, cinematographer

Joris Ivens Special Jury Prize, International Documentary Film Festival Amsterdam, 1989; Sundance Film Festival, 1989; Special Mention, Berlin International Film Festival, 1989; San Francisco International Film Festival; Telluride Film Festival; Special Jury Prize, Bombay International Film Festival; Sydney International Film Festival; Jerusalem International Film Festival; Yamagata International Documentary Film Festival; "Stalker," Special Human Rights Prize of Memorial, Russia, 1995; Best Documentary, Sverdlovsk National Festival, USSR, 1988

Mikhail Ulianov (Central Television, Moscow, 1988)
  Director, writer, cinematographer

Tumbalalaika in America (Central Television, Moscow, 1987)
  Director, cinematographer

For the Theater to Be . . . (Oleg Efremov) (Central Television, Moscow, 1987)
  Director, cinematographer

Arkhangelsk Muzhik (Central Television, Moscow, 1986)
  Director, cinematographer

Grand Prix, International Electronic Cinema Festival, Cannes, 1987; top state national prize for best documentary, USSR, 1989

Spain Forever (Central Television, Moscow, 1985)
  Cinematographer

Hello, Byadulya Speaking (Central Television, Moscow, 1985)
  Director, cinematographer

The Center of Gravity (Central Television, Moscow, 1984)
  Director, cinematographer

Before the Harvest (Central Television, Moscow, 1983)
  Director, cinematographer

At Pushkin's Home (Central Television, Moscow, 1982)
   Cinematographer

Russian Legends (Central Television, Moscow, 1983)
   Cinematographer

Monday, a Day Off (Central Television, Moscow, 1983)
   Director, cinematographer

Exploring Antarctica (5 films; Central Television, Moscow, 1983)
   Cinematographer

Tvardovsky's Home (Central Television, Moscow, 1982)
   Cinematographer

The Eighth Director (Central Television, Moscow, 1981)
   Director, cinematographer
Best Documentary, USSR TV Festival, Erevan, Armenia, 1981

Pushkin and Pushchin (Central Television, Moscow, 1980)
   Director, cinematographer

The Beginning (Central Television, Moscow, 1979)
   Director, cinematographer

Kornej Chuckovsky (You're a Fiery Man) (Central Television, Moscow, 1979)
   Cinematographer

The Ordeal (TV Kazakhstan, Alma Ata, 1978)
   Director, co-writer, cinematographer
Best Documentary, Leipzig International Documentary Film Festival, 1978;
Best Documentary, National TV Festival, Erevan, Armenia, 1978; Best Film of
the Year (top national award of the Young Communist League), 1978

Mikhail Bulgakov (Central Television, Moscow, 1977)
   Cinematographer

Nickolaj Tikhonov: Life and Times (Central Television, Moscow, 1977)
   Cinematographer

Vladimir Tatlin (What an Interesting Personality) (Central Television, Moscow, 1977)
    Cinematographer

Deniska-Denis (Central Television, Moscow, 1976)
    Director, cinematographer

Alexander Tvardovsky (Central Television, Moscow, 1976)
    Cinematographer

Arkady Raikin (Central Television, Moscow, 1975)
    Director, cinematographer

Valentina Tereshkova (Central Television, Moscow, 1974)
    Director, cinematographer

This Is Our Profession (Central Television, Moscow, 1973)
    Director, cinematographer

Yury Zavadsky (Central Television, Moscow, 1971)
    Director, co-writer, cinematographer

Raissa Nemchinskaya, the Circus Actress (Central Television, Moscow, 1970)
    Director, co-writer, cinematographer

Surgeon Vishnevsky (Central Television, Moscow, 1969)
    Cinematographer
Grand Prix for Best Cinematography, Leningrad Television Festival, 1969

The Weavers (banned; Central Television, Moscow, 1968)
    Cinematographer

Sergey Smirnov (Central Television, Moscow, 1966)
    Cinematographer

Where the Sun Does Not Set (Central Television, Moscow, 1964)
    Cinematographer

Appendix: Notable Figures in Soviet Filmmaking and Other Arts

ABULADZE, TENGHIZ (1924–1994), Georgian film director, one of the founders of the Georgian "new wave." In his early works (*Lurdzha Magdany, Strangers' Children,* and *I, Grandmother, Iliko, and Illarion*), he created a Georgian version of neorealism. However, his international fame is due to the trilogy *The Plea, The Tree of Desire,* and *Repentance,* bringing a painterly metaphorical style and parable form to replace his former realism.

AKHMADULINA, BELLA (b. 1937), Russian poet. According to Joseph Brodsky, she is "the heir of the Lermontov-Pasternak line in Russian poetry." Gaining fame at very young age and becoming part of the Thaw movement of "stage poets," she nonetheless never changed the interiority of her poetry for accessibility. Combining passion and intellect, her style is far from oratorical fire or superficial sensuality; the subject of her meditations is the inner world and the inner logic of culture.

ANTOKOLSKY, PAVEL (1896–1941), Russian poet and translator. One of the last heirs of the Silver Age of prerevolutionary Russian culture, he found a niche in the overwhelming Soviet realism of the period—he dealt with the history of culture, expressed in flawless, often markedly old-fashioned poetic forms.

BAIBAKOV, NIKOLAI (b. 1911), Soviet statesman. Appointed people's commissar of the oil industry in 1944, he found his career going downhill under Khrushchev but was made chairman of Gosplan under Brezhnev and continued in that position until perestroika. In the late 1960s he was one of the initiators of developing oil fields in western Siberia, thereby building the planned Soviet economy around oil production. Raw materials remain the base of the country's economy to this day, despite all the market reforms.

BASKAKOV, VLADIMIR (1921–1999), Soviet film official who was first deputy chairman of Goskino USSR during 1962–1974. As cinema minister Romanov's right hand (the gray cardinal), he determined the fate of Soviet film. Armed with unusual aesthetic sensitivity, he often censored and even banned films not for plot or ideas but for "unneeded aesthetic tendency."

BATALOV, ALEXEI (b. 1928), Russian actor. He embodied the intelligentsia for Soviet film of the Thaw period: smart, modest, decent, tender and loyal in love, and uncompromising in questions of honor. Extremely selective in his projects, the actor never betrayed that image, no matter the era his characters lived in: contemporary (*Nine Days of One Year,* 1962), the recent past (*My Dear Man* and *The Cranes Are Flying,* 1957), in the nineteenth century (*The Lady with the Dog,* 1960), or the whirlwinds of the Civil War (*The Flight,* 1971). He is the rare Soviet actor to have created his own screen niche.

BIRMAN, SERAFIMA (1890–1976), Russian actress. The strongly etched characterizations of her roles often held deep dramatic bitterness. Her best part was Efrosinia Staritskaya in Eisenstein's *Ivan the Terrible* (1944–1946), where precision took on a lapidary manner and drama reached classical levels.

BOLSHAKOV, IVAN (1902–1980), took over in June 1939 from Dukelsky as head of film under Stalin. He turned out to be right for the job, since he could foresee the dictator's desires and knew how to placate him. Bolshakov is known for his usual remark to directors: "I don't know yet what I think about your film." Like his boss, Bolshakov saw film as a profoundly ideological matter. Film production under him fell to ten a year by 1950, because Stalin personally read all the screenplays and censored all the films. After Stalin's death, Bolshakov worked in prominent positions in various ministries until he retired.

BORISOV, OLEG (1929–1994), Russian actor. Using a small palette of effects, he created deep, paradoxical, and often unattractive characters obsessed by a single passion, be it lofty or base. His best films include *Workers' Settlement* (1966), *The Marriage* (1978), *The Train Has Stopped* (1982), *Adolescent* (1983), *Parade of Planets* (1984), and *The Servant* (1988).

BUKHARIN, NIKOLAI (1888–1938), Soviet statesman, active organizer of the October 1917 Revolution, in Lenin's words "the Party's favorite and its most valuable theoretician." Bukharin led the left-wing faction of Communists in 1917–1918 (protesting against the conclusion of the Brest-Litovsk Peace Treaty and calling for world revolution). He was editor in chief of the two main national newspapers of the Soviet Union: Pravda, 1918–1929, and Izvestiya, 1934–1937. In the late 1920s he spoke out against extremism in collectivization and industrialization, creating the right-wing opposition to Stalin's policies. The arrest and execution of the members of the opposition was a key moment in Stalin's Great Terror.

BULGAKOV, MIKHAIL (1891–1940), Russian writer. A doctor by training, he showed Chekhov's influence in his early book, *Notes of a Young Doctor;* but in later works Chekhovian taciturn realism gradually gave way to another tradition—Gogolian phantasmagoric grotesque (*Diavoliada, Theatrical Novel*). His play *The Flight,* his novel *White Guards,* and the stage version of *Days of the Turbins,* devoted to the fate of the White movement (against the Communist Reds) and imbued with nostalgia, led to years of conflict with the Soviet regime and with Stalin personally. Enormous popularity belonged to another of his novels, *Master and Margarita,* a cult work for the intelligentsia of the Thaw and later recognized as a Russian twentieth-century classic.

CHACHAVA, VAZHA (b. 1933), Georgian pianist, professor, head of accompanist department at the Moscow Conservatory. Elena Obraztsova's accompanist. Other singers who worked with him include Arkhipova, Kasrashvili, Sotkilava, Andruladze, Palm, and Pisarenko.

CHUKOVSKY, KORNEI (1882–1969), Russian poet, literary historian, and translator. In the prerevolutionary period he was one of the most fashionable and prestigious literary critics in Russia. He began translating then, too, primarily from English (Wilde, Whitman, Twain, Chesterton). However, to most Russians he is best known for his children's stories in poetry, written mostly in the 1920s and remaining to this day the first books for Russian children.

DORONINA, TATIANA (b. 1933), Russian actress. Her performance as Nastasya Filippovna in *The Idiot* (1957), a production of the Leningrad BDT (Bolshoi Drama Theater), determined many of the roles she would later play, vivid, strong, willful women unable to control their passions. Her best films include *Big Sister* (1967), *Once More about Love* (1968), and *The Stepmother* (1973).

DOVZHENKO, ALEXANDER (1894–1956), Ukrainian film director. One of the principal figures in Soviet silent film, he received international fame for his unique style and epic power of the images he borrowed from the Ukrainian national cultural tradition and applied to postrevolutionary reality. His greatest masterpiece is *Earth* (1930), which manages to combine organically natural-philosophical metaphysics with the spirit of socialist construction. The same features distinguish his sound films (despite the yoke of Soviet imperial censorship) and even his diaries. The epic Dovzhenko style had a strong influence of later Soviet auteur film, particularly on Andrei Tarkovsky and Larissa Shepitko.

DUKELSKY, SEMYON (1892–1960), successor of Shumyatsky as head of the Cinematography Committee under the Council of People's Commissars of the USSR. A former agent of the secret police, he was one of the organizers of the Red Terror in Ukraine during the Civil War and an active participant and organizer of mass repressions in the 1930s–1940s. He was in charge of Soviet cinema for only fifteen months, March 1938–June 1939, but managed to leave a negative impact by doing away with royalties. This led to an even greater dependency of filmmakers on the state and to a loss of feedback from the audience. The box office was no longer a measure of a film's success; only ideological criteria mattered.

EFREMOV, OLEG (1927–2000), one of the great stage and film actors of the second half of the twentieth century. In 1956 he founded the Studio of Young Actors, which later became the Sovremennik Theater. It became the symbol of the Thaw era in its theatrical version: its productions reflected the dreams and hopes of the young generation. His own persona, the intellectual optimist, fit the theater's symbolic function. In 1970 he became the chief director of the Moscow Art Theater.

EVSTIGNEYEV, YEVGENY (1926–1992), Russian actor. He came to acting at a mature age and quickly became a leading stage and screen actor of his day, thanks to his mastery of psychological grotesque elements. He stole the show in every part with actorly fireworks, not only brilliant in form but imbued with meaning. His best films include *Welcome, or No Unauthorized Admittance* (1964), *Watch Out, Cars!* (1966), *The Flight* (1971), *Seventeen Moments of Spring* (1973), and *A Dog's Heart* (1989).

GABRILOVICH, YEVGENY (1899–1993), Soviet screenwriter. He built most of his screenplays on a single model: a "little" person finds himself in a historical cataclysm. This paradigm, on the one hand, made his films seem timely no matter how the political winds blew and, on the other, allowed him to avoid underlining the required ideology by paying attention to the personal life, which he filled with subtle and multilayered psychological understanding. His best films include *Mashenka* (1942), *The Dream* (1943), *Communist* (1958), *Lenin in Poland* (1966), *No Ford in a Fire* (1968), *Monologue* (1973), and *Declaration of Love* (1978).

GALANTER, BORIS (1935–1994), Russian documentary director. His very first films brought him fame: *Boomerang* (1964) and *The Horizon beyond the Mountains* (1965). In the late 1960s he was the unofficial leader of the documentary school at the Sverdlovsk Film Studio, making *The Best Years of Our Lives* (1967), *Where Your House Is* (1971), and *Julietta* (1974). In the late 1970s he made feature television films, primarily biographies like *Life of Beethoven* (1978) and *I Am with You Again* (1981).

GERASSIMOV, SERGEI (1906–1985), Soviet film director and actor. For half a century (from the mid-1930s), his films were considered—by the Communist Party and by Soviet art historians—as perfect examples of socialist realism (*Seven Brave Men*, 1936; *Komsomolsk*, 1938; *Young Guards*, 1948; and *Quiet Don*, 1958). A genius at teaching, he trained a long line of outstanding actors and directors in his studio at VGIK: Sergei Bondarchuk, Nikolai Rybnikov, Liudmila Gurchenko, Nikolai Gubenko, Nonna Mordukova, Frunzik Dovlatyan, Kira Muratova.

GOLOVNYA, ANATOLY (1900–1982), one of the founders of the Soviet school of cinematography. With Vsevolod Pudovkin he created the famous trilogy: *Mother* (1926), *The End of St. Petersburg* (1927), and *Storm over Asia/The Heir of Genghis Khan* (1928), in which the powerful dynamic of angle changes expressed the dramaturgy. Author of several books on cinematography: *Light in the Art of the Cameraman* (1945) and *The Mastery of the Cinematographer* (1965). For almost a half century (from 1925), he was head of the cinematography department at VGIK.

GRUSHIN, BORIS (b. 1929), Russian sociologist. In 1960 he created and headed the first Institute of Public Opinion in the USSR, and in 1989 he founded the country's first Center for the Study of Public Opinion, Vox Populi. In the mid-1990s he was a member of the President's Council and today remains one of the most influential sociologists in Russia. His major work is a four-volume *Four Lives of Russia Mirrored in Surveys of Public Opin-*

ion: Sketches of Mass Consciousness of Russians in the Time of Khrushchev, Brezhnev, Gorbachev, and Yeltsin, two of which have already been published.

GUBENKO, NIKOLAI (b. 1941). People's Artist of Russia, laureate of the State Prize, actor and director, minister of culture of the USSR in the late Gorbachev period (1989–1991), member of the State Duma from the Communist Party (1996–2003), head of the Duma Committee on Culture (2000–2003), and now artistic director of the Association of Actors from the Taganka Theater in Moscow. His best-known roles include those in *I Am Twenty,* 1964; *Nest of Gentlefolk,* 1969; *They Fought for the Homeland,* 1975; and *May I Have the Floor,* 1975. His most famous film as director is *Winged Birds,* in which he told the story of his homeless childhood.

IOSELIANI, OTAR (b. 1934), Georgian film director. He developed his own film language (Buster Keaton was a distant prototype): mathematical severity and refined form are combined with a light nostalgia tone and a unique unruffled Georgian humor. After his conflicts with Soviet apparatchiks, he emigrated to France, where he lives and works.

KARETNIKOV, NIKOLAI (1930–1994), Russian composer. In the late 1950s he joined the growing avant-garde movement, based on the revolutionary innovations of Arnold Schönberg and Edgar Varese. He used the twelve-tone system for his operas *Till Eulenspiegel* (1985) and *Mystery of Apostle Paul* (1987), his ballets *Vanina Vanini* (1962) and *Tiny Tsakhes Called Tsinnober* (1964). In the 1980s he wrote a lot of church music, and his most popular work is the cycle *Six Religious Songs* (1993). He wrote many scores for film and theater.

KARMEN, ROMAN (1906–1978), Soviet film director considered for several decades as the "chief official documentary filmmaker of the USSR" (especially for international film propaganda). He filmed the Civil War in Spain, headed the frontline filmmakers during World War II, directed the filming of the Nuremberg Trial (*Judgment of the People,* 1946). In the 1950s–1970s he filmed in Vietnam, India, and Latin America (Cuba, Chile). The peak of his career was the documentary epic *The Unknown War* (1978), filmed in the USSR for Air Time International.

KAUFMAN, BORIS (1906–1980), cinematographer, brother of Dziga Vertov. He studied at the Sorbonne in Paris and was cameraman for all of Jean Vigo's films, including *A propos de Nice* (1929), *Zéro de Conduite* (1933), and

L'Atalante (1934). In the early 1940s he moved to the United States, where
he became famous for his work on films by Elia Kazan (*On the Waterfront,*
1954—Oscar; *Baby Doll,* 1956; *Splendor in the Grass,* 1961) and Sydney Lumet
(*Twelve Angry Men,* 1957; *Long Day's Journey into Night,* 1962; *The Pawnbroker,*
1964).

KHESSIN, BORIS (1920–2002), Russian television official and journalist. The
true father of Soviet television film, enthusiast and workaholic, he headed the
Ekran Studio for twenty years. Thanks to his tireless activity, Soviet television
had a premiere almost nightly of a new documentary or animated, musical, or
feature film. He founded the magazine *Krugozor* (View), which, by including
a flexible plastic record, anticipated multimedia print magazines.

KHUBOV, NIKITA (b. 1936), Russian film director. He started out as cinematographer and director in documentary films (*Daily Life in the Salt Mines,*
1965; *Frank Discussion,* 1966; *Tula Sketches,* 1970). In the early 1970s, he moved
to feature films: *Will Trade Dog for Locomotive* (1975), *Squadron of Flying
Hussars* (1980), and *The Body* (1990).

KLIMOV, ELEM (1933–2003), Soviet film director. His early films *Welcome, or
No Unauthorized Access* (1964), and *Sport, Sport, Sport* (1971) were marked by
a turbulent and brilliant inventiveness in film language (particularly the grotesque and collage). In the mid-1970s, however, his intonations grew darker
(due in great part to the tragic death of his wife, Larissa Shepitko, in 1979):
after *Agony* (1981) and *Farewell* (1983), Klimov made one of the most powerful and unbearable films in world cinema—*Go and See* (1986). Then he left
film: his brilliant plans for a screen version of *Master and Margarita* did not
come to pass, due to the collapse of Soviet film production.

KONCHALOVSKY, ANDREI (b. 1937), Russian film director. Each of his films
made under the Soviet regime was an experiment in cinematic form; and
each experiment was successful in its way—be it cinema verité (*The Story of
Asya Klyachina,* 1967, released in 1987), filmmaking in a painterly style (*Nest
of Gentlefolk,* 1969), a rock ballad happening (*Romance about Lovers,* 1974), or a
national epic (*Siberiade,* 1979). He emigrated to the USA in 1980 and made several films that tried to combine the psychological subtlety of his early works
with the demands of Hollywood (*Runaway Train,* 1985; *Tango and Cash,*
1989). He returned to Russia in the early 1990s and continues to work in film,
theater, and television. His film *Inner Circle* is based on the story of Stalin's

projectionist, Alexander Ganshin (called Ivan Sanshin in the film). Bolshakov is one of the characters in the film.

KOZINTSEV, GRIGORY (1905–1973), Soviet film director. In 1921 he and Leonid Trauberg founded FEKS—the Factory of the Eccentric Actor—which yielded a number of outstanding actors and directors for early Soviet cinema (Zheimo, Kuzmina, Gerassimov, Zhakov) and became one of the most important stylistic movements in Soviet silent film. In such movies as *The Overcoat* (1926), *Devil's Wheel* (1926), and *New Babylon* (1929), eccentricity (in acting, editing, and camerawork) was presented as the highest form of cinema. In the 1930s, when Communist Party pressure was very strong, he made a film in a traditional realistic style (thanks to the natural charm of Boris Chirkov as Maxim) called *Trilogy about Maxim* (1935–1939), which the authorities considered a great achievement in socialist realism. Of his late films, the most interesting are the screen versions of Shakespeare's *Hamlet* (1964) and *King Lear* (1971), distinguished by great expressiveness and acting and the scores by Dmitri Shostakovich.

KRAVCHENKO, LEONID (b. 1938), Russian journalist. He was editor in chief of *Stroitelnaya Gazeta* (1975–1980) and of *Trud* (1980–1985). The peak of his career came during perestroika: he was first deputy minister of the State Committee for Television and Radio (1985–1988) and head of TASS (1988–1990) and was then appointed chairman of Ostankino television and radio. After the attempted coup in August 1991, he was fired from television and went back to newspapers.

KULIDZHANOV, LEV (1924–2002), Soviet film director. Several early films, fundamental in the aesthetics of the cinema of the Thaw, brought him fame: *The House I Live In* (1957) and *When the Trees Were Big* (1962). Of his late films, the screen version of Fedor Dostoevsky's *Crime and Punishment* (1970) is outstanding for his work with brilliant actors.

KUZMINA, ELENA (1909–1979), Soviet actress. Her basic characterization lay in the contrast between her comedic appearance and the tender drama of inner life. She played her best roles in films by her husbands, who were Grigory Kozintsev (*New Babylon*, 1929; *Alone*, 1931), Boris Barnet (*Outskirts*, 1933; *At the Edge of the Blue Sea*, 1936), and Mikhail Romm (*The Dream*, 1943; *Russian Question*, 1948; *The Secret Mission*, 1950).

KVASHA, IGOR (b. 1933), Russian actor. One of the founders of the Sovremennik Theater, he continues to perform there. His best role in film was
Yakov Bogomolov in *Premature Man* (1971), which gave full rein to his talent and favorite type: the intellectual who cannot deal with his own complex
inner life. He is active in film and television.

LADYNIN, ANDREI (b. 1938), Soviet film director, son of Ivan Piriev and
Marina Ladynina. He worked primarily in detective and adventure films, cre-
ating well-built films that lacked artistic subtlety but enjoyed popularity: *The
Victor* (1975), *Colonel Zorin's Version* (1978), and *Five Minutes of Fear* (1985).

LAKSHIN, VLADIMIR (1933–1993), Russian literary critic. In the 1960s, he
was the leading critic of *Novy Mir,* but when editor in chief Tvardovsky was
dismissed, he moved to *Inostrannaya Literatura,* which became one of the
very few liberal journals during the stagnation period in literature. During
perestroika, he wrote the first serious study of the work of Mikhail Bulgakov.

LAPIN, SERGEI (1912–1990), Soviet official. He worked in radio propaganda from 1942 (chief editor, 1949–1953), then worked in diplomacy until
1967 (including a stint as ambassador to China at the height of the Cultural
Revolution) and as director of TASS (1967–1970), and then until the start of
perestroika was in charge of Soviet television. Through numerous personnel and structural reorganizations, he formed a television and radio system
(Gosteleradio) that was an ideal response to the ideological and political
needs of the Brezhnev era.

LEVENTAL, VALERY (b. 1938), Russian stage designer, graduate of VGIK. In
1965 he became a designer for the Bolshoi Theater (chief designer, 1988–1995).
He also did a lot of work at the Moscow Art Theater. Among his best works
are Alexander Gelman's *We, the Undersigned* (1979), executed in a hyperreal-
istic style, and Chekhov's *Seagull* (1980) and *Uncle Vanya* (1985), in which
he combined a massed painterly impressionism with laconic constructivist
methods. He also worked for La Scala and Communale theaters in Italy.

LEVITSKY, ALEXANDER (1885–1965), Russian cameraman. He started in 1910
(two years after Russian cinema began) and was quickly one of the most famous masters. He specialized on screen version of literary classics (*Nest of
Gentlefolk,* 1914; *War and Peace,* 1915). His best work, according to descrip-

tions, was apparently the lost film of Vsevolod Meyerhold, *Portrait of Dorian Grey* (1915), which was a forerunner of the aesthetic of German expressionism. He worked on the first Soviet films (*The Extraordinary Adventures of Mister West*, 1924). A master of artistic lighting, he taught some of the best cinematographers of the first Soviet generation: Golovnya, Volchek, Monakhov, and many others.

LITERATURNAYA GAZETA, Izvestiya, Moskovskie Novosti, and *Komsomolskaya Pravda* were the widely read newspapers among the intelligentsia during perestroika. They actively supported Gorbachev's reforms and the tendencies in society that led to the rejection of the Communist Party's monopoly on power.

LUBYANKA, the popular name for the infamous building in Moscow on Lubyanka Square, which became the home after the October 1917 revolution for Dzerzhinsky's Extraordinary Commission (Cheka), which was empowered by the Communist Party to perform all punitive functions. In all its subsequent transformations and renaming (OGPU, NKVD, KGB, MGB, and so on), this agency remained the main instrument of suppression of all forms of opposition, free thinking, and freedom of the country's people. Numerous cultural figures, military leaders, economic administrators, and often Communist leaders, including foreign ones whom Stalin considered a threat or whose loyalty he doubted, were held, tortured, or executed in the internal prison at Lubyanka.

LUMIÈRE, LOUIS (1864–1948), French engineer. With his brother, Auguste, he solved the problem of quality projection of a moving photo image onto a big screen. On December 25, 1895, on the Boulevard des Capucines, the Lumière brothers held the first cinema session in the world, showing several of their brief films (52 seconds), including *Arrival of a Train at the La Ciotat Station, Workers Leaving a Factory,* and *Feeding a Baby.* For the next several years, the Lumière brothers sent their cameramen to every corner of the globe, building the foundation of documentary film and the system of film screenings. However, they themselves considered their invention merely a sideshow attraction and saw no aesthetic potential in it. They made more than two thousand films and left film production in 1900, devoting themselves to the development of equipment for still photography. In the history of film, they are considered to be "fathers of the cinema."

MAKAROVA, TAMARA (1907–1997), Soviet actress. Thanks to the combination of restrained ("realistic") acting and a heightened emotional level, she was one of the major stars of psychological films in the Stalin era. Her best parts were in the films of her husband, Sergei Gerassimov: *Komsomolsk* (1938), *The Teacher* (1939), *Young Guards* (1948), and *People and Animals* (1962).

MAKASEYEV, BORIS (1907–1989), Soviet documentary cameraman. One of the first (back in 1935) to film the Civil War in Spain, he stayed there to the very end. He also participated in the filming of the Nuremberg trials. He is one of the most decorated documentary filmmakers of the Stalin era—in the first six years after World War II he received four State Prizes of the USSR.

MALENKOV, GEORGY (1902–1988), Soviet statesman. In the 1930s he was formally chief of personnel of the Central Committee of the Communist Party, which did not keep him, as a close friend of Yezhov and Beria, from playing an important role in the mass repressions of the Stalin Terror. After the war, he participated actively in the state anti-Semitic campaign, and by the early 1950s he was the number two man in the Party. After Stalin's death he became chairman of the Council of Ministers. However, the internal Party intrigues placed Malenkov (with Kaganovich and Molotov) in the "anti-Party group," and he was expelled from the government and, in 1961, expelled from the Communist Party.

MAMEDOV, ENVER (b. 1923), Soviet official, who for many years (and under several chairmen) was first deputy chairman of the State Television and Radio Committee of the USSR. He performed the classic function of a top manager: smart and relatively liberal among the hard-liners who reported directly to the Communist Party Central Committee, he took on the task of softening the ideological and psychological tensions in the team.

MANSUROVA, TSETSILIA (1896–1976), Russian actress, prima of the Vakhtangov troupe, who premiered the lead in the legendary production of *Turandot* (1922). Her acting style involved defined gestures and a grotesque plasticity that harmonized in a strange way with her deep singsong voice. Her most important roles included Zoyka in *Zoyka's Apartment* (1926), Beatrice in *Much Ado about Nothing* (1936), Roxanne in *Cyrano de Bergerac* (1942), and Filumena in *Filumena Marturano* (1956).

MARETSKAYA, VERA (1906–1978), a talented Russian theater and film actress. In the Stalin era, her looks (typical ordinary Russian) made her a film "idol." Her characters were used to show that the USSR was the state of workers and peasants. The most vivid symbol of this demagogy was the film *Member of the Government* (1940), in which her character travels the radiant path from illiterate village girl to congresswoman.

MIKHOELS, SOLOMON (1890–1948), the great Jewish stage actor and (from 1929) artistic director of the Moscow State Jewish Theater. Incomparable interpreter of plays based on the works of Sholom Aleichem (Reb Alter in *Mazltov,* Shimele Soroker in *200,000,* Menakhem Mendel in *Man of Air,* and Tevye in *Tevye the Milkman*). He won worldwide acclaim for his King Lear. In August 1941, Stalin appointed Mikhoels head of the Jewish Antifascist Committee, and he traveled all over the world, meeting Einstein, Wells, Dreiser, and Chaplin. When the anti-Semitic campaign began in the USSR, Mikhoels, with his world fame, was the greatest obstacle in its way; on January 13, 1948, Mikhoels was killed in a faked automobile accident. His assassination gave wings to a government anti-Semitic campaign, which was stopped by Stalin's demise on March 5, 1953.

MYAGKOV, ANDREI (b. 1938), Russian actor. One of his first roles was Alyosha Karamazov in *The Brothers Karamazov* (1969), but later he preferred to play "insignificant" but whole people. His greatest fame comes from his roles in Eldar Ryazanov's popular comedies (*After the Bath, or Irony of Fate,* 1975; *Office Romance,* 1977; and *The Garage,* 1980).

NABOKOV, VLADIMIR (1899–1977), writer in Russian and English. He left Russia in 1919 and lived in Cambridge, Berlin, and Paris. In 1945 became a U.S. citizen; in 1960 he moved to Switzerland. The erudite, refined, and ironic writer was a great individualist. His most famous works include *Invitation to a Beheading, The Gift,* and *The Luzhin Defense.* He garnered international fame for his lectures in American universities and his literary research, crowned by his gigantic annotated translation of *Eugene Onegin,* by Pushkin. He also found notoriety when Stanley Kubrick filmed his novel *Lolita.* Nabokov appeared on the cover of *Life* and was nominated for an Oscar for the screenplay; the term "Lolita" became commonly used.

NEVINNY, VYACHESLAV (b. 1934), Russian actor. Thanks to his stocky build and accent, he usually plays simple folk, either good-natured bumpkins or rude slobs. His best films include *The Garage* (1980), *Dead Souls* (1984), and *The Shadow* (1991).

OBRAZTSOVA, ELENA (b. 1937), Russian mezzo-soprano. Her unusually beautiful voice, velvety and juicy, is coupled with her powerful dramatic talent and nuanced phrasing. She performs both in opera and chamber music. She has sung in the leading opera theaters of the world (Vienna, La Scala, the Metropolitan, Covent Garden). Her best roles include Marina Mnishek (*Boris Godunov*), the Countess (*Queen of Spades*), Amneris (*Aida*), Azucena (*Il Trovatore*), Carmen (*Carmen*), Dalila (*Samson et Dalila*), and Jocasta (*Oedipus Rex*).

OVANESOVA, ARSHA (1906–1990), Soviet documentary film director. In 1931 she began a monthly documentary film magazine, called *Pioneriia,* which was for and about children. She developed the genre subsequently: *Salute to the Pioneers of Spain* (1946), *Story of Our Children* (1945), and *Youth of the World* (1949). In 1958 she made *Unusual Meetings* about the grown characters from her early film diary.

PILIKHINA, MARGARITA (1926–1975), Soviet cinematographer, one of the trendsetters in camerawork in the era of the Soviet new wave. Her best films include *Two from One Block* (1957), *Foma Gordeyev* (1959), and *Tchaikovsky* (1970). Her incontrovertible masterpiece is *I Am Twenty,* directed by Marden Khutsiev in 1964, which became the aesthetic manifesto of the cinema generation. Her light, dynamic, and documentary style was an innovation that influenced many films of the period. She died of cancer during the filming of her directorial debut, *Anna Karenina.*

PIRIEV, IVAN (1901–1968), Soviet film director. In the late 1930s and 1940s he was considered the best comedy director in Stalin's empire, creating an overly emotional and crudely pompous style. His particularly popular films were *A Rich Bride* (1938), *Tractor Drivers* (1939), *The Swine Girl and the Shepherd* (1941), *At Six O'clock after the War* (1944), and *Kuban Cossacks* (1950). In his later years he made several film versions of works by Fedor Dostoevsky: *The Idiot* (1958), *White Nights* (1960), and *The Brothers Karamazov* (1969). For many years he was head of Mosfilm, the main film studio of the USSR.

PLYATT, ROSTISLAV (1908–1989), popular and beloved Russian theater and film actor. Endowed with incredible charm and velvety voice, he played kindly eccentrics. His charm increased with age, his characters gradually turning into wise men who loved life and believed in human goodness. His best films include *The Dream* (1943), *Seventeen Moments of Spring* (1973), and *Afterword* (1983).

PRUDKIN, MARK (1898–1994), Russian actor. His career is among the longest in world theater. He performed on the stage of the Moscow Art Theater for seventy years, from 1924 until his death. His best roles include Chatsky (*Woe from Wit*, in the Stanislavsky production of 1925), Shervinsky (*Days of the Turbins*, 1926), Breve (*Resurrection*, 1930), Basov (*The Cynics*, 1953), Khmelik (*Solo for Grandfather Clock*, 1973), and Prince K. (*Grandfather's Dream*, 1981).

PTUSHKO, ALEXANDER (1900–1973), Soviet film director. For several decades he was considered the best Soviet film director of fairy tales; he did pioneering work in puppet animation (*Master of Life*, 1932) and combining actors with animation (*New Gulliver*, 1935) and experimentation with color (*Stone Flower*, 1946) and sound (*Ilya Muromets*, 1956, the first Soviet widescreen film with stereo sound). With almost every film, Ptushko opened a new chapter in the art of special effects.

PUSHCHIN, IVAN (1798–1859), Russian poet and social activist. Pushkin's closest friend in school, he soon joined various secret societies for reforming the monarchial state that sprang up in Russia after the victory over Napoleon in 1815. In 1825 he participated in the Decembrist insurrection and was given a death sentence, which was commuted to hard labor in Siberia. He was amnestied in 1856. A year before his death he wrote *Notes on Pushkin*, which became the basis of Russian Pushkin studies.

PUSHKIN, ALEXANDER (1799–1837), Russian poet who completed the formation of literary Russian language (therefore considered without a doubt "the greatest Russian poet"). Imbued with the influence of frivolous eighteenth-century French poetry and early English Romanticism, he developed an individual, strong poetic style. His phenomenal improvisational ease combined with precision of phrasing and clarity of thought: his markup drafts are an inexhaustible treasure trove of interpretations for Pushkin scholars and for young Russian writers a model of authorial striving for perfection. His prose (particularly *Belkin's Stories*) was a precursor of realism in Russian literature.

RAIKIN, ARKADY (1911–1987), Soviet stand-up comedian. A master of getting into character, he was the most popular and beloved actor of the USSR for many decades. His monologues were quoted and became part of the vocabulary of quite different social strata, from the intellectual elite to the "ordinary people." Soviet ideology turned Raikin into the classic buffoon who could say out loud things others only dared to think, but it meant that he was scrutinized all the more closely.

RAIZMAN, YULI (1903–1994), Soviet film director. During his incredibly long creative life in film, without ever—under all the political changes—acting in opposition to the regime and always reflecting the required ideology in his films, he nevertheless quietly managed to bring the personal lives of his characters to the forefront. The subtle nuances of love and not-love interested him much more than official dogmas. His best films include *The Earth Thirsts* (1930), *Pilots* (1935), *Mashenka* (1942), *Communist* (1957), and *Personal Life* (1982).

REMIZOVA, ALEXANDRA (1903–1989), Russian actress and theater director who played her first famous roles in productions of Vakhtangov (*Miracle of St. Anthony, Turandot*). In the late 1930s she moved into directing. She worked at the Mossoviet Theater under Zavadsky. Her best productions include *Before Sunset* (1954), *Dear Liar* (1961), *Millionairess* (1964), and *Playing with the Cat* (1973).

ROMM, MIKHAIL (1901–1971), Soviet film director. He received fame and official recognition in the late 1930s after his two-part film on Lenin (*Lenin in October* and *Lenin in 1918*). However, his smaller films are of greater interest artistically: *Pyshka/Boule de Suif* (1934), *The Thirteen* (1937), and *Dream* (1943), which are distinguished by sensitive work with actors and inventive camerawork. During the Khrushchev Thaw, he made one of the period's greatest works, *Nine Days of One Year* (1962), followed by two masterpieces of documentary film: *Ordinary Fascism* (1966) and *Yet I Still Believe . . .* (1975, completed by his former students). His work as a teacher was extraordinarily successful; his students included Tarkovsky, Abuladze, Shukshin, Talankin, Smirnov, Konchalovsky, and many others.

ROSHAL, GRIGORY (1898–1983), Soviet film director. Graduate of Vsevolod Meyerhold's Theater Studio. He earned a reputation in the unspoken hierarchy of Soviet film as a good average filmmaker. There are no masterpieces among his films, but they are distinguished by an ability to work with actors and a good literary base—he specialized in doing screen versions of literature: *A Petersburg Night* (1934), *The Oppenheim Family* (1939), *The Artamonov Case* (1941), and the trilogy *The Road to Calvary* (1957–1959).

SAPPAK, VLADIMIR (1921–1961), Russian theater critic and journalist. His witty and readable book *Television and Us* was one of the first in Russia to analyze the television's potential from a historical point of view, formulating such fundamental concepts as "character X-ray" and "presence effect."

SAVELYEVA, ERA (1913–1985), Soviet cinematographer. She began in the mid-1940s as second camera for Volchek in films directed by Romm. Her greatest fame came in the 1950s on two films shot in a vivid, expressive manner: *Ballad of a Soldier* (1959, with V. Nikolayev) and *Resurrection* (1960, part 1).

SHOSTAKOVICH, MAXIM (b. 1938), Russian conductor, son of composer Dmitri Shostakovich. In the mid-1970s he was in charge of the Symphonic Orchestra of Central Television and All-Union Radio. He moved to the United States in 1981. In recent years he has been active in the Russian religious and patriotic movement.

SHPALIKOV, GENNADY (1937–1974), Soviet screenwriter. His poetic, subtle, and wise screenplays, which ignored the school rules of construction, set the tone of the "cinema thaw": *I Stride through Moscow* (1963), *I Am Twenty* (1963), and *I Come from Childhood* (1965). In 1967 he directed his own screenplay, *A Long Happy Life,* which forecast the coming "stagnation" period and bid a wrenching farewell to the romantic ideals of his youth. He committed suicide on November 1, 1974.

SHUMYATSKY, BORIS (1886–1938), prominent Soviet official, fought for Soviet power during the Civil War in the Far East. In 1933, he was appointed head of the cinema industry. He dreamed of creating a Soviet Hollywood and in fact did modernize the technology of Soviet film and introduced Soviet filmmakers to world film. He initiated numerous films that became Soviet classics. In January 1938 he was arrested, tortured, and executed.

SIMONOV, KONSTANTIN (1915–1979), Soviet poet, writer, playwright, and screenwriter. His greatest literary success came in war-related works—he spent several years as a war correspondent, first in Khalkhin-Gol and then at all the fronts of World War II; he ended up as a colonel. His poetry collection *With You and Without You* (1942)—particularly the poem "Wait for Me," which became an anthem of sorts of lyric patriotism during the war—and the epic trilogy *Living and Dead* (1954–1959), brought him national popularity.

SMIRNOV, ANDREI (b. 1941), Russian film director. His greatest success was *Belorussian Station* (1970), devoted to the fate of frontline soldiers in the peacetime period of "stagnation" in the USSR: their lofty wartime ideals were in painful conflict with the swamp of unprincipled consumerist indifference. In 2000 he starred as Ivan Bunin in *Diary of His Wife*.

SMIRNOV, SERGEI (1915–1976), Russian writer. His basic theme in his books, plays, and screenplays was the unknown heroes of the World War II, primarily the defenders of Brest Fortress. His research in documents and oral histories took many years (*Brest Fortress*, 1957–1964; *Heroes of Brest Fortress; Family;* and others).

SMOKTUNOVSKY, INNOKENTY (1925–1994), one of the great stage and film actors. His role as Prince Myshkin in the Leningrad BDT's production of *The Idiot* (1957) brought him an honored place in theater history; and in film history, it was his portrayal of Hamlet in Kozintsev's film (1964). With his mastery of movement, gesture, expression, and speech, he created indelible images with infinite range. His best films include *Nine Days of One Year* (1962), *Watch Out, Cars!* (1966), *Crime and Punishment* (1970), *Uncle Vanya* (1971), and *Dead Souls* (1984).

SOLOVYOV, SERGEI (b. 1944), Russian film director. He changed his cinematographic style several time: refined atmospherics of the 1970s (*The Station Master*, 1972; *One Hundred Days after Childhood*, 1975), documentary, cinema verité manner (*Someone's White and Bay*, 1986), avant-garde rock kitsch (*Assa*, 1988; *House under a Starry Sky*, 1990), and neoclassical (*Three Sisters*, 1994; *Tender Age*, 2000).

SOLZHENITSYN, ALEXANDER (b. 1918), Russian writer. He became famous in 1962 with the publication of "One Day in the Life of Ivan Denisovich," which described a day in the hard-labor camps (the author had spent 1945–1953 in the camps). In the late 1960s his novels *First Circle* and *Cancer Ward* were published in the West, and he was awarded the Nobel Prize in Literature in 1970. KGB persecution led up to the charges of treason and his expulsion from the Soviet Union. In the mid-1970s, he was the thought leader among émigrés and, during perestroika, among much of the post-Soviet intelligentsia. His sharp and uncompromising statements (especially after his return to Russia) changed many people's attitudes toward him from adoring to skeptical and even hostile.

STEPANOVA, ANGELINA (1905–2000), Russian actress who worked at the Moscow Art Theater from 1924 until 1988. She added sharpness of characterization and a note of skeptical intellectualism to Stanislavsky's classic severity, which had dulled in Stalinist times. Her best roles include Mariette (*Resurrection,* 1930), Irina (*Three Sisters,* 1940), Betsy (*The Fruits of Enlightenment,* 1951), Stella (*Dear Liar,* 1962), and Arkadina (*The Seagull,* 1968).

STRIZHENOV, OLEG (b. 1929), Soviet actor. He gained fame and adoration (particularly from female audiences) in the late 1950s in a series of films in which he had the romantic lead: for example, *Gadfly* (1955), *Forty First* (1956), and *Voyage beyond Three Seas* (1958). As he aged, he endowed the leading man part with psychological overtones.

SVILOVA, ELIZAVETA (1900–1975), Soviet editor. She began in film before the revolution of 1917, as a teenager in the laboratory of the Pathé brothers. In the 1920s, she was part of the "kinoks"—the Russian abbreviation from "cinema" *(kino)* and "eye" *(oko)*—a group of young filmmakers created by Dziga Vertov. She was his wife and assistant editor, and she was involved in all his silent documentary masterpieces. In the 1940s, when the cinema ideological bosses kept Vertov from working, she became a director and made the films *In the Foothills of Alatau* (1943), *Auschwitz* (1945), and *Atrocities of the Nazis* (1946). After her husband's death in 1954, she was the guardian of his legacy, and for another twenty years she edited and whenever possible published his articles, diaries, studies, and letters.

TARKOVSKY, ANDREI (1932–1986), Russian film director. After the triumph at the Venice Film Festival of his feature-length debut, *Ivan's Childhood* (1962), and then his many years of struggle with the Soviet ideological machine over all his subsequent films—*Andrei Rublev* (1966–1969), *Solaris* (1972), *The Mirror* (1975), and *Stalker* (1979)—Tarkovsky became a symbol for Russian film of spiritual resistance to compromise. His films unite the basic values of Russian religion, philosophy, and metaphysics. They defined his very special and unique film language: long shots, slow panning, and other elements permitting him to capture the flow of time through nature and man. His last two films, *Nostalgia* (1983) and *The Sacrifice* (1986), were made abroad.

TATLIN, VLADIMIR (1885–1953), Russian artist, a leader (with Kasimir Malevich) of the Russian avant-garde. He exhibited with art groups in the 1910s (World of Art and Jack of Spades). His style was close to cubism and futurism, but he was one of the founders of Russian constructivism. His greatest work is the never-realized *Tower of the Third International* (1919–1920), a gigantic complex of cylinders turning at different speeds around a tilted axis; the tower was supposed to become the cultural propaganda center of world revolution. After the crackdown on "formalism" in the 1930s, he went back to easel art.

TISSE, EDUARD (1897–1961), Soviet cinematographer. He was the cameraman on all of Sergei Eisenstein's films (except for the stage set work on *Ivan the Terrible,* done by Andrei Moskvin); he and Eisenstein developed a unique, perfect visual style distinguished by gigantic energy of scale and based on rigid graphic elements and bold, almost paradoxical placement of planes of varying depth in a single shot.

TROYANOVSKY, MARK (1907–1967), Soviet documentary cameraman. In the 1930s he filmed almost every "epic historic" event: the enormous building sites of Communism, the conquest of the North Pole, and expeditions to the Antarctic. During World War II, he led documentary groups at the front.

TSVETAYEVA, MARINA (1892–1941), Russian poet. Her poetry and plays were revolutionary; she invented more forms of versification than all nineteenth-century Russian poets put together. Her poetry is marked by romantic maximalism, the themes of solitude, tragic love, and rejection of daily life. She left Russia in 1922 but returned to the USSR in 1939, following her husband and daughter, who wanted to move back home. She committed suicide in Elabuga, after the arrests of her husband, sister, and daughter.

TVARDOVSKY, ALEXANDER (1910–1971), Russian poet. His narrative poem *Vassily Terkin* (1942–1945) brought him national fame and love: the soldier hero became a natural part of contemporary folklore. He was editor in chief of *Novy Mir* (1950–1954 and 1958–1970), the main literary journal of the Thaw intelligentsia, which published (thanks to his personal appeal to Khrushchev) "One Day in the Life of Ivan Denisovich," by Aleksandr Solzhenitsyn. However, with the advent of Brezhnev's stagnation period, the journal's liberal tendencies were unacceptable, and he was replaced as editor. An officially recognized poet with three Stalin Prizes, he was also author of the poem "By Right of Memory," which circulated only in samizdat and was not published until Gorbachev's perestroika in 1987.

ULYANOV, MIKHAIL (b. 1927), Russian film and stage actor. After several successful roles, he achieved national stardom in the film *Chairman* (1964). His roles always reveal the might and breadth of character, turbulent passions held in check. His best parts include Dmitri Karamazov (*The Brothers Karamazov,* 1969), General Charnota (*The Flight,* 1971), Marshal Zhukov (*Liberation,* 1970–1972), and Richard III (*Richard III,* 1976). Since 1986 he is the artistic director of the Moscow Vakhtangov Theater.

URUSEVSKY, SERGEI (1908–1974), Soviet cinematographer. An adherent of radical innovation in camerawork, and with a rare painterly talent, he turned films into visual poems, saturated with extreme angles, expressive movements of the subjective camera, and, when he began work in color, with a brilliant color palette. He achieved national fame with *Village Schoolteacher* (1947) and international fame with *The Cranes Are Flying* (1957, Grand Prix of the 1958 Cannes Festival) and *I Am Cuba* (1964). In the early 1970s, he directed two films (*Trotting,* 1970; and *Sing a Song, Poet!* 1973), in which his visionary poetics found an auteurial avant-garde realization.

UTESOV, LEONID (1895–1982), Soviet pop singer. He was the most popular performer in the USSR for many years, thanks to his sly ("Odessa") charm and unusual voice. In the Stalin era, his band played an important role, bringing modified versions of jazz culture, which was banned by the Communist Party for being "bourgeois" and "decadent," to his Soviet audiences. Perhaps the blind eye turned by the authorities to his music was due to Stalin's love for his film *Cheerful Fellows* (1934).

VERTINSKAYA, ANASTASIA (b. 1944), Russian actress. Her fame came with two romantic roles, Assol in *Red Sails* (1961) and Gutierre in *Amphibious Man* (1962). Her refined aristocratic beauty and manner, unusual for the Soviet screen, allowed her to play Ophelia (*Hamlet,* 1964) and Princess Mary (*War and Peace,* 1966–1967) early in her career. The "noble" parts (sometimes lyrical, sometimes played for irony) continued to make up the majority of her repertoire.

VERTOV, DZIGA (Denis Kaufman; 1896–1954), director, screenwriter, theoretician, and classic of world documentary film, one of the creators of its language. He came to Soviet documentary film in 1918, inspired by the ideas of the revolution, and became known as a vivid innovator and experimenter. He was close in spirit to LEF (Left Front of the Arts) and its masters and leaders—Mayakovsky, Eisenstein, and Tatlin. Vertov's films *One Sixth of the World* (1926), *Symphony of the Donbass* (*Enthusiasm*, 1930), *Three Songs about Lenin* (1934), and especially *Man with a Movie Camera* (1929) remain models for generations of documentary filmmakers. Despite his attempts to toe the party line—as in *Lullaby* (1937), which glorified Stalin—he was too free and independent to become a protégé of the leader. In his final years he was kept from his own film work, branded as a formalist and cosmopolite; the only thing he was permitted to do was the newsreel. He wrote articles and manifestos that reveal his accurate vision of the future of documentary film.

VISHNEVSKY, ALEXANDER (1906–1975), Russian surgeon, member of the celebrated dynasty of doctors; in 1956 became chief surgeon of the Soviet Army. He was the first to perform heart surgery with a local anesthetic, which was the main topic of his scientific works, along with artificial circulation and the use of polymers in surgery.

VOITSIK, ADA (1905–1982), Soviet actress. She had a powerful dramatic personality that allowed her to play women with ruined lives. Her talent was not required in the era of the Stalin empire, which sought simplification and schematic presentation. Among her best films are *Forty First* (1927), *Party ID* (1936), and *The Dream* (1943).

VOLCHEK, GALINA (b. 1933), Russian actress and stage director, daughter of cinematographer Boris Volchek. She took over as chief director of the Sovremennik Theater after Efremov left for the Moscow Art Theater in 1970, and she kept the troupe together through that difficult period. She is a vivid character actress and a talented and strong-willed director.

VYAZEMSKY, PETR (1792–1878), Russian poet and critic. His style combined British lapidary precision and skepticism (his mother was English) with Russian patriotism (the influence of Karamzin, who frequented his boyhood home). A European-style intellectual, he was part of the most elite circles of the Russian Empire, but perhaps his wisdom and skepticism kept him from giving free rein to his creative energy and doomed him to the auxiliary role of "the friend of Pushkin" and "the friend of the Decembrists."

YEVTUSHENKO, YEVGENY (b. 1933), Russian poet. A leader of the generation of Thaw poets (with Andrei Voznesensky, Robert Rozhdestvensky, and Bella Akhmadulina), he imbued post-Stalinist poetry with the spirit of human dignity. The idol of the intelligentsia (especially students), he nevertheless managed to avoid the total crackdown of the authorities: his rebelliousness—intentionally or not—never crossed the line to dissidence and open protest. He wrote the screenplay for *I Am Cuba*. He began teaching in the United States in the mid-1990s.

YUSOV, VADIM (b. 1929), Russian cinematographer. He is rated as one of the greatest professionals of the Soviet school. He worked with the best directors of various generations (Tarkovsky, Shukshin, Danelia, Bondarchuk, Dykhovichny) and now is head of the cinematography department at VGIK.

YUTKEVICH, SERGEI (1904–1985), Soviet film director. For many years (with a hiatus during the anti-Semitic campaign in the late 1940s–early 1950s), he was one of the most influential figures in Soviet cinema, as both practitioner and theoretician.

ZAVADSKY, YURI (1894–1977), Russian theater director and actor, from the school of Vakhtangov, who became chief director of the Mossoviet Theater from 1940. He began as a romantic lead and, as a director, tried to create a subtle and lyric atmosphere in a single style, from set design to the ensemble acting. Sometimes, however, this desire for aesthetic perfection turned into monotony. His best productions include *Death of a Squadron* (1934), *Masquerade* (1964), and *Petersburg Dreams* (1969).

Index

Lightning Source UK Ltd.
Milton Keynes UK
UKHW020428300820
368968UK00027B/1111